DON'T HIRE A SOFTWARE DEVELOPER UNTIL YOU READ THIS BOOK.™

From idea to launch: a survival guide for non-technical entrepreneurs, small businesses & startups. Learn how to manage the software creation process & transform your mobile app or SaaS concept into a commercial product.

Now an Amazon **international best seller** in multiple book categories in the US, UK, Canada, Brazil and Australia.

Author
K.N. Kukoyi

Copyright © 2016 by K.N. Kukoyi. All rights reserved.

Don't hire a software developer until you read this book.™

From idea to launch: a survival guide for non-technical entrepreneurs, small businesses & startups. Learn how to manage the software creation process & transform your mobile app or SaaS concept into a commercial product.

Copyright © 2016 by K.N. Kukoyi. All rights reserved. Cover copyright © 2016 K.N. Kukoyi. All rights reserved.

The right of K.N. Kukoyi to be identified as the author of this work has been asserted in accordance with the Copyright, Designs and Patents Act 1988. All rights reserved.

No part of this publication may be reproduced, or transmitted in any form or by any means whether copied, photocopied, emailed or stored in a retrieval system, without the prior written permission of the author except in accordance with the provisions of the Copyright, Designs and Patents Act 1988 and for the quoting of brief passages by reviewers.

Disclaimer and limitation of liability: This book contains information about software development, project management and product development and a wide range of other topics relevant to start-up businesses and entrepreneurs. The information and strategies contained herein may not be suitable for every situation and this book is not intended to provide personalised advice, whether legal, business, financial, accounting or taxation related and you must not rely on the information in this book as an alternative to advice from qualified legal or finance professionals. You should perform your own due diligence before making business decisions. The author and publisher will not be liable to you in respect of any loss or risk, personal, business or otherwise, that is incurred as a consequence, whether special, direct or indirect from the use and application of any of the contents of this book and whether from acting or refraining to act based on reading the material contained herein and do not represent, warrant, undertake or guarantee that the information and use of the guidance in the book will lead to any particular outcome or result.

Although the author and publisher have made every effort to ensure that the information in this book was correct at the time of publication, the author and distributors do not assume and hereby disclaim any liability to any party for any loss, damage, or disruption caused by errors or omissions, whether such errors or omissions result from negligence, accident, or any other cause. All information and links included herein have been provided in good faith. Readers should be advised that websites or links provided may change or cease to exist in future. The reference to companies or websites within this book does not constitute an endorsement of the information the company or website may provide, the services it offers or the recommendations it may make, nor is this book affiliated with or endorsed by any of the companies referred to herein.

FREE RESOURCES

There are many downloadable resources that come free with this book. Here's the full list and links to where you can find them:

- **Free resource 1:** *Chapter challenges workbook.* A summary of all the challenges that appear in this book. Note down the actions you wish to take and set yourself due-dates to complete them!
  http://www.mylanderpages.com/donthireasoftwaredeveloperuntilyoureadthisbook/Free-resource-1
- **Free resource 2:** *10 x Trello boards*, for you to copy and use, including boards to help you manage the build of your project, project management boards, a road map board, customer service boards and task prioritisation boards – just choose the ones you want.
  http://www.mylanderpages.com/donthireasoftwaredeveloperuntilyoureadthisbook/free-resource-2-trello-boards
- **Free resource 3:** *My personal version of the PMI Log which is great for reviewing information, organising your thoughts and making decisions.*
  http://www.mylanderpages.com/donthireasoftwaredeveloperuntilyoureadthisbook/Free-resource-3-pmi-log
- **Free resource 4:** *NFR checklist.* Very important when building professional apps!
  http://www.mylanderpages.com/donthireasoftwaredeveloperuntilyoureadthisbook/free-resource-4-nfr-checklist
- **Free resource 5:** *Customer profile template.*
  http://www.mylanderpages.com/donthireasoftwaredeveloperuntilyoureadthisbook/5-customer-profile-avatar
- **Free resource 6:** *Sample job advert for back-end / full-stack developer with crib notes.*
  http://www.mylanderpages.com/donthireasoftwaredeveloperuntilyoureadthisbook/resource-6-sample-job-advert
- **Free resource 7:** *Developer Interview Log* to help you keep track of your interviews.
  http://www.mylanderpages.com/donthireasoftwaredeveloperuntilyoureadthisbook/resource-7-interview-log

- **Free resource 8:** *Issue log for the beta launch of your MVP.*
  http://www.mylanderpages.com/donthireasoftwaredeveloperuntilyoureadthisbook/resource-8-issue-log-for-beta
- **FREE GIFT:** 2 x bonus chapters*: 1. Presales and raising funds for your business* and *2. A brief time out.*
  http://www.mylanderpages.com/donthireasoftwaredeveloperuntilyoureadthisbook/free-gift-2x-free-chapters

HOW TO USE THIS BOOK

You will come across the following conventions within this book:

Chapter summaries. The start of each chapter contains a preview of what's to come in bullet-point form, so you can zoom in on key areas of interest.

Chapter challenges. At the end of some chapters, there are challenges. They are tasks that will help you make progress towards specific goals in your product's development. If a chapter includes a challenge, this will be highlighted in the summary at the start of the chapter.

Free resources. These are available in some chapters for your convenience and may include *scripts, templates and other documents* that you can download, or copy to save time. If a chapter includes free resources, this will be highlighted in the chapter summary. Please see the *Free Resources* pages at the start and end of the book for the full list.

Boxed text represents a *professional ("pro") tip, project pitfall* or general *tip* or warning. These occur throughout the book to highlight important points.

Italics are used to identify business or technical concepts, terms, products, tools and company names. If you're doing research and need facts on specific technical topics, you'll find much better quality information if you search using the correct "techie" terminology. The IT community usually write to communicate to others *within* the industry and use industry-standard words and phrases, so knowing the jargon will really help. The way you communicate has the potential to save you a *lot* of frustration and wasted time…and time is money when you're developing software! It will become easier and quicker to communicate with a developer when you speak a common language.

Exercises. Some chapters contain exercises for you to complete. Some will involve web research and others sitting down with a pen and paper to do creative work! If it's not a convenient time for you, you may wish to use your Kindle device or Kindle reader app to bookmark exercises so you can come back to them when it suits you.

Naming conventions for different types of app. Many types of app exist, so when "apps" or "products" are mentioned in this book, this is a reference to software applications in general, otherwise I will specifically refer to *mobile apps* and *web apps* and occasionally to *desktop apps*. Many of the tips, tools, processes and techniques contained within this book are universal, and will be relevant regardless of the type of app that you wish to build.

Links. Many chapters contain links to tools, resources, and products to assist you in managing your project or delivering your software. Most the tools listed in this book are free or low-cost, as I appreciate that you may be on a tight budget. There are also links to sources of information such as legal websites, business resources and guides for mobile app development.

Examples and case studies also exist within this book. Where present, they are highlighted in the relevant chapter summaries.

Chapters and sections

The 25 chapters of this book have been grouped into sections, beginning with starting your business, through to your first product release.

You do not need to read this book in order. However, if you are new to these topics or are starting a business for the first time, this may be useful to ensure you don't miss out on key points, chapter challenges or exercises along the way. If you are reading the book out of sequence, please be aware that you may "jump in" at a point where specific topics have already been discussed. I recommend using your Kindle device or Kindle reader app to run keyword searches on topics of interest, and italicised keywords, so you have easy access to all the information available.

To assist readers who are dipping in and out of the book, I refer to both previous and forthcoming chapters to identify related topics that were mentioned earlier in the book, and related topics still to come.

Table of Contents

DON'T HIRE A SOFTWARE DEVELOPER UNTIL YOU READ THIS BOOK.™ 1

Don't hire a software developer until you read this book.™ 3

FREE RESOURCES 5

HOW TO USE THIS BOOK 7

Table of Contents 9

INTRODUCTION 12

SECTION 1 YOUR BUSINESS, YOUR IDEA & YOUR CUSTOMERS 19

CHAPTER 1 Protecting your interests 20

CHAPTER 2 How to develop your idea…and 5 market research exercises 36

CHAPTER 3 Creating customer profiles, and your first customer interviews 56

SECTION 2 TECHNICAL AND SOFTWARE DELIVERY BASICS 75

CHAPTER 4 An introduction to Agile principles 76

CHAPTER 5 How to identify the skill gaps in your team…and what to do about them 86

CHAPTER 6 The insider secrets of the IT industry 98

CHAPTER 7 What type of app should you build? 112

SECTION 3 MONETISATION AND MARKETING 125

CHAPTER 8 Generating revenue from your software 126

CHAPTER 9 App marketing basics 140

SECTION 4 PROTOTYPING, USER EXPERIENCE AND CHOOSING YOUR MVP 155

CHAPTER 10 Prepare to prototype! 156

CHAPTER 11 Creating a positive "user experience" for your customers 169

CHAPTER 12 Your prototyping options 189

CHAPTER 13 How to test your prototype 204

CHAPTER 14 How to select and prioritise your MVP 214

SECTION 5 FINDING A DEVELOPER 225

CHAPTER 15 Finding developers with the right skills 226

CHAPTER 16 How to hire a developer 238

CHAPTER 17 The interview process 254

SECTION 6 PEOPLE, PITFALLS AND PROJECT LIFE-SAVERS 265

CHAPTER 18 People management, and productive working relationships 266

CHAPTER 19 Project management, pitfalls and perils 276

SECTION 7 BUILD AND TEST IT **293**

CHAPTER 20 How to estimate the cost of your MVP 294

CHAPTER 21 Preparing to build your product 304

CHAPTER 22 How to manage your software project 314

CHAPTER 23 Break your app - before your customers do! 338

SECTION 8 LAUNCH IT! **353**

CHAPTER 24 How to launch your MVP (as a beta) 354

CHAPTER 25 Life after Launch 372

THANK YOU 379

DEDICATION 380

ABOUT THE AUTHOR 381

CREDITS 382

INTRODUCTION

"Everyone can tell you the risk. An entrepreneur can see the reward."
- Robert Kiyosaki

This book tells a story.

It's the story of an idea. Your idea, and its transformation into a tangible product.

It's a story about starting, or expanding your business based on that product, and bringing a commercial software application to market. It's about the world of software delivery and how it works; the "big picture" and the small but critical details, its cycles and working practices, and making good software development decisions in order to achieve your goals.

It is a story about you, a "non-technical" business person with a technical job to do!

There is no question that software development is a complex activity, but you'll find it far easier to manage the process with a survival guide to assist you and show you how to get started.

You will discover more about what's involved in building and launching a web or mobile app, whether you've started building your product, or are considering your options.

There are more types of app, or "application" than you might expect, and we'll consider the wider trends in software, including strategies, tactics, and data to help you make informed, strategic decisions about the options available and the software that is best for your business, and your customers.

If you've already hired a developer, it's not too late! You'll find plenty of information about how to avoid mistakes and unnecessary issues as your software is developed. You will be shown techniques and processes to help you successfully manage your project, and you'll discover how to build a productive working relationship with the person, or people responsible for building your product.

INTRODUCTION
* * *

What else will you learn?

You will expand your knowledge in some areas and discover many "unknown unknowns" in others!
You don't know what you don't know, as the saying goes. Would you agree that the things we *aren't* aware of often cause us the most difficulties?

It's impossible to prepare for situations you can't see coming. However, in software development there are challenges which are very likely to arise on *every project*.

Wouldn't it be nice to get a heads-up right now to find out what they are, and how to deal with them?

There are also those queries that you already know you need answers to. You may be asking yourself questions such as:

"What contractual agreements should I have in place?"

"How should I go about interviewing and selecting a developer?"

"How often should I pay them?"

"What if I'm unhappy with the product that's delivered to me?"

"How will I keep a software project on track when I don't know how to code?"

You'll receive answers to all these questions and more! There are many important topics for us to cover, so let's get specific, so you can see *exactly* what benefits you'll get from reading this book:

You will learn about product development and software delivery, but in addition to that, we'll cover other subjects that will contribute to your progress and success. These include the **practicalities of starting a business, company formation, freelancer and confidentiality agreements and legal and Intellectual Property considerations.** (Chapter 1.)

Following this, we'll move on to **market and consumer research and interviewing your target customers, assessing different types of app and**

INTRODUCTION

income generation strategies, creating prototypes and considering user experience (UX) and running user testing sessions, so you can be confident that your product is going to be a hit. (Chapters 2, 3 and 7, 8 and 10-13.)

Next, we'll look at **ways of finding developers with the skills you need at a price that suits your budget,** (Chapters 15-17) and **how to communicate with your developer** in ways that will help you get your product built more quickly and with less confusion and wasted resources. (Chapters 10, 14, 19, 21 and 22.) We'll also talk about **Agile development roles and principles,** and how to make them work for you. (Chapters 4, 5 and 22.)

Building high-quality software will be critical to the success of your product, so we'll review the **measures that software professionals** take when building software and preparing it for release to customers, (Chapters 5, 6 and 21) and you'll learn how to test for defects. The essentials of **project management, avoiding project pitfalls that will waste your time and money,** and the **practicalities of managing the development of your software** will also be covered in detail. (Chapters 14, 18-23.)

The **launch of your product** will be an important and exciting time, but around this time it will also be important to think about **setting up simple, but effective customer care processes**.

Once you have your product you'll need to promote and sell it, so

basic marketing and sales will be covered too; both online and in the app marketplaces. (Chapters 9, 24 and 25.) All the necessary activities will be explained and broken down into practical steps that you can follow.

Throughout the book, I'll share **insights** and **professional tips** to help you avoid the mistakes and perils that you may be unaware of if you're new to this topic, and we'll cover the "techie" and commercial subjects needed to manage your venture. There are also **hundreds of links** to **free, and low-cost tools and resources** perfect for entrepreneurs starting software ventures and building their businesses. You'll also be given access to 8 free documents that you can download to save yourself time.

There is a *lot* of information in this book! Including such a wide range of information and topics has made it more challenging to write, but this is also where the value lies.

INTRODUCTION

*After reading this book, you'll understand **what** you need to do, **why** it's important to do it, **how** to do it and **when** to do it, with no mystery, or guesswork involved. The **tools** you'll need are also provided, and you can get started with this one book, instead of having to begin by reading ten!*

This is *your* software survival handbook and you will be able to tap into the specific information you need, based on the stage you're at.

* * *

From speaking to entrepreneurs like you, I know you want to get positive results and to avoid making mistakes wherever possible. CB Insights, a tech market intelligence platform, ran a "post-mortem" analysis on the failure of 101 startups based on feedback from the founders,

https://www.cbinsights.com/blog/startup-failure-reasons-top/

Fig 1. Source: CB Insights - Top 20 Reasons Startups fail

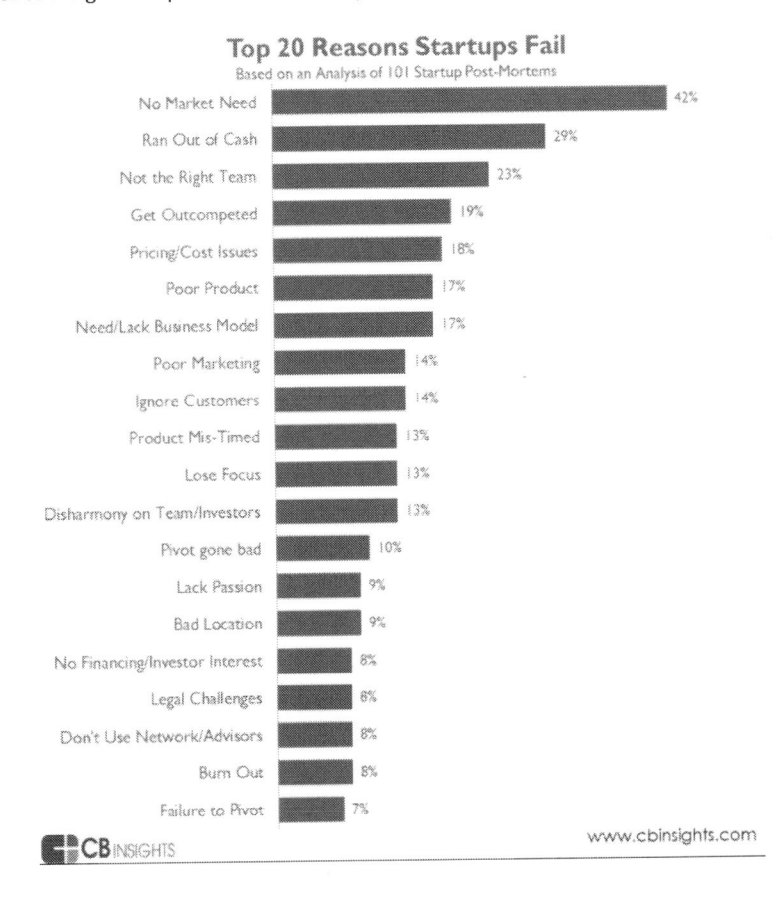

Top 20 Reasons Startups Fail
Based on an Analysis of 101 Startup Post-Mortems

Reason	%
No Market Need	42%
Ran Out of Cash	29%
Not the Right Team	23%
Get Outcompeted	19%
Pricing/Cost Issues	18%
Poor Product	17%
Need/Lack Business Model	17%
Poor Marketing	14%
Ignore Customers	14%
Product Mis-Timed	13%
Lose Focus	13%
Disharmony on Team/Investors	13%
Pivot gone bad	10%
Lack Passion	9%
Bad Location	9%
No Financing/Investor Interest	8%
Legal Challenges	8%
Don't Use Network/Advisors	8%
Burn Out	8%
Failure to Pivot	7%

CB INSIGHTS   www.cbinsights.com

INTRODUCTION

This book addresses a number of the common reasons for failure provided by the founders that were interviewed, including the top 9 items in the reasons for failure table. It will also help you:

- **To increase your knowledge, and reduce the risks involved in starting your tech business.** *Hiring a developer, or agency to build your app, and then "leaving them to get on with it" is a common rookie mistake.* Your product will be evolving on a daily basis, and your input will be needed, so you should be checking-in with the builder of your app to see that the plans you agreed have not gone off track! Getting started will be a bumpy road without adequate knowledge about the things you'll need to *know, ask,* and *do* to make your venture a success.
- **To increase your confidence.** This book provides information on the warts-and-all of software development. Having a better understanding of the processes involved in building software will reduce your reliance on the people you hire, who may, or may not be helpful in giving you the right information, or providing guidance as you start your software creation journey.
- **To get easy access to the information you'll need.** Traditional technical textbooks are written for professionals already in the industry. They require a level of existing knowledge and have a narrow focus. They don't cater for the needs of entrepreneurs and startups who need a breadth of skills and knowledge across multiple topics to cover all the bases. They are also likely to assume that your software will be built with the assistance of a full software delivery team.

This book can be used even if you *don't* have the luxury of a large team to assist you and requires no pre-existing knowledge. You'll be provided with all the information you need to get started and to progress right though to product launch. Regardless of the size of your team, or your resources, I'll show you how you can benefit from having a well-managed development project.

* * *

In case you were wondering, this isn't theoretical knowledge!

I know how rewarding it is to make the journey from idea to working software and this is something that I have done repeatedly since 2004. Working as an IT Consultant I have delivered commercial-grade software for multi-national clients used by people all over the world and I have led and worked within numerous Agile software delivery teams. My experience spans across business, as well as

INTRODUCTION

"tech" and covers: business strategy, product development, testing and software quality, project management, market research, customer care and the translation of ideas into technical requirements, and this is what I'll be sharing with you!

If you'd like to know more, please see the *About the Author* page.

Visit the Free Resources page to pick up the documents, tools, scripts and tables that come free with this book to help you with your venture. I'd love to hear about your experiences. You can reach me with any questions at:

hello@purposefulgroup.com

Good luck!

SECTION 1

YOUR BUSINESS, YOUR IDEA & YOUR CUSTOMERS

CHAPTER 1
Protecting your interests

In this chapter:
- Software and Intellectual Property
- Freelancer employment contracts
- Contracts and non-disclosure agreements
- Trademarks
- Choosing a legal status for your company
- Insuring your business
- Accounting, budgeting and keeping financial records
- Finding an accountant
- A brief word about VAT

If you're already familiar with Intellectual Property and the legal aspects of dealing with freelancers, please continue on to Chapter 2. If not, let's discuss these fundamentals!

IMPORTANT: Most the topics in this book are international, however, laws and procedures may differ according to your state, or country of residence. Please contact the equivalent bodies in your own country and when seeking professional advice, always use the services of lawyers and chartered or certified accountants authorised and qualified to practice in your country.

Intellectual Property

In order to protect your interests, you'll need to know about Intellectual Property (IP).

IP is an umbrella term which covers copyrights, patents, designs, trademarks and the laws and codes of practice related to them.

CHAPTER 1
Protecting Your Interests

Fig 2. Types of IP. Source: The Intellectual Property Office (IPO)

Intellectual Property (IP) concerns creations of the mind. IP can be:

- An invention
- A literary or artistic work
- A name, symbol or image used in business
- A design

The Intellectual Property Office (IPO) is the government body responsible for intellectual property rights in the UK. It's well worth contacting the IPO (or its equivalent in your own country) for some free advice. However, you may still need to seek advice from a solicitor. Their familiarity with relevant trademark case law, recent disputes and an understanding of how these might relate to your individual case will be important, so if you hire a law firm, confirm that they are *specialists* in IP.

Copyright and other sources of information

Software is *usually* protected under *copyright law*. The information below, provided by the IPO, provides one example where software is considered to be a *copyright* matter and when it may require a *patent*.

Fig 3. Patents and computer programs. Source: The Intellectual Property Office (IPO)
http://www.ipo.gov.uk/blogs/iptutor/stem-patents-and-trade-secrets-part-1/

> **Patents and computer programs**
>
> Computer programs are normally protected by copyright although patents are available in the UK for the majority of inventions that involve computer programs.
>
> For example, a washing machine run by a software program to use less water and at lower temperatures would be patentable, whereas general application programs such as word processing software or an app for a smartphone may not be patentable. Therefore, it is important to get legal advice on patent applications in this technical area.
>
> Don't forget that other forms of intellectual property rights can be important in protecting your innovation – for example, protecting the trade mark used for the app you have developed.

This page from the IPO contains an IP overview, as well as links to specific IP topics: https://www.gov.uk/government/organisations/intellectual-property-office

The IPO have produced a short video called "What's intellectual property got to do with me?" You can access it here: https://youtu.be/PMab4oRGaZc. It's just over 1 minute long and packs in a lot of information which is relevant regardless of your location.

Freelance employment contracts

Having a solid contractual agreement in place is a sensible idea for several reasons:

- It's a legal document that both parties must take seriously.
- It's a reference in case of disputes.
- Things run more smoothly when everyone knows where they stand!

Your contractual agreement should clearly state what the person or company you hire will do and what happens if either party fails to fulfil their contractual obligations.

CHAPTER 1
Protecting Your Interests

Here are some clauses you may wish to cover in an agreement:

A clear description of the work to be done. Describe what you are hiring the developer to do, for example: "Develop a Social Media mobile app for Android devices, including all tasks associated with the build of the app and its launch, which should follow good industry practice and be delivered to a professional standard."

Obligations. Whether you hire an individual or an agency to take responsibility for the build of your product, you should include any obligations that you expect them to fulfil. Obligations might include agreeing to behave in an honest manner, to follow your instructions and to work with reasonable care and skill. Include your obligations to the developer too. An example might be to make payments on a certain day each week, or to pay an agreed number of days after your project (or a milestone within it) has been delivered to your satisfaction.

Working hours. Do you want to agree on specific days of the week which will be worked? Will working hours be fixed, or flexible? Should there be a minimum or maximum number of hours to be worked each week?

Payment cycles. Are you going to pay daily, weekly, monthly, or per project on a fixed fee basis? Will you pay an hourly rate, or would you consider staged payments based on reaching specific project milestones? If staged payments are to be made, you might agree to split the development work into segments and pay based on the successful completion of each one. This may benefit both parties; your developer knows when they should be getting paid and you are assured of progress before you make payment. If you agree to use milestones, you'll need to list the work to be delivered for each one to avoid future disputes (or confusion) about what was to be included or excluded at each stage.

Time sheets and invoicing. When should time sheets or invoices be submitted to you for payment, and in what format? (We'll talk about tools for logging the hours worked by your developer using *time tracking tools* in chapter 16.)

Termination and Serving notice. What are the terms (or scenarios) under which either party can end the agreement? How must this be done and how much notice is needed? Under what circumstances would you wish to end the contract immediately? Would you like your agreement to include a probationary period?

CHAPTER 1
Protecting Your Interests

Intellectual property rights. Once you know all the types of Intellectual Property that you have within your business, then you will better understand the points that you will need to cover in your contract. Employers often write into their contracts that all IP generated whilst working for their company belongs to them exclusively. You will want to protect your *idea*, your product's *source code* and *any other IP linked with your venture*.

Confidentiality / Non-disclosure. This is a requirement to keep any material, knowledge, processes or information confidential. Please refer to the section about *Non-Disclosure Agreements* covered in the next section.

Restrictions on either party. Are there any restrictions that need to be put in place? If so, it should be clear what these are and when they apply. Examples of restrictions may include stating that an employee cannot set up and compete with your company in the same market after working for you, or that they may not approach your clients. Seek legal advice regarding which restrictions would be considered "reasonable" and legally enforceable.

Absence. Make it clear how your developer should give you notice of any absence they wish to take from the project and decide how you would like to be notified if your developer is unwell or has a personal emergency and is unable to work.

Expenses. Will expenses be allowed? If so, what type(s)?

Final deliverables. At the end of the project, (or whenever you and your developer agree to part ways), there will be some final deliverables that you should receive and be given access to. These may include *source code, designs,* and *digital assets (*such as *logos* and *images, files, databases and data)* and any *user names, passwords and access codes* that your developer holds.

Insurance. Business insurance is discussed later in this chapter, however it's important to be aware that freelancer contracts often state that the freelancer must have *their own* insurance cover and that a copy of their policy is provided as evidence *before* they start work. It will be useful to have these details available should an issue arise that would require some form of insurance claim.

CHAPTER 1
Protecting Your Interests

Legal documents and services

Non-disclosure agreements (NDAs)

Before you discuss your idea, make any verbal or written agreements, or hire anyone to join your project, **make sure you know where you stand in terms of Intellectual Property.** The IPO offers this advice:

Fig 4. Discussing your invention. Keeping Schtum! Source, The Intellectual Property Office (IPO)

If you have previously revealed your invention publicly in any way, you cannot patent it.

However, this does not mean that inventions cannot be discussed before a patent application is made.

There may be people you will need to discuss your invention, with such as:

- the development team
- an investor
- an IP professional (such as a Patent Attorney)

Before you discuss the details all parties should sign a 'Non-Disclosure Agreement' which can help to protect the secrecy of your invention.

You do not need a Patent Attorney to sign a **non-disclosure agreement** as they are subject to legal privilege.

NDAs (also described as secrecy or confidentiality agreements) are legal contracts which give you grounds to take action in court against those who break their terms. They can also be used if you want to share your idea in order to get feedback, but wish to keep information about your company and its plans confidential. The entrepreneurial community is divided about NDAs – some believe ideas are worthless and it is the *execution* of the idea that matters, whilst others believe that ideas can be valuable. You will need to decide where you stand on this matter and what you will do if people refuse to sign. Will you work with them, or choose to walk away?

There are a number of places online where you can access legal documents. *Docracy* describes itself as "The web's only open collection of legal contracts and the best way to negotiate and sign documents online" and has contracts and agreements for hiring developers and designers, which you can find here:

CHAPTER 1
Protecting Your Interests

http://www.docracy.com/4754/contract-for-mobile-application-development-services

http://www.docracy.com/2817/standard-agreement-for-design-services-interactive-web-works-full-assignment

SEQ Legal offer a selection of free and pay-as-you-go legal documents for IT, Internet and Business Law, including documents for those creating mobile apps, NDAs, SaaS agreements, software license agreements and more: http://www.seqlegal.com/

Elance, an online marketplace for freelancers has some sample NDA, project and freelancer agreements that you can review: http://help.elance.com/hc/en-us/articles/203735913-Sample-Contract-Agreements

Contractstandards.com, offers "standardized contracts, checklists, and clauses built with analysis of thousands of public documents" and has a software development agreement that you can review: https://www.contractstandards.com/contracts/software-development-agreement.

If you're UK based, *Lawbite* offers access to a range of legal documents on a pay-as-you-go basis for a one off cost of £99 + VAT including e-signing facilities and two free fifteen minute legal advice sessions: https://www.lawbite.co.uk and *Rocket Lawyer* charges £25 a month for access to legal documents and the ability to ask questions; https://www.rocketlawyer.co.uk/

The UK Government's gov.uk website has several versions of NDA available to view and download at: https://www.gov.uk/government/publications/non-disclosure-agreements.

A few words of caution about contracts:

These links have been provided for your convenience.

*If in doubt, please seek legal advice t*o ensure that your contract includes all the necessary clauses and caveats and is suitable for your specific situation.

You may also wish to seek advice to find out how an NDA might be enforced if you and your developer are not based in the same country. In this case, you

CHAPTER 1
Protecting Your Interests

may need to confirm whether the laws of your home country are applicable to people living and working elsewhere.

There are software agreements, website terms and conditions and other legal resources available in chapter 6. Look for the section *Legal and compliance related requirements.*

Trademarks

A *trademark* is defined as a design, graphic, logo, symbol, word or phrase or any combination of these used to identify your business or product. If your trademark application is approved, this will allow you to use the registered trademark symbol, ®.

A list of trademark specialists can be found on *The Institute of Trade Mark Attorneys* website: http://www.itma.org.uk/members/

To see whether the company, product or brand name(s) you have in mind have already been trademarked, check the database of existing names and keywords here: https://www.ipo.gov.uk/tmtext.htm. Companies House has a page to help you check whether the limited company name you want has already been taken - you cannot pick a name that has already been claimed. You can find it here: http://wck2.companieshouse.gov.uk//wcframe?name=accessCompanyInfo.

If you haven't got a name for your business or product yet, there's a thought-provoking process outlined here: http://www.nickkolenda.com/naming-process/. Do a search on the page for the words *table of contents,* which will show you the process broken down into sections.

Choosing a legal status for your company

There are a number of "business structures" or "legal statuses" you can choose, including *limited company, sole trader, partnership and social enterprise:*

CHAPTER 1
Protecting Your Interests

A *limited company structure* "limits" your personal liability because the company is a legal entity - your finances and the company's finances are separate. This protects personal assets such as your home, car or other personal property in the face of legal action or bankruptcy, (although it's still essential to have the right insurance cover in place.)

A *sole trader's* assets *aren't* protected in this way - the individual and the business are not separate legal entities.

The Director(s) of limited companies are obliged by law to submit or "file" *annual returns* and *annual accounts* (replaced by *confirmation statements* as of June 2016) to Companies House; the UK body that forms and dissolves limited companies and registers and manages their data. As a limited company, you face fines and other penalties if you or your accountant do not file the required paperwork on time. Sole traders do not need to perform these tasks.

For more information about director's responsibilities, visit:

https://www.gov.uk/running-a-limited-company/directors-responsibilities and https://www.gov.uk/running-a-limited-company/company-annual-return.

Overall, limited companies have more paperwork and legal obligations to fulfil. It may be for these reasons that limited companies can be seen as more professional - they are subject to more "checks and balances."

Partnerships and *Limited Liability Partnerships.* These businesses consist of two or more individuals sharing profits, management and legal responsibilities.

Social enterprises are set up to help people or communities and can register as sole traders, limited companies, partnerships, charities, co-operatives or CICs (Community Interest Companies) if the necessary criteria are met. Visit http://www.socialenterprise.org.uk/ for more information.

Registering your business with the correct organisations

Both sole trader and limited companies must contact *HMRC* (Her Majesty's Revenue and Customs) and register for *Self-Assessment;* HMRC's process for collecting taxes from the self-employed. *Self-Assessment tax returns* can be completed online or on paper. You'll be given more time to complete yours if you choose the online option. There's a time limit for registration, based on when you started your business. The link below explains how to calculate your *registration deadline:* https://www.gov.uk/set-up-sole-trader/register. Don't get on the wrong side of the tax man, confirm your deadline and avoid issues!

If you wish to form a limited company, you can approach Companies House directly via the Gov.uk website: https://www.gov.uk/register-a-company-online and register your company and its name for a fee of £12, or pay a *company formation agent* anything from around £15 - £150 to set the company up for you. Gov.uk lists a number of formation agents on its website - using one of these may be a better plan than trawling the web: http://bit.ly/1OtJe2p

Additional sources of information

HMRC offers information at: https://www.gov.uk/government/news/webinars-emails-and-videos-if-youre-self-employed which includes dates of forthcoming webinars on record keeping and filing tax returns, links to advice based videos on YouTube, plus email services and several e-learning guides. There's a Self-Assessment tax guide here:

http://www.hmrc.gov.uk/courses/SYOB3/syob_3/html/syob_3_menu.html and a guide to business expenses here:

http://www.hmrc.gov.uk/courses/SYOB3/syob_3_exps/html/syob_3_exps_menu.html

Business insurance

There are a range of insurance policies you can take out to protect your enterprise against legal action and claims for damages.

Costs will vary depending on factors such as your age, location and the nature of your business.

Levels of cover range from around £500,000 into the millions, depending on the size of your business, the level of risk you're exposed to, and the amount of cover you require. Let's look at a few examples:

Business contents insurance. Don't assume that your home insurance policy will cover business items, such as expensive computer or home office equipment. Check with your home insurer to make sure you're covered.

CHAPTER 1
Protecting Your Interests

Public liability insurance covers you and your business for compensation claims and legal expenses in the event that a customer or member of the public makes a claim against you for property damage, personal loss or injury.

Employer's liability insurance protects your employees and covers you against damages if a claim is made against you by an employee. Employer's liability insurance is required by law if you hire staff, however, this may not be required if the worker:
- Is based in a different country, or is in the same country, but does not work in your office
- Uses their own equipment
- Has their own insurance
- Does not have a long-term contract
- Is not directly supervised by you

Professional indemnity insurance cover will help you defend claims relating to inadequate advice, negligence or errors and the cost of rectifying mistakes, including legal costs, compensation and expenses.

Selecting a reputable insurance company

https://www.comparethemarket.com,
http://www.gocompare.com/,
http://simplybusiness.co.uk/insurance and
http://www.confused.com/ are some of the larger online price and quote comparison sites for business insurance. Axa;
https://us.axa.com/small-business/
(US) and http://www.axa.co.uk/insurance/business
(UK), Hiscox; http://www.hiscox.com/small-business-insurance/
(US) and https://www.hiscox.co.uk/business-insurance/
(UK) and Direct Line for business https://www.directlineforbusiness.co.uk/ are some of the big names in the general insurance market.

Policy inclusions and exclusions can vary significantly between companies.
Read the small print carefully and if necessary, request clarification before signing up!

Accounting, budgeting and keeping financial records

CHAPTER 1
Protecting Your Interests

It's a good idea to keep a log that you can continually update as you learn more about the running costs associated with building, owning and maintaining a software application. You can use this to create a rough budget for the initial project to get your app built, and for running it on a monthly basis thereafter. After your initial product is developed, you may wish to enhance or add new functionality to it, so keep that in mind when budgeting. Log any one-off, monthly and annual costs, and any other expenses that arise. There is information about project costs and ongoing expenses related to app ownership in chapter 21.

Keeping financial records

Make sure you claim the cost of hiring staff and other allowable businesses expenses. Keep your receipts, invoices and bank statements as evidence of your business transactions and for your self-assessment tax returns and pass copies to your accountant, if you plan to use one.

In the UK, financial records must be kept for a period of six years.

Bookkeeping, (financial record keeping), will help you keep track of all your receipts and expenses. This can be done using spreadsheets, mobile apps or accountancy software such as *Xero*, https://www.xero.com/uk/ or *Freshbooks*, https://www.freshbooks.com. You can do your own bookkeeping, or hire a bookkeeper or accountant to help you.

You can confirm which expenses you may claim via your accountant, HMRC or the Gov.uk website. Here is a list of common business expenses that you can claim for if you go down the self-employment / sole-trader route; https://www.gov.uk/expenses-if-youre-self-employed/overview.

According to the Gov.uk website, the major categories of expenses you can claim for include:

- Office costs, e.g. stationery or phone bills. You may also be able to claim some expenses if you work from home.
- Travel costs, e.g. fuel, parking, train or bus fares.
- Staff costs, e.g. salaries or subcontractor costs.
- Financial costs, e.g. insurance, accountant's fees and bank charges.
- Costs of your business premises, e.g. heating, lighting and business rates.

- Advertising or marketing expenses, e.g. costs related to running your website and online advertising.

Expenses for limited companies work differently and you can find out more about the accounting process for limited companies and the expenses that can be claimed here:

https://www.gov.uk/running-a-limited-company/company-and-accounting-records

https://www.gov.uk/prepare-file-annual-accounts-for-limited-company/overview

Expense management apps

If you choose the do-it-yourself route for bookkeeping or accounting, there are some excellent free and paid apps available under "receipts", "expenses" or "accounting" searches via Google Play, The App Store and other app marketplaces. A few examples include *Toshl*; see http://apple.co/2adDKS9 for Apple device users and http://bit.ly/LGBgtG for Android users, https://toshl.com/ and *Finance PM* for Android, http://bit.ly/2aj9cxT via the Google Play store.

These are great time-saving devices because they make it so easy to log expenses as soon as they arise, so your bookkeeping is always up-to-date.

CHAPTER 1
Protecting Your Interests

Fig 5, images i-iii. The Toshl mobile app

i)   Adding expenses

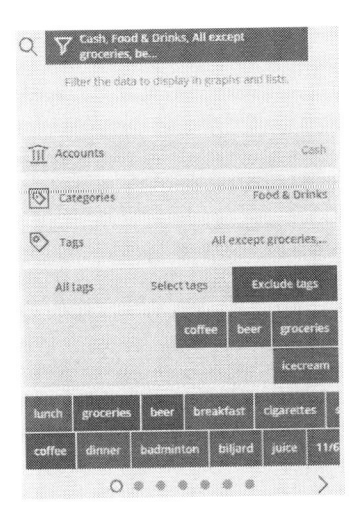

The labels in the apps are quite versatile, so you can customise them to suit your own purposes.

ii) Setting a budget

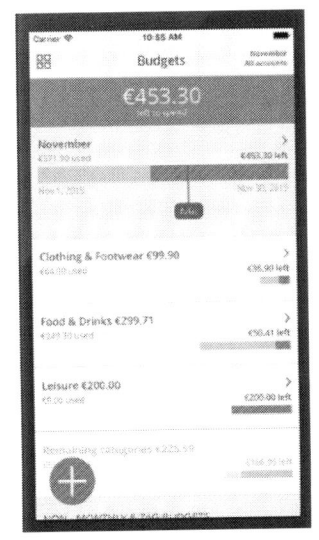

Budgets can be set within some apps, so the app subtracts your expenditure from the funds you have available.

CHAPTER 1
Protecting Your Interests

iii) Exporting or printing your expense and accounting records.

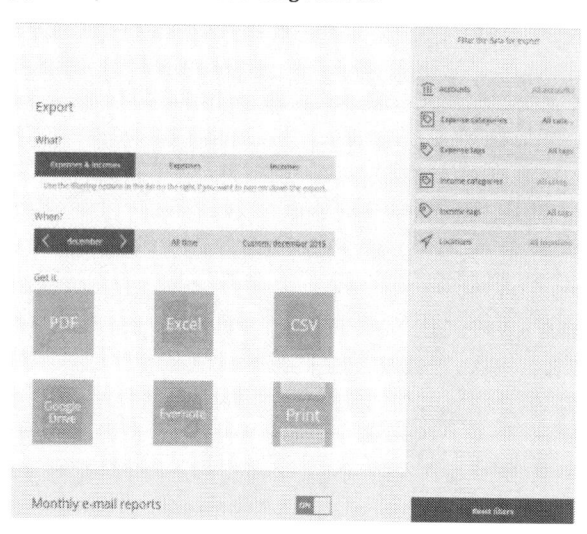

In most cases, expense apps will allow you to generate a spreadsheet based on all the expense entries logged in the app. *Abukai expenses,* http://bit.ly/2axnWpd will let you photograph an expense and will turn this into a line item in a spreadsheet, which can be emailed to you. You can see from the example that Toshl offers several ways to export your data.

Finding an accountant

Many accountants offer free initial consultations to discuss their services and charges. You can find an accountant via the ICAEW - the Institute of Chartered accountants in England & Wales at http://www.businessadviceservice.com/.

A brief word about VAT

I won't go into a great level of detail about *VAT (Value Added Tax)* and *VAT registration* here, except to mention that sole traders and limited companies must become *VAT registered* once the business begins earning over £83,000 (correct as of March 2016.) Being VAT registered involves collecting and paying VAT to HMRC on a quarterly basis. There are some advantages to registering to pay VAT, even if you haven't hit the £83,000 threshold. These include creating the impression that you are a larger company, (possibly making it easier to do business with larger VAT registered organisations) and being able to claim VAT back on your own business expenses. In January 2015, a new type of VAT, *VAT*

CHAPTER 1
Protecting Your Interests

Moss, (VAT mini one-stop-shop), was introduced. As a result, VAT due on the sales of digital services from businesses to consumers based in the EU must be charged at each customer's local rate of VAT. The £83,000 threshold applies to VAT Moss too. There is also a simpler, *flat rate VAT scheme* for businesses: https://www.gov.uk/vat-flat-rate-scheme/overview.

VAT and VAT Moss overviews can be found here: https://www.gov.uk/vat-returns/overview.

Next, let's explore your idea...

CHAPTER 2
How to develop your idea...and 5 market research exercises

"Learn from yesterday, live for today, hope for tomorrow. The important thing is not to stop questioning."
- Albert Einstein

In this chapter:
- Why do people pay for products and services?
- Guided market research exercises: competitor research, market positioning and more!
- Google search secrets
- Project pitfalls
- Creating simple business plans
- Free resources
- Chapter challenges

Why do people pay for products and services?

When people pay money to a business, they're paying for services or products that give them what they *want* or what they *need* by either: i) solving a painful problem that they'd like to get rid of, or ii) bringing them a benefit or result that they would like to receive.

The more wants and needs your product fulfils, the more powerful your *proposition* (the idea you're intending to bring to market) becomes. Usually, the bigger the problem you solve or benefit you help people to obtain, the more you can charge for delivering it.

Can I share another quote with you? It comes from an American businesswoman called Alice Foote MacDougall, who once said:

"In business, you get what *you* want by giving other people what *they* want."

CHAPTER 2
How to develop your idea...and 5 market research exercises

Which problems and "wants" can you solve, and solve well?

Make customers your obsession

Walking in the shoes of your customers is essential when creating software products. For over ten years I've managed and been part of teams that have delivered websites and digital products used by members of the public and specific consumer target markets; including pregnant women, people trying to manage debt and people trying to buy their first home.

I've delivered many types of software for business users too, including applications used by journalists, accountants, administrators, sales teams, human resource departments, trainers and customer service functions!

I have spent countless hours observing and interviewing people as they use software, getting a feel for *what* they do and *why,* and trying to understand the relationships they have (or would like to have) with the software they use:

- What annoys them?
- What makes their lives easier?
- What are their needs, priorities and preferences?
- *Why* are those things so important to them?

Study the people that you hope will become your customers, startups so you can understand how they think and behave - the goal is to transition from *your* way of thinking to *theirs.*

Question, listen, observe, understand and *then* create a solution that fits.

Someone representing your business should spend time with the people who are eventually going to use your product, because:

- *You can't create a product to satisfy a group of people if you don't understand what they want, what they value and why they value it.*
- *If your product isn't useful, usable or valuable enough, you won't be able to build a solid customer base of people who will use or pay for it – and without that, you will find it difficult to build a viable business.*

In the Introduction, we saw that the number 1 reported reason for failing in the *CB Insights* study was a lack of real need for the product and reason number 9 was ignoring the customer! Neglecting your customers is one of the biggest pitfalls and ways to lose money on your venture. Seek to understand them, carry out market research and take into account their wants and needs. Regularly check-in with your target market as your product evolves to be sure that you are still on track to deliver a product that pleases them.

Have you ever been given a gift that wasn't right for you? Maybe it was something that the person who gave it to you would love to receive. Trying to sell a group of people the wrong product is similar, but not only is the "gift" not right, but you're also expecting them to use *and* pay you for it!

To "nail" the perfect gift, you either need to know and understand the other person well, or ask them what they want directly! We'll talk about how to interview potential customers, also known as *prospects* in Chapter 3.

You are at the start of an ongoing scientific experiment...

To maximise interest and sales, you'll want to make sure that you have:

- Identified a *problem* to solve - ideally a large or very painful one!
- Identified a group that needs a solution to that problem (i.e. your *target market*.)
- Come up with a *solution* that is *attractive and acceptable* to your target market.
- Identified a *method* to deliver the solution to your target market (either yourself or via a 3rd party) in an effective, economical and profitable manner.

Try not to assume that you have the 100% "right" product idea straight away, confirm that your theories and assumptions are correct.

Does your solution lend itself best to a web app that people will use on a desktop computer with a larger screen when they're at home and are less time-pressured, or is it a quick-fire, do "on-the-go" type of activity better suited to a mobile app? Are both relevant at different times of day?

Investigate different ways of delivering your solution to your target market and keep fine-tuning until the point where your idea is "ready" to be transformed into software delivered just the way your users want it.

Let your customers shape your vision.

CHAPTER 2
How to develop your idea...and 5 market research exercises

One definition of entrepreneurship is "organising and managing an enterprise, usually with considerable initiative and risk." You can reduce the uncertainty and risk linked to your venture by *gathering data, seeking evidence, asking questions* and *making decisions based on what you learn.*

Don't rely on assumptions or guesswork!

Let's review some key questions...
Here are 5 questions to ask yourself about the market that you're considering:

- **What is the size of your market?** Is it big enough to support a business?
- **How sustainable is your idea?** What kind of longevity do you think your idea has?
- **What is the health / stability of your market?** Is the market experiencing growth, or declining? If you only have one product and a small budget, look for opportunities that will provide your business with a good foundation for growth.
- **Who are your competitors?** How many are there? What do they charge? How well are they are serving the market? (Note that if there are a lot of competitors in the market, this can be a good sign as it means there's a lot of demand.)
- **What about the bigger picture?** Your business will be impacted by events in the wider world. What impact could external factors have on your business venture and what could you possibly do about this?

In the market research exercise below, we will review ways that you can start to gather the answers to all these questions.

A guided market research exercise

Initial assessment of demand and validating your idea

Here are some simple, but powerful market research exercises you can do to assess the idea and market that you're considering. (If you've done a lot of research relating to your idea, that's fantastic - try scanning down to see if there are any other angles you can cover off that you haven't considered yet.)

Are you ready to get started? If this isn't a good time, please set yourself a bookmark and come back to this section later.

CHAPTER 2
How to develop your idea...and 5 market research exercises

Time required: 30+ minutes, per exercise, depending on how long you spend on each one.

Materials required:

- A device connected to the Internet and a web browser for searching (e.g. Internet Explorer, Google Chrome, Safari, Firefox, etc.)
- A pen and paper, spreadsheet or other method for recording notes.

Objectives: To assess the levels of demand, opportunity and risk associated with your product idea, before investing too much money and effort into it. By following the steps here, you will be able to gather information that could be used to refine your initial idea further.

Here's a worked example. It can be applied to any idea, but let's imagine that you wish to build some **computer game** software. You want to see what types of computer game are most popular before you decide on a course of action. Follow along with me using this example, or complete the exercise based on your own ideas and area(s) of interest.

Google Trends and keyword tool exercises

Google Trends, https://www.google.co.uk/trends displays *trends* in the use of search terms over time (rather than providing specific figures). It's possible to search for global trends and local trends by changing the search filters available at the top of the page. You can compare up to 5 different *search terms* at once and can search within a specific time-frame.

At the top of the screen, you can see that I've set my regional search to United Kingdom. My search covers the last 12 months and I've chosen to look at Web Search trends as opposed to image, news or the other search options available. (See the blue bar at the top of the image, far right.)

CHAPTER 2
How to develop your idea...and 5 market research exercises

Fig 6. A comparison search using Google Trends, based on web searches from July 2015 - July 2016

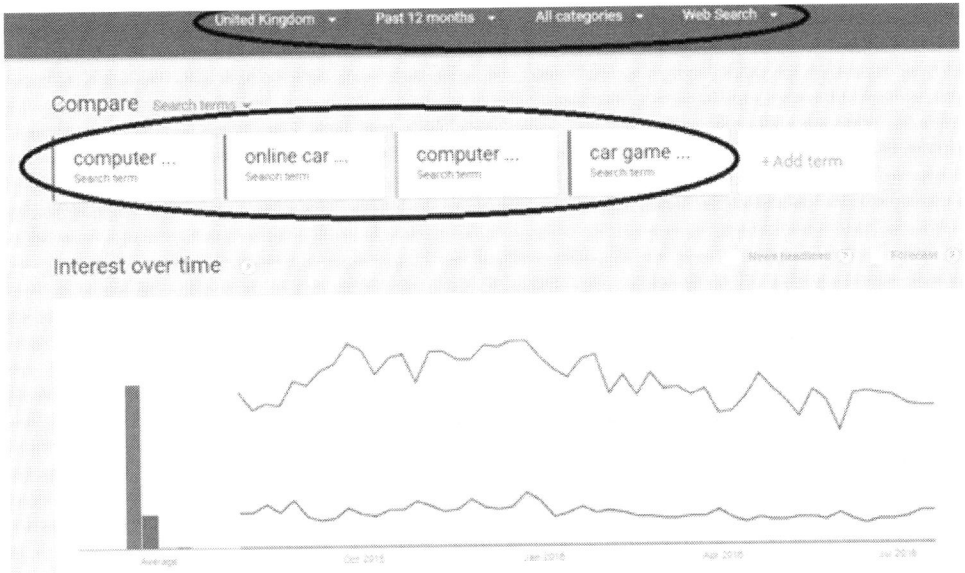

The boxes with the blue, red, yellow and green bands represent the four terms I've decided to compare and the bar and line graphs give an instant visual of their relative popularity.

In this example, I searched for computer games (with the blue band) as a benchmark and then decided to search for different types of computer game to see which search terms are most popular.

You can see that the term online car games (the red band) is the second most popular term, whilst the search terms represented by the yellow and green bands barely register on the graphs.

Persevere with your research until you are able to select a computer game or car game sub-genre that looks promising. There are many combinations of search terms you could try if you were looking for car games; "formula 1 racing games", "road race games", "car simulation games" etc.

Look for ones with a consistent or upward trend in popularity over time.

Keyword tools

There are tools you can use to check the relative popularity of *keywords* used in searches on the web. These tools are generally used for *SEM (Search Engine Marketing)*, which companies use when they wish to pay a search engine like Google or Bing to advertise their businesses by displaying them in people's search results. However, they can be used to gather a lot of useful information, even if you're not intending to pay for *SEM*.

The services below all provide *keyword volume data,* so you can see the phrases that individuals and businesses are searching for online, and the numbers of people running those types of searches. Do further research (and new keyword searches) on any phrases that you find interesting. A few examples of these tools include:

Instakeywords; http://www.instakeywords.com/

The *Google Keyword Planner* tool, which is part of *Google AdWords;* used for *SEM,* paid advertising to help companies rank highly on Google, https://adwords.google.co.uk/KeywordPlanner. (You may need Gmail and AdWords accounts to access this tool.)

Wordtracker; https://www.wordtracker.com/?splash=true

Wordstream.com; http://www.wordstream.com/keywords/

CHAPTER 2
How to develop your idea...and 5 market research exercises

Fig 7. Running a keyword search for the term "computer games" using the Wordtracker tool

Keywords	Volume	IAAT	Comp.	KEI
computer games	1121	7991	19.46	60.73
free computer racing games	443	0	0	100
free computer games	330	290	9.47	69.23
children s educational computer games	173	1	2.77	85.59
school computer games	94	1	2.77	84.02
computer zombie games	93	...	...	...
pc games computer games	78	0	0	100
educational computer games for kids	56	3	3.51	79.26
jobs4u computer games	38	---	---	---
childrens educational computer games	34	1	2.77	81.12

Before we move on, let's clarify the meaning of the column headings shown in the Wordtracker example above:

Volume. The number of times a keyword has been searched for in the previous month.

IAAT (in anchor and title) shows how many web pages have a given keyword in both the title tag (the title of each search result) and anchor text (the clickable text in a link).

Competition. This number ranges between 1 and 100, and represents the number of optimised pages on the internet for each keyword. (The higher the number, the more web pages there are that contain the keywords.)

A high *KEI* indicates keywords which a lot of people are using when they search, but which have a lower *competition* in terms of the number of web pages that contain these keywords, measured on a 1 to 100 scale.

CHAPTER 2
How to develop your idea...and 5 market research exercises

Competitor research and market positioning exercise

There are other quick ways to assess your competition or to refine your idea. Let's start with a 5-step process for the mobile app market, then we'll do the same for web apps.

Researching the mobile app market

1. **Review some app categories.** If you are considering different product ideas, it can be helpful to see all the options that exist! Take a look at the *categories* of app available at Apple's App Store, https://itunes.apple.com/en/genre/ios/id36?mt=8 or Google Play Store, (click the "categories" button in the top menu area); https://play.google.com/store/apps?hl=en_GB, or alternatively, visit the app stores via your smartphone.
2. **Look for gaps or areas of dissatisfaction.** Run a keyword search and look at the apps that are a close match to your area(s) of interest. Select 3 or more competitor apps with *overall* ratings of between 3 and 4.5. These are apps in the range from "O.k." to "very good." For each one, drill or scroll down and look at the proportion of ratings from 5* to 1*. The 5* reviews tell you what pleases users most about the app, 3* and 4* reviews reflect positivity, but indicate that some users feel the product "could be better" or has just fallen short of the ideal for some reason. Look at what needs improvement and *note the reviews with specific information included:* what disappointed the user or stopped them from giving a better review? The 1* and 2* reviews obviously reflect dissatisfaction. What do reviewers really dislike, or consider to be significant issues with the product and why? Look out for trends. *From what you have observed, is there an opportunity to offer a superior product or to position a new app so it covers functionality or services that have been neglected or overlooked?*
3. **Assess how good your competitors are at customer service.** Do they respond positively and professionally to customers' feedback? Do they even respond at all? Could you offer better customer care than them? Is there any sign that planned upgrades or bug fixes on the way to deal with the issues that you identified?
4. **Where do you fit into this picture?** Now that you have this information, you'll have more ideas about how to *position* your app. This may include

things you should do (and avoid doing), the likes and dislikes of users of the app and what is important to them. These could be functional gaps - the app doesn't do all the things that users would like, or in the *way* that they would like, or technical issues such as app crashes, bugs, complaints about too many adverts in the app, or other elements that annoy people. You may even be able to see reviewers' photos - this will give you an idea of the demographic that use the app, their ages and whether they are male or female. Does there seem to be a *type* of person that uses these apps? What do they say they use the app for? *This information is all absolute gold in terms of market intelligence and consumer research!*

5. **Review, reflect and take the next step.** Keep a record of your observations and ideas so you can easily review and compare all the information you've gathered. Armed with this information, there is an opportunity to build an app which is appealing in all the right ways, but avoids the worst elements of your competitors' products. In addition to quality, also consider what new or exciting twists you could provide to make your app unique, so it stands out within its category.

Fig 8. Star ratings for a game available in the Google Play Store

REVIEWS

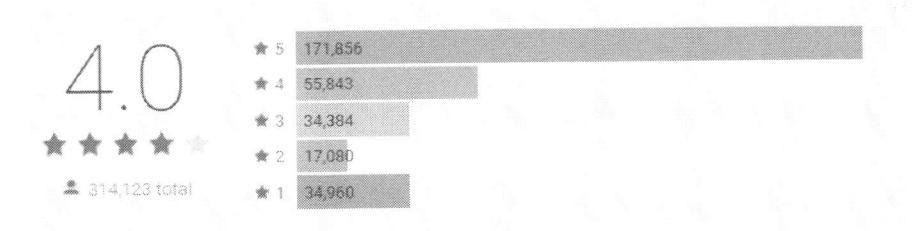

4.0
★★★★★
314,123 total

★ 5 171,856
★ 4 55,843
★ 3 34,384
★ 2 17,080
★ 1 34,960

To research a web (or desktop app), repeat a similar process:

1. **Run a Google search** for "apps" or "software" or "web app" or "SaaS" + [your area of interest]. Look at the results and the products that come up and investigate any relevant ones. (We'll talk more about different types of app in Chapter 7.)
2. **Look for product reviews** using Google and some of the big software comparison review sites such as *Capterra*, http://www.capterra.com, *G2crowd* https://www.g2crowd.com and *TrustRadius*, https://www.trustradius.com.

3. **Repeat steps 2 - 5 from the *mobile apps* section** above, using Google and the review sites to collect your data.

There is no reason why you can't review web apps when developing your product idea for a mobile app and vice-versa. The more data you can collect about functionality and customer preferences, the better.

Google research secrets

Get the most from Google with these less well-known search tools:

Get serious about searching with the *Google advanced search,* https://www.google.com/advanced_search. Include exact words or phrases, or choose to exclude specific keywords from your search results. You can add a + (plus) sign next to words that must appear, and a – (minus) sign next to words that you *don't* want to see in your search results.

Turn Google into your personal research assistant with *Google Alerts,* https://www.google.co.uk/alerts, useful for monitoring the latest news on your topic of interest. Put it to work collecting data from across the web for you 24 hours a day, 7 days a week!

Enter the keywords you're interested in, enter an email address, click on the "show options" menu and specify how often you want to receive notifications and you're set. Once your app is "live" you could set up an alert to see who's talking about it!

CHAPTER 2
How to develop your idea...and 5 market research exercises

Fig 9. Put Google Alerts to work for you and receive alerts via email or RSS

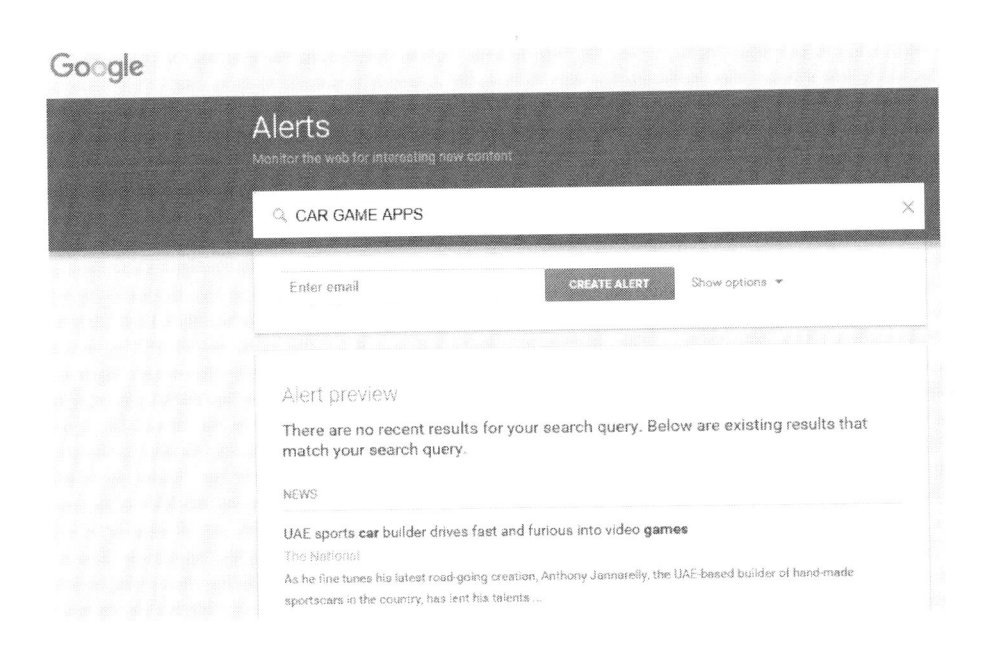

Google Scholar, https://scholar.google.co.uk/schhp?hl=en&as_sdt=2000b will help you locate research published on your topic of interest including journals and research from leading institutions. Set up an *alert* so you can receive email notifications about your preferred topic(s).

CHAPTER 2
How to develop your idea...and 5 market research exercises

Fig 10. Find the latest academic research on your topic of choice using Google Scholar

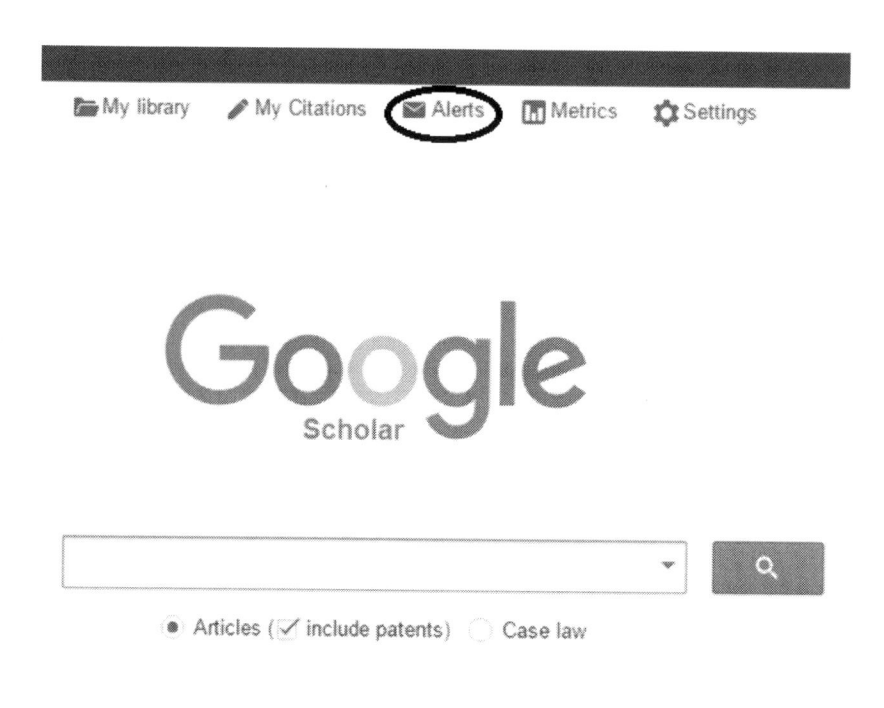

Stand on the shoulders of giants

Google's *Consumer Barometer* can be used to review high-level trends across populations. It also provides insights into different consumer groups and their behaviour and usage trends across smartphones, desktops and tablets: https://www.consumerbarometer.com/en/

Other sources of market and business intelligence data

Libraries can be a fantastic source of market data that may not be free online. Some have access to the databases of big players in the business intelligence and market data industries. Contact your local library to see whether you can access it for free. If not, some of the companies offer an initial free trial:

Bureau Van Dijk provides company information and financial data for the UK, Europe and Australia via their *Fame* and *MINT* products, http://www.bvdinfo.com/en-gb/our-products/company-information/national-products.

CHAPTER 2
How to develop your idea...and 5 market research exercises

To find global data, including the USA and Asia Pacific, consider using the *Orbis, Amadeus, Osiris* or *Mint Global* databases: http://www.bvdinfo.com/en-gb/our-products/company-information/international-products and http://www.bvdinfo.com/en-gb/our-products/company-information/international-products.

COBRA provides thousands of business guides, factsheets and reports, http://cobra.cobwebinfo.com/.

IBISWorld provides market research data, business and industry reports, http://www.ibisworld.co.uk/.
Key Note is a leading business intelligence company, https://www.keynote.co.uk/.

MarketLine Advantage profiles major companies, industries and regions, http://marketline.com/.

Analysis tools for businesses: PESTLE and SWOT exercises

PESTLE analysis
External factors beyond your control can have a big impact on your business. Products should evolve as customer demands and preferences change, but also as the business environment changes. Larger companies will make sure they have staff, (often people like me) to do research and analysis to make sure they are aware of and prepared for impending challenges, but there is no reason why small businesses can't take precautions too!
The *PESTLE* acronym covers 6 types of external factor that you should consider and stands for - *Political, Economic, Social, Technological, Legal and Environmental.*
You may wonder how these factors might affect you, but at any time your customers' ability to buy from you might be affected as a result of changes in the landscape in any of these 6 areas. Changes of government can mean changes to the laws which affect business operations. *Technological* advances can have a big impact on businesses, so watch out for new trends. These may result in software needing to be modified or updated in order to keep pace with, or to take advantage of changes, or to comply with new laws.

Changes can affect businesses significantly - every time Google, Amazon or Facebook change their algorithms or policies, companies of all sizes scramble to adapt and restore the status quo. Businesses must also pay attention to *legal* requirements and compliance with rules and regulations. See Chapter 6 for more information about the regulations that you may need to consider.

Using Google to carry out PESTLE research

You can't necessarily control external events, but keeping an eye on events and changes in the wider world *might* give you enough advance warning to take the necessary precautions. To make sure you're aware of any important factors or changes that will affect the market you're interested in, run some Google searches in the following areas and select the variation(s) that you are most interested in:
- "Compliance" or "legislation" or "law" or "regulations" + [your area of interest]
- "Technological advances" or "technological trends" or "latest technologies" or "new technologies" + [your area of interest]
- "Economy" + [your area of interest]
- "Growth industry" or "growth market" or "growth sector" + [your area of interest] and "industry decline" or "market decline" or "sector decline" [your area of interest]
- "Demographics" or "statistics" or "trends" or "data" + [the current or previous year] + [your area of interest].

You can see where I'm going with this. These keyword combinations will retrieve useful information, but you can experiment with other phrases too.

Project pitfall

Any developers that you hire will be counting on you to provide them with the correct information relating to any rules, regulations and legislation that must be adhered to when building your software and running your business.

Make sure you do your research in this area well in advance! In Chapter 6 we'll look at some of the rules and legislation which may apply to your business.

CHAPTER 2
How to develop your idea...and 5 market research exercises

SWOT analysis

Another quick but effective tool you can use for assessments or decision making is the *SWOT analysis*. Grab a sheet of paper and write down the *Strengths, Weaknesses, Opportunities and Threats* (SWOT) associated with the topic you wish to review and then assess the positive and negative factors associated with it.

SWOT analyses can be used to review:
- A product or service
- Your own skills and abilities
- Your idea(s)
- Different competitors
- Different customer groups or markets

They can also be used to make comparisons. When you do your SWOT analysis, remember to include any new information you have gathered whilst reading this chapter.

An example
Strengths might include receiving consistent positive feedback about your product, or product idea and its features.
A lack of experience in the car gaming industry might be classed as a *weakness*.
An *opportunity* could be that you've discovered a gap in the market that you believe your product could fill.
A *Threat* might be a limited budget to build your software, or discovering that an existing player has also identified the gap and will be developing or upgrading a product to meet the demand.
If you get your keywords right, *Google Alerts* can be great for notifying you about opportunities and threats. You could even monitor competitors by name!

CHAPTER 2
How to develop your idea...and 5 market research exercises

Fig 11. SWOT analysis table. https://commons.wikimedia.org/wiki/File:SWOT_en.svg, Xhienne

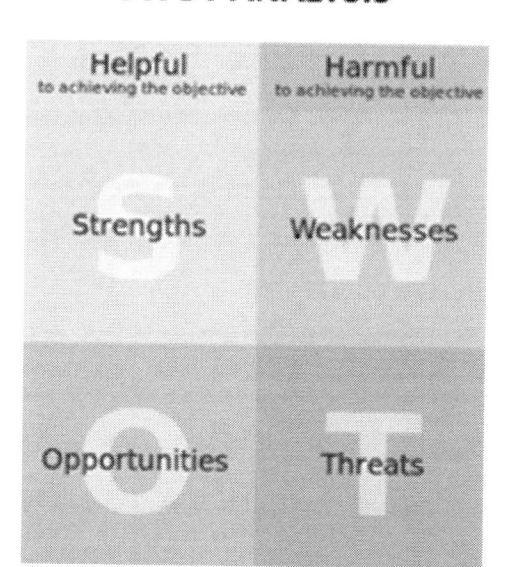

SWOT ANALYSIS

	Helpful to achieving the objective	Harmful to achieving the objective
	Strengths	Weaknesses
	Opportunities	Threats

Comparing SWOT analyses for different ideas can provide insights you might not otherwise have had. Dig into this further - some weaknesses or threats may make an idea a non-starter, so you'll need to think about:
- Your ability to deliver a quality product
- The resources you have to get your product out to the market quickly (financial, or otherwise.)
- Whether your opportunities outweigh your threats
- Whether weaknesses can be overcome
- Whether there are enough strengths to make your venture worthwhile
- How your strengths can be maximised

Creating a business plan

Consider writing a business plan if you haven't done so already! If you're planning to go to the bank for a loan, expect to be asked to produce one.
In contrast with traditional business plans, the *Lean Canvas* and *Lean business model canvas* are quite interesting and thought-provoking documents to complete. They're short and to the point, yet contain enough detail to help you understand how you will build a successful business around your product. I've included several of the "lean" style of business plan here. I've worked on them

CHAPTER 2
How to develop your idea...and 5 market research exercises

with clients and for my own ventures and I think they're brilliant. The bank may still require a traditional plan, but you can transfer the information you've gathered into one later if you need to.

- Business model canvas; https://strategyzer.com/canvas/business-model-canvas?url=canvas/bmc
- Lean canvas; http://3daystartup.org/wp-content/uploads/2014/04/lean-canvas.jpg
- Business model canvas; http://www.witszen.com/wp-content/uploads/2013/05/Business-Model-Canvas.png

In the next chapter, I'll explain how to go beyond the figures that the keyword and business intelligence tools provide and gather insights directly from "real" people.

Get them done and check them off! Chapter 2 challenges:

- ☐ If you weren't ready or able to complete the market research exercises, set yourself a reminder to come back to them.
- ☐ Create at least 1 "lean" business plan. Give them a try - they'll really get you thinking.
- ☐ Reflect on what you've learned in this chapter. What conclusions can you draw and what action(s) will you take as a result?
- ☐ Commit to trying to think like a scientist and consistently seek data and evidence to confirm that all is really as it seems. Does your idea need to be adapted in any way(s) to make it more useful, or relevant? How?
- ☐ Note the action(s) you'd like to take, based on the market research that you've done during this chapter and set due dates for them.

Everything you've learned will be wasted knowledge if you don't follow up! Download the entire set of chapter challenges for this book in the form of a work book, with an activity log to help you keep track of important tasks:

http://www.mylanderpages.com/donthireasoftwaredeveloperuntilyoureadthisbook/Free-resource-1

CHAPTER 2
How to develop your idea...and 5 market research exercises

CHAPTER 3
Creating customer profiles, and your first customer interviews

"The more you engage with customers, the clearer things become and the easier it is to determine what you should be doing."
- John Russell, former VP, Harley-Davidson Europe

In this chapter:
- Identifying your target customers
- Customer profile creation exercise
- Finding customers to help you validate your idea
- Top 10 do's and don'ts for running customer interviews
- Sample customer interview questions
- Free resources
- Chapter challenges

In the previous chapter, we talked about approaching the development of your product like a scientific experiment. You can advance forwards, or stop to make corrections based on what you've learned, and use data and evidence to help shape your ideas. Now, we're going to look at how to gather data that will identify the right customers for your product and help you understand what their priorities are.

Creating customer profiles

When developing a product, creating profiles that represent your target customers is a beneficial exercise, whether you're planning to serve consumers or other businesses.

You may have come across avatars before - they are usually cartoon-style representations of people. *Customer avatars* (a.k.a. *customer profiles* or *customer personas*) may be paired with a written profile to help you visualise your *target customer*. This is a person that you have identified as being *most likely* to buy from you. Your target customer has *exactly* the type of problem(s) that you can solve and their wants and needs fit well with your product. Your *target market* is a broader group of potential customers. Imagine looking at a huge crowd (your target market) from a distance through a telescope, and then zooming in on one individual (your target customer.) It's much easier to try and understand one person's needs than it is to focus on a multitude of people at once. Another common term for people who might buy from you is *prospects*.

CHAPTER 3
Creating customer profiles, and your first customer interviews

Here are some examples from *YouGov*, an international market research firm. Note how they combine the image of the avatar with written details to create the overall customer profile. They have a fantastic profiling tool, https://yougov.co.uk/profileslite#/ which looks at audience profiles across different companies. Here are some YouGov profiles for readers of *The Independent* and for *Instagram* customers:

Fig 12. YouGov customer profile for customers of *The Independent* newspaper.

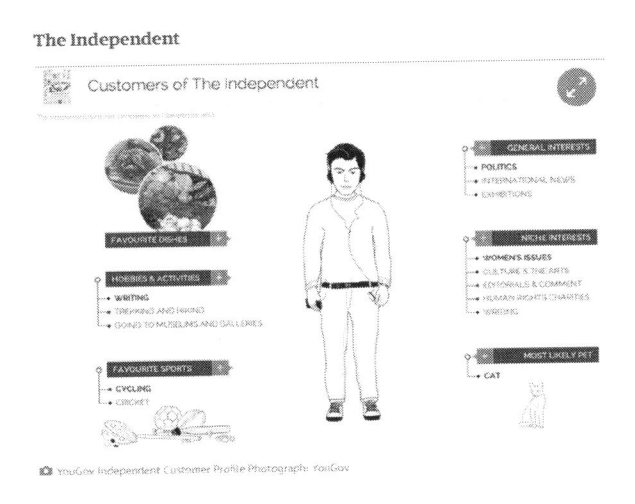

Fig 13. YouGov customer profile for Instagram customers.

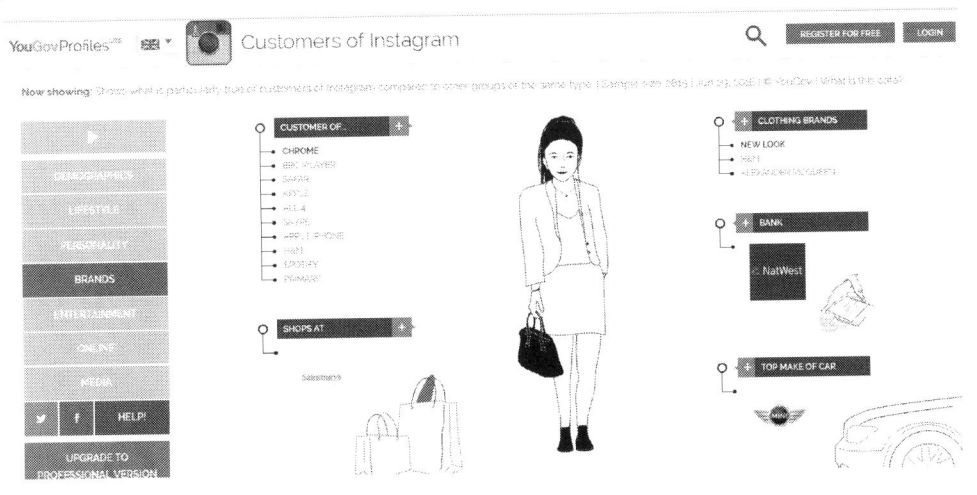

Companies pay agencies thousands of pounds to create customer avatars for them, because they create a focal point which helps them hone their products. You have an opportunity to get these benefits free of charge!

CHAPTER 3
Creating customer profiles, and your first customer interviews

A strong customer profile will help you focus on the types of people that you need to serve and communicate with to build your business. The insights you gain will make it worth the effort.

Consumer classification tools

You may find it helpful to approach this activity from several angles. There are companies that analyse and segment consumer populations and help businesses understand how to "speak" to their audiences in the right ways via marketing and advertising. They achieve this by providing *consumer classification* data.
US and general classifications:
http://www.strategicbusinessinsights.com/vals/ustypes.shtml
UK focused classifications: http://acorn.caci.co.uk/downloads/Acorn-User-guide.pdf

Consider the classifications that both these links identify and use them as inspiration as you create your own customer profile(s). As you look through them, you may be drawn to certain descriptions or may recognise that your target customer comes from a group that has already been "classified." If this is the case, there may be a wealth of information about that group online that you can use to augment your knowledge. Look for research, statistics and trends, news articles, blogs and academic papers as a starting point. Use the Google search tricks from Chapter 2 to do some advanced searching and to set yourself alerts.

Customer profile creation exercise

Now it's your turn! There are a few things to note before you start:
- You can create profiles for multiple avatars. If this feels like the right thing to do, create them, take a careful look at them all, decide which ones feel like the *best fit* for your product and focus on those.
- If anyone you've spoken to so far has been enthusiastic about your product idea (especially if they say they would consider buying it), capture as much information as possible about their hobbies, habits, and lifestyle and consider using them as one of your avatars, at least until you have reason to believe that there are other profiles that would be more suitable.
- Use the YouGov profiler tool to search for products or brands close to your vision of your own product and see what you can learn! Remember

CHAPTER 3
Creating customer profiles, and your first customer interviews

that everyone lives within a context. What customers are doing when they *aren't* using your product also matters. *Learning about their preferences and the products and services that they like to use could have a bearing on* how you present and position your own product.

Now start to imagine the type of customer that you wish to attract. Really try and see them in your mind's eye. Don't be shy - let's get into the spirit of this!

Fig 14. Customer profile form.

Review the forms below and complete the relevant parts:

Full name of avatar	Create a realistic name for your avatar which you feel suits their personality.
Gender	Could your avatar be of any gender or are you targeting a specific gender group? Does any particular gender feel like a better fit for your product?
Age	How old are they? State a precise age. Your target market will have an *age range*; your target customer should have an *age*.
Family / Relationship status	Are they single, married or cohabiting? Do they have children? If so, how many and how old are they? Depending on what your product is, even the gender of their children could be important.
Education	Did they finish school? Attend college or university? Do they have a degree or more advanced level of education such as a master's degree or Doctorate?
Occupation	What do they do for a living? Are they "blue collar" workers, elite professionals or somewhere in between?
Job title	This will be useful if you're planning to create a B2B (business to business) product rather than one for consumers (B2C) and want to target

CHAPTER 3
Creating customer profiles, and your first customer interviews

	specific people such as HR Managers, CEO's or Marketing Directors.
Annual income	How much do they earn and how much disposable income do they have available to spend on products and services like yours? Are they looking for budget products, mid-range or luxury ones?
Home life	Where in the world does your avatar live? Do they live in an urban area, in a commuter town or out in the countryside? What kind of neighbourhood do they live in? Do they rent or own their own home?
Hobbies, groups, community activities and memberships	What do they do in their free time? Do they have any hobbies, or belong to any online, or offline groups, clubs or societies? (Once you know this, you'll have a much better idea of where to find your target customers, where to advertise or market your product and where to go when you need to gather feedback on your idea or product.)
Favourite newspapers and magazines	Which newspapers and magazines do they read? Is this done on or offline? (If you're considering paying for ads in newspapers, this information could be very useful. News publications know their reader demographics, so ask for their reader statistics before you pay for advertising space.)
Favourite websites	Where can they be found online? Which social media platforms do they use? (This will give you an idea of where to find your target group, where to advertise or market your product and where to find people to help with market research and product testing.)
You might also wish to consider the following:	
Vehicle	Does your target customer own a car? Ride a scooter or a bicycle? What make and model? How many vehicles do they own?

CHAPTER 3
Creating customer profiles, and your first customer interviews

Industry sector	This may be relevant if your customers will be other businesses.
Company size	If you are looking to sell to businesses, what size of business are you targeting?

The inner world of your target customer

Let's spend a little time thinking about your target customer's inner world. This is another exercise to help you get "in tune" with your customer's problems, and how they think and feel.

Fig 15. The inner world of your target customer.

What are your avatar's problems, frustrations and challenges?	
What are their fears and concerns? What, if anything troubles them?	
What benefits are they hoping to receive?	
What are their hopes, goals and aspirations?	
How well does your product fit into this picture? *Does your product idea need to be adapted to better suit the target market?* *Or is there a target market that would better suit your product?* If you've had any a-ha moments, that's excellent! Please write them down.	

You can download a copy of this form and the customer profile form, with space to add your own avatars' details at:

http://www.mylanderpages.com/donthireasoftwaredeveloperuntilyoureadthisbook/5-customer-profile-avatar

CHAPTER 3
Creating customer profiles, and your first customer interviews

Creating an avatar to represent your target customer

Here are some examples of avatars that can be used to represent consumers or business customers:

Fig 16. Freepik avatar creator tools. Male avatar creator.

http://www.freepik.com/free-vector/male-avatar-creator_822151.htm

Fig 17. Freepik avatar creator tools. Female avatar creator.

http://www.freepik.com/free-vector/woman-avatar-creator_824042.htm

CHAPTER 3
Creating customer profiles, and your first customer interviews

Fig 18. Freepik avatar creator tools. Business team avatar examples.

http://www.freepik.com/free-vector/business-team-avatar-collection_874660.htm

You can choose a cartoon-style avatar as seen in the Freepik designs, but you can also use an image that you feel represents your target customer, or even do a hand drawing.

Practical applications

You should now have version 1 of an avatar and customer profile to work with!

Understanding what they want, value and hope for will help you to create a product well-suited to their needs and an effective and targeted marketing plan in the future.

Now, you can start making decisions that take your avatar(s) into account, including shaping the way your product evolves. This might feel a bit odd at first, but thinking like this will allow you to make some very clear decisions about what is and isn't right for your target customer(s). You can ask yourself:

- "How would my avatar, [insert avatar name] feel about this? What would they expect?"
- "How would my avatar like to perform this task?"
- "How could my product make life easier and more convenient for my avatar?"
- "What part(s) of my product will my avatar value the most?"

- "How could I make using my product a more enjoyable experience for my avatar?"
- Would my avatar like this social media post?

Continue to update your customer profile(s) as you learn more about your target customer(s). They should evolve over time. This is just the beginning!

Remember that you're testing theories...

Remember to consider everything you *think* you know about your customers to be a theory or assumption until you have enough evidence to be sure. The earlier you find out that things may not be as they first appeared, the easier it will be to adjust your plans and make your product into what it needs to be. Stop and reflect, then work out what to do next. You may need to make some adjustments, or abandon certain plans altogether. This could be disappointing, but it isn't a failure - you could have lost time and money in pursuing the wrong type of customer or building the wrong type of product. Agile and Lean principles support the concept of "failing fast", then making adjustments based on what has been learned, and trying again. This is what entrepreneurs do!

Finding target customers to interview

Evaluating an idea or product using customer interviews or user testing sessions can cost as much as several thousand pounds *per session,* if set up by professional *recruitment* or *market research agencies.*

These agencies will find people from your target market that are willing to be interviewed. Some agencies will run the tests for you, others will expect you to run them yourself.

This may or may not include venue hire costs (if you would like a venue to be provided for the testing sessions) plus an incentive payment ranging from between £30-100 for each person that is interviewed as payment for their time.

If you don't have the budget to hire a specialist company, then you'll need to find your own participants and run your own interviews.

Now you've gone through the avatar creation process you'll have a list of possible places where your target customers might be found, including membership groups and profiles on social media sites. At the time of writing, these were the most popular social media sites in the US and UK:

- Facebook
- YouTube

CHAPTER 3
Creating customer profiles, and your first customer interviews

- Twitter
- LinkedIn
- Instagram
- Pinterest
- Google+
- Snapchat
- Tumblr
- Reddit
- Flickr
- Meetup.com

If you know of any specialist membership sites, forums or groups that might be relevant, try those too. If not, try Googling for "top membership sites, forums or groups" and add your area of interest.

Ease into the task of finding people to interview by starting with friends and family and asking for introductions to *their* friends and family. Consider attending networking groups and events where you can speak to people who may be in your target market face-to-face. Meetup.com https://www.meetup.com/ and Eventbrite, https://www.eventbrite.com/ may be able to help you find local events in your area, regardless of where you're based.

When reaching out to people you know, or have been connected with:
Create social media posts, let people know what you need and ask them to share your messages.

When people respond, try and get at least some face-to-face interviews arranged if you can - it will be easier to build rapport in person and you will be able to observe people's facial expressions and body language as you talk to them about your product idea. You could offer to treat people to a beverage or lunch when you ask for their time.

When reaching out to people you don't know:
Try joining relevant groups on each social media platform that you use. Post within the group, and if possible drop people in the groups short messages which are relevant to them, using their name if possible, so your communication doesn't feel impersonal and generic. Explain who you are and what assistance you're looking for. If there is anything you can exchange in return for their time and effort, let them know that too. Some people will be willing to help; others

will want to know how getting involved will benefit *them.* Not everyone will have the time or even the interest in helping, but from a statistical perspective, the more people you ask, the more will say yes!

This article contains some useful tips for reaching out to people online: https://www.linkedin.com/pulse/20130624114114-69244073-6-ways-to-get-me-to-email-you-back.

Ask people how they'd prefer to be contacted and try to be as flexible as possible. Be prepared to make contact via phone, Skype, Google Hangouts or using other methods.

What should you ask your target customers?

Gather as much data as possible, so you can refine your product idea or *proposition* (your proposed solution to the problem) through:

- Understanding more about their needs and problems.
- Learning whether the target customers you identified *really are* your ideal customers - are your avatar(s) accurate or not?
- Discussing *how* you might solve the problem (if you already have an idea of how the product might work.)
- Looking for trends - specific likes and dislikes, and any commonalities. What do people strongly agree or disagree about?
- Testing the waters to see if people would pay for the product. If so, how much and if no, why not? Under what circumstances *would* they pay for it?

It's not just what you ask, but how you ask it...

Training as a coach and working as a market researcher forced me to work on getting rid of some of these commonplace habits. Do your best to avoid them when you're interviewing, and you'll get much better-quality responses.

Here are my top 10 do's and don'ts when running customer interviews, testing prototypes and standard user tests:

- **DO be organised.** Have a notepad to hand or ask for permission to record the conversation. Listening to recordings will also help you improve your interview technique. Prepare a set of questions to ask in the form of a script. Ideally you should be consistent, asking *every customer the same* *set of questions* so you can compare them more easily later. However, changing the *order* of questions can be beneficial to the interview process. Do a few interviews, see what works, then update and reorder your script if needed. Run through any exercises and questions you've prepared a few times to check for issues before your first interview and read your script out loud too - interestingly, you'll pick up on different issues via your auditory sense than you will just by reading it.

- **DO put people at ease before you start.** Explain there are no right or wrong answers and that you would appreciate their honest opinions and feedback. (When testing a prototype or product, assure them that you are testing *it*, and not them!) Ask some warm-up questions; a summary of who they are and their occupation can be a good way to start. Ask them how they are or how their day was, then recap on why you're speaking to them. Don't tell them *exactly* why until the end, otherwise you risk introducing *interview bias*. This happens when an interviewee says what they *think* you want to hear to please you, or to avoid offending you. That would count as a *false positive*.
- **DO be prepared to repeat yourself.** Let people know that they should ask you to repeat any questions that they feel are unclear.
- **DO ask open questions...and ask for full explanations.** There's nowhere left to go if someone responds with a "no," so ask *open questions* and start your sentences with *Who, What, When, Which, Where, How* and *Why* and not "Do you?", as this can close conversations down quite quickly. Other good questions include, "How often do you...?", "When was the last time you...?", "What made you say that?", "How does that work?", "Can you tell me about...?"
- **DO be encouraging.** Keep saying things, like "Uh-huh", "Keep going", "Tell me more." This is especially important if you're on the phone, to confirm that you're listening and are still there! If people don't explain the reason for their comments, ask "What makes you say that?" or "How come?" to prompt them to go into more detail.
- **DON'T lead people.** *This is very important.* Saying things like "Would you like a [your product]?" and "Would you pay £4.99 for an app that does [whatever your product does]?" are pushing someone in the direction you want them to go in. You could end up with false positives if you lead people to the answers you want. You want to know what they would *really* do and what they *honestly* think.
- **DON'T fill the silence.** Ask a question...*and then stay quiet!* Don't try and fill in the silence by asking another question, or ten! If you know anyone

who has a habit of asking many questions on top of each other, I'm sure you'll agree that it can be a bit maddening after a while, *so give each person space and time to think.* If you ask multiple questions at once you'll break their concentration, which disrupts the process. Silence may make you feel a little nervous, but over time you'll feel less self-conscious about it. *Nothing fatal happens during a silence and some great insights can come during those moments.*

- **DON'T fire questions at people - or interrupt them.** Don't direct questions at people like machine gun fire, or make them feel like they're on trial and facing a prosecuting lawyer! Create a calm atmosphere, listen carefully and don't interrupt! If another question pops into your mind, write it down so it doesn't distract you and get back to listening, otherwise you might miss something important.
- **DO push for negative feedback.** Always ask what people *don't* like, what isn't clear and what's annoying or confusing. You want to find out as many negatives about your proposition as possible, *before* you invest in building a product and to allow you to make essential adjustments.
- **DO make it a positive experience.** As the product develops you will need regular feedback to stay on track. Try to make the interview experience as pleasant, professional and interesting as possible so people are happy to talk to you again in future when you have more to discuss or show to them.

Running customer interviews

To begin, create a set of interview questions to help you gather *information* and *evidence*. Shall we start with a few examples?

A customer interview about computer games
The benefits of games and the problems they solve include alleviating boredom, escapism, relaxation (or stimulation) and social contact and a sense of belonging in the case of team games. These are my *hypotheses* on why people play games. Now I'll need to prove them *and* decide how the things I learn should shape my product development decisions.

When starting the interview:
Take down the person's details - name, age (or age bracket), job title and details of hobbies and websites visited regularly to help you build up a picture of each

customer. Compare these with your avatar and customer profile. What do you learn?

Begin with some general questions about the problem that your product solves as a "warm up." It would probably be inappropriate to ask people directly whether they play games for escapism or social contact, but you could ask how people spend their free time and when they play games and expand the conversation from there.

Ask about people's daily schedules - do they drive or take public transport to and from work? How do they spend their time during the commute? When they get home, what happens? If they try to relax and wind down, how do they do this? What hobbies and activities do they pursue after work and at weekends? Find out where gaming fits into their life currently.

In this example, you're looking to identify all the free time and windows of opportunity for playing games and how long each window lasts, because you want to know *how much time people have to play* your game and to understand their *current gaming habits*. There's no point creating an immersive game that needs an hour to complete if your target customers have just 15 minutes of free time here and there throughout the week and don't have much time to play at weekends.

Next, ask them to tell you about *the last time* they played a computer game. Asking about the last time that a user performed an activity is a question used by professional researchers. It's a great question because the answers you receive should be purely based on fact and what people really *have done,* rather than what they *might do*.

Topic of discussion	Sample questions
Regular habits	*How many* games did they play in a row? Which day of the week did they play? Find out if this is the norm, or not. What time of day was it? Find out if this is the norm, or not. *How often* do they play during the week? What about at weekends? *How long* do they play for?

CHAPTER 3
Creating customer profiles, and your first customer interviews

Preferred devices	Which device did they use to play the game? Do they play on any other devices? Which, if any, is their preferred device and why?
Specific questions about the game	What type of game was it? What happened? What was the result of the game? (Win, loss, draw, level reached etc.) Which options and settings available within the game did they use? Ask them to tell you all the ones they use on a regular basis. This may lead to you gathering other information on the topic.
Preferences, motivations and competitor research	What do they like about gaming in general? What are the pros and cons of the games that they play? What are their *favourite* types of games? Why do they like those games? What do they like the least about them? What do they find most annoying or frustrating? What is most important to them about these games?
Further exploration	If people can show you their games and walk you through how they play them, and their strategies, even better - this exercise is also about understanding the mindset, motivations and inner world of the person you're speaking to.
Gathering feedback about your own idea	If you're ready to do so, talk about your idea directly or indirectly and note the reactions of the person you are interviewing. Ask them to tell you what they like and dislike about the idea and why.

These questions can be adjusted to suit most topics, just insert your area of interest.
Of course, products can be very different, so here's a second example:

CHAPTER 3
Creating customer profiles, and your first customer interviews

A customer interview about a mobile app for scanning documents
Here's another example. If you wanted to create a document scanning mobile app, which allows the user to take pictures of documents with their phone and then share, upload or email them, you might start out by asking people what kinds of documents they receive and where they come from. From here, discuss each item they mention in turn, gathering as much information as you can.

You might also ask how they manage physical paperwork at home, how many letters they get each week, what types of letters they get, what they do with them and where they keep them. You'd explore what annoys or frustrates them about managing post and documents and investigate if there is anything time consuming about doing this.

Then you might ask about *the last* set of paper documents they received, what happened and how they dealt with them, what was complicated about the situation, how they solved the problem and what would have made the situation easier for them - take down the names of any products they mention, so you can investigate any competitors. Ask for an opinion about these products and note down their strengths and weaknesses.

If you are ready to do so, talk about your idea directly or indirectly and note the reactions of the person you are interviewing. Ask them to tell you what they like and dislike about the idea and why. Note down all the ideas and suggestions that come up.

Note the words people use when they converse with you and stay alert for any slang or jargon used. As well as helping you to learn more about your customers, this information will be useful for marketing later. Use terminology that your target market is familiar with to grab their attention.

Log and analyse your feedback
There's a simple analysis technique you can use to review all the feedback received, called Plus, Minus, Interesting, which I've adapted into an easy to use record sheet. You can download a copy of the Plus, Minus, Interesting (PMI) log:

http://www.mylanderpages.com/donthireasoftwaredeveloperuntilyoureadthisbook/Free-resource-3-pmi-log

Fill in each column as follows:
Plus. Note down all positive feedback and expressions of interest. Strong positive feedback would include comments like: "I really like it!" "That would be useful, because…", "How much would you charge for this?" and "When can I get it?"

CHAPTER 3
Creating customer profiles, and your first customer interviews

Minus. Write down all negative feedback or signs of disinterest in the product idea. If people say the idea would *not* be useful or solve their problem and if they dislike *the way* you propose to solve the problem, note this down.

Interesting! Note down any surprising feedback or information. This could relate to how people would like to use the product, insights gained or new ideas and suggestions that you receive. What do people value or get most excited about? Which devices do they prefer, mobile or desktop? *How* do they want to use the product? Also, note down the other products mentioned and any other information you gain from them, both good and bad.

General notes. If you wish to create a product for businesses, note the industry sector, number of employees, turnover and age of the company. Note down what people say word for word and even the phrases they use. This is all excellent information to help you understand your customers. Keep a record of who seemed most interested in the idea and their age, gender and other things you know about them, so you can start to build up a profile of what type of person (or business) likes your product the most.

Get them done and check them off! Chapter 3 challenges:

- [ ] Download a copy of the customer profile and customer inner world forms and complete them. Create your customer avatar(s) and customer profile(s).
- [ ] Prepare yourself mentally for all types of feedback. How will you manage less positive feedback or suggestions, yet remain motivated, and open-minded enough to take away useful information?
- [ ] Create a plan for yourself and start doing customer interviews, so you can gather feedback about the product and test out the theories about your target market and avatar(s). Create a list of people you will interview, starting with people you know and decide if you will reach out to others via social media or other channels that you have identified.
- [ ] Evaluate the feedback you've gathered. What have you learned?
- [ ] What "a-ha" moments have come from reviewing all the data in your PMI log? (Get a copy of the log via the download link provided earlier in the chapter.)
- [ ] What customer problems have you identified? How will you use this information?
- [ ] Do you need to adjust your idea to make it fit in more with customers' needs?
- [ ] Store all this information. Some of it may need to be turned into requirements and discussed with your developer later. Perhaps you could create a business research folder to hold your data...

CHAPTER 3
Creating customer profiles, and your first customer interviews

- ☐ Update your avatar(s) as you learn more about how your market thinks and feels.
- ☐ Write down the actions you need to take based on feedback from your customer interviews.

Download the entire set of chapter challenges for this book in the form of a work book, with an activity log to help you keep track of important tasks:

http://www.mylanderpages.com/donthireasoftwaredeveloperuntilyoureadthisbook/Free-resource-1

SECTION 2
TECHNICAL AND SOFTWARE DELIVERY BASICS

CHAPTER 4
An introduction to Agile principles

"Agile means…to be nimble and adaptable. To embrace change and become masters of change, to compete through adaptability by being able to change faster and cheaper than your competition can."
- Craig Larman, author and co-creator of LeSS (Large Scale Scrum)

In this chapter:
- An overview of the Agile philosophy
- User stories and product backlogs
- The software development life-cycle; and a few sports analogies!
- Why Agile is a great framework for startups and entrepreneurs
- The benefits of hiring developers with quality Agile experience
- Chapter challenges

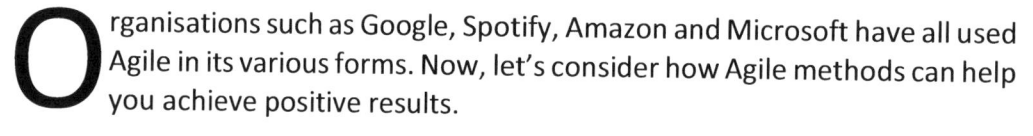

Organisations such as Google, Spotify, Amazon and Microsoft have all used Agile in its various forms. Now, let's consider how Agile methods can help you achieve positive results.

Agile teams believe that:
Focusing on delivering value for customers,
Seeking feedback and making incremental improvements,
Taking time to reflect on what works and what doesn't,
Controlling the duration of tasks and activities,
Maintaining effective team communication and
Keeping things simple, all increase the chances of projects succeeding.

Agile is actually an umbrella term, the Agile family includes XP (eXtreme Programming), Scrum, Kanban, Lean and DSDM (Dynamic Systems Development Method) frameworks. It is usually contrasted with Waterfall, a more traditional software development methodology.

Agile frameworks emerged from a desire to overcome some of the issues known to plague "traditional" software development projects - long wait times for software to be delivered to customers, a lack of flexibility from the customer

CHAPTER 4
An introduction to Agile principles

paying for the software or the technical teams delivering the software and unsustainable working practices.

The Agile mindset reflects a more pragmatic approach to building software *in the real world*. There is an acceptance that we will always have the *least* amount of knowledge at the start of a project. However, over time we will learn more about what our product should become - which could be very different from the original vision! Making adjustments as we learn requires change, and Agile allows us to manage this flexibly *and* efficiently.

There is an *Agile Manifesto* (see the link at the end of this chapter) that focuses on *putting people, customer interaction* and *communication* first.

Timeboxing is a time management tool used regularly in Agile teams to keep tasks, meetings and non-development activities focused. Agile makes use of *timeboxed,* recurring development cycles called *iterations* (meaning "to repeat"), which usually last anything from a week to 30 days before they end and then begin again. At the end of each iteration there is an expected output from the development team, which was defined at the start of the iteration. Agilists believe in making frequent releases of software (a mantra usually referred to as "release early, release often.")

The terms "to iterate," or "iterate over" are used to describe the process of improving *something* (in our case, a product, or idea) in stages. Agile teams add functionality *incrementally*, over a period of time to enhance or extend software applications. This is in contrast with the *"big bang"* style of release associated with Waterfall, where a large amount of functionality, usually built over a longer time period is delivered all at once.

There is often some degree of "learning on the job" that goes on in development projects - especially if the type of product or the technologies being used are unfamiliar. This is normal, but the balance should be more towards coding than learning, most of the time. Agile teams use *development spikes* (which are timeboxed technical investigations), to gather information so that decision can be made, or to undertake research that answers questions such as: "Can we do it?", "Should we do it?" and "*How* should we do it?"

See Chapters 20 and 21 for more about using timeboxing to help you manage your project.

CHAPTER 4
An introduction to Agile principles

XP, Scrum, Kanban, Waterfall?

I agree, the names are a bit unusual. Allow me to cut through all the jargon!

I wholeheartedly believe in using Agile principles to guide the software delivery process, and I have followed Scrum, Scrumban (a Scrum/Kanban hybrid), Kanban and XP practices throughout my software delivery career. Agile is ideal for the fast changing, "suck and see" world of entrepreneurship. It is well-suited to environments that are unpredictable or uncertain, markets which are competitive, those where change happens very rapidly or where there is fast growth.

I'll explain, (and demonstrate) how to create a simple software development process based on Agile principles in Chapter 22, so that you can get off to a solid start when you begin to build your product.

Each member of the Agile family has its own set of practices. Let's look at each in turn:

Scrum's repeating development cycles are called *sprints. These are* usually 2 or 4-week release cycles, where the team *prepares and then builds a defined set of functionality* pulled from a product to-do list called a *product backlog.* This is a prioritised set of requirements and tasks, and includes user stories, features, requirements, enhancements, technical tasks and bugs. The order of items can be changed and work can be prioritised and de-prioritised. We'll talk about capturing requirements for your backlog in Chapters 11, 14 and 22, and I'll explain what user stories are later in this chapter.

At the end of the sprint cycle, the team demonstrates the work to their customers. The team then reflects on the highs and lows during the sprint and brainstorms ways to make improvements for the next one. The cycle then starts again.

Scrum has four "ceremonies", *sprint planning meetings, daily scrums (*often called *stand-up meetings), sprint review meetings, and sprint retrospective meetings (*commonly known as *retros).* Stand-up meetings are daily micro-meetings that focus on what has been done, what will be done and raising any issues that prevent or impede progress, known as *impediments,* or *blockers,* which we will discuss in Chapter 22.

CHAPTER 4
An introduction to Agile principles

There are several key *Scrum roles* including:

ScrumMaster, (this spelling is correct, but you'll see it spelled Scrum Master too) servant leaders who act as facilitators, sometimes perform project management duties, but always help the team operate efficiently and effectively and shield them from distractions.

Product Owner, those responsible for setting the vision of the product and the prioritisation of tasks on the *product backlog; the product to-do list*.

The Scrum team. The technical staff, (including developers) who work together to deliver the functionality.

It's important to be aware that there will be skill-gaps on a project with a small number of team members. If you understand what and where these gaps are, you'll have a far better chance of making sure that important tasks get done at the right times and aren't overlooked or forgotten.

For that reason, we'll review these roles and others in more detail in Chapter 5.

XP (short for eXtreme Programming), is known for the practice of *pair programming* This involves two developers working on a single task on a shared *computer,* writing code and solving problems together.) "Two heads are better than one," as the proverb goes! Followers of XP believe that together, developers will come up with better solutions than they would do alone and that quality will increase as the paired developers pick up on each other's mistakes. XP has iterations (not sprints), which usually last 1 or 2 weeks.

Kanban, which means "card" in Japanese, emerged from the working practices at the Toyota car manufacturing plants. It favours JIT, (Just In Time planning - not planning *too* far in advance due to the possibility of change) and setting limits on the number of tasks that each team member can have in their work queue, in order to control throughput and avoid bottlenecks in the software development production line. There is also a strong emphasis on eliminating waste, which includes factors such as how well the team passes tasks between members without creating time lags, and how disruption and distractions can be minimised within teams.

Scrumban is a hybrid of Kanban and Scrum, whilst **Lean,** like Kanban emerged from the manufacturing sector and places an emphasis on customer value and eliminating waste.

CHAPTER 4
An introduction to Agile principles

User stories and The Product Backlog

It can be challenging to explain what your requirements are - especially in great detail, but this is very important. *User stories* are used across all the Agile frameworks as a way of breaking down requirements into very small components that can be more easily understood, managed and built because they have been simplified as much as possible.

User stories are small, self-contained units, or "building blocks" of functionality. When added together and assembled, they result in a larger body of functionality, a system or a product.

User stories focus on the people that will use the software, who have specific roles or tasks to perform. These are our *users*. In the user story context, these are also called *actors,* and the user story should describe *what* the actor (or user) wants to do and *why*.

As long as user stories contain all the important elements and can be understood by your team, they can be written in any format, although some teams will use the GWT (Given-When-Then) approach to write them, which can make it easier for developers to translate each user story into code.

A common format for summarising, or describing user stories at a high-level is:
As a [insert type of customer / user / actor]
I want to be able to [insert the goal]
So that I can [insert the benefit]

This helps the person writing the story to think about who the functionality is for, what the functionality should do, and what the benefit is.

For example...
If you were building software to help media companies display content on their websites, one of the many user stories you would require would include one to allow articles to be published online. The story might be described something like this:

As a journalist
I want to be able to publish an article.
So that readers can view it on the website.

If you were to develop software for the construction industry, you might have a story like this one:

As a builder
I want to be able to search for a list of wholesalers by postcode.
So that I can find a wholesaler based close to my place of business, where I can buy building supplies.

This is just an overview of the stories, there is still a lot more detail that needs to be provided! User stories are kept on the product backlog, along with additional information about the functionality required for the story and how it should work.

For the purposes of this book, I will be focusing on clarifying the sorts of information you'll need to gather for your developer in order to save money and time during the build process, rather than focusing on the intricacies of user story writing and the use of specific guidelines and conventions. We'll keep all the benefits that come with creating good user stories, though!

In Chapter 14 we'll talk about the types of information that your developer will need from you and there's a reminder in Chapter 22 that you can use as your app is being built.

The Software Development Life Cycle (SDLC)

Software development has a life-cycle, and to stay on top of your project, you'll need to be aware of what stage of the cycle you're at, what needs to be done at each stage and why each stage is important. The basic elements of the cycle vary slightly in terms of terminology and where the cycle "officially" starts and ends, before it continues again, but it is generally the same regardless of whether you follow the Waterfall methodology, or Agile principles. What differs is how frequently the cycles repeat, the mindset of the team(s) involved and how they organise themselves and approach the way they build the software.

I'm going to talk you through the cycle. Look out for the jargon - as usual, it will be useful when you need to talk to developers or other technical people:

- **Concept.** This stage includes the birth of the initial idea, the exploratory work needed to decide whether the idea should be pursued and the development of the idea through customer interviews, market research and data analysis. (Some also call this the *Discovery* phase.) If you've read Chapters 2 and 3 - you'll recognise that you've worked through the concept stage already. Great news!

- **Requirements gathering and analysis** includes taking the initial concept and producing a set of *requirements* (the description of what the users of the software will need to be able to do, as well as the technical tasks that must be actioned if the software is to run reliably.) This stage involves mapping out the steps and processes involved in helping users get from "A to B" using your product, (these steps are called *user journeys*), and how the system will need to behave in different scenarios and under different conditions.
- **Design** looks at how the system needs to be *architected* to fulfil the requirements. It takes the components of the system; their structure and organisation and the flow of data within it into consideration. It also considers the hardware to support the product and the programming language(s) that might be used to build the product.
Strangely, the SDLC does not always explicitly mention the user experience (UX) and visual design elements of the process. This would include the creation of wireframes (which outline the layout of the screens that users will interact with), and the design of the product, so it is easy and pleasant to use. Colour schemes and other visual elements of the product's design will also need to be planned in advance of the build stage and handed over to those building the product, to be sure that they build it according to the visual design that has been prepared. See Chapters 5, 11 and 12 for more information on these topics.
- **Build** (also called the *development* or *coding* stage.) This involves writing code to fulfil the requirements gathered together during the requirements gathering and analysis stage, integration work; to ensure that all the functionality that is part of the product behaves as one cohesive unit and solving any technical problems related to this.
- **Test**. This covers the discovery of issues, faults and parts of the product that don't behave, or work together as intended. Testing also involves getting feedback from users via user testing, usability testing, user acceptance testing and beta testing. There are many different types of testing for different purposes and in Chapter 23, we'll review several these that you will need to be aware of. Testing is an *absolutely critical* part of the cycle which is often denied the respect and attention it deserves. The amount of testing you do and how thoroughly you do it can have a *significant impact on the quality of your product.*
- **Release**. *Releasing, going live, deploying, pushing to live* or *shipping* all mean the same thing - getting a public version of a product, or specific

CHAPTER 4
An introduction to Agile principles

functionality out to *customers* or *users*. Developers will also need to make *internal releases* so that functionality can be tested by the team.

- **Maintenance** happens after the initial project to create the software has come to an end. Once a product is live and being used by customers, it needs to be maintained to ensure that it continues to deliver service consistently and to a high standard. Things can go wrong or break and the technological landscape may even change, as we discussed in Chapter 2, so the period *after* building your initial product may be quite eventful too!

When you decide to build new functionality, or to update your product, the cycle will begin again.

According to the Waterfall methodology, the software development life cycle moves through the following stages one-by-one, in order, cascading down like a waterfall until the project is completed, however, Agile projects run through the analysis to release stages *in every single iteration.*

Fig 19. The Waterfall model. The concept stage marks the start of the project and the release stage marks the end, with maintenance following after. Each stage is completed only once within an entire project.

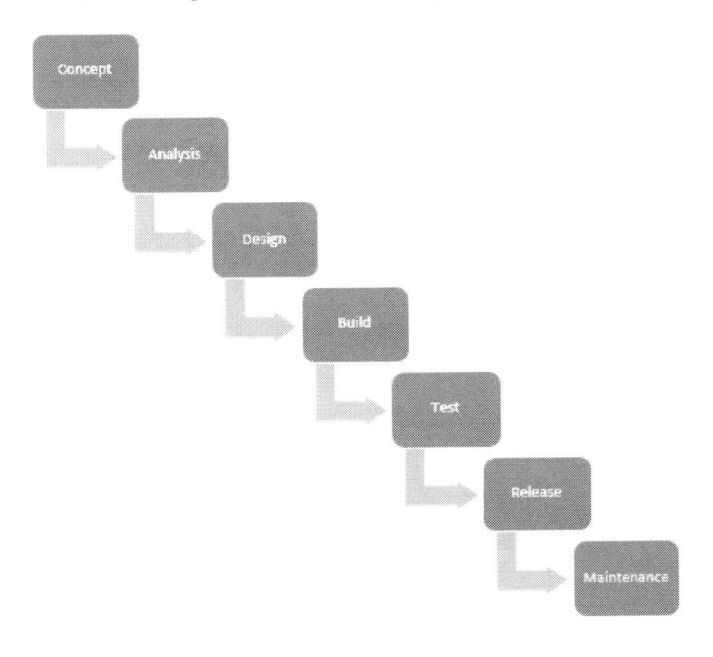

Fig 20. The Agile development cycle. A single iteration includes all the stages from requirements gathering and analysis to release.

CHAPTER 4
An introduction to Agile principles

https://upload.wikimedia.org/wikipedia/commons/5/50/Agile_Project_Management_by_Planbox.png. Aflafla1,Iterative development model V2.jpg,

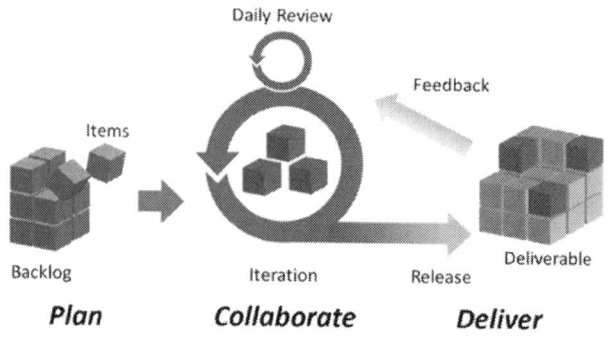

Agile Project Management: Iteration

The Agile cycle, and a few sports analogies!

Scrum is actually named after the Scrum formation in rugby. In Agile teams, professionals with a mix of different technical skills work together and operate as a single unit, instead of being grouped together based on their skills or working on only one stage of the project a time. The team constantly pass the ball (i.e. the software) back and forth to each other, and they attempt to score; (in other words, to make software releases) often during the course of a project. They do not cross the finish line once, like the Waterfall teams do. The Waterfall process is more like a relay race with the baton (the software), being passed between different stages and teams once and crossing the finish line just once during the project, with those whose tasks come towards the end of the race under pressure to make up any time lost by those who completed their parts of the project at an earlier stage!

Individuals on Agile teams can communicate easily and share their specialist knowledge with each other throughout the development cycle. There is a lot of activity happening at once, but the team members provide each other with feedback and take care not to cause delays for other team members. Agile teams are also *self-organising,* which means that teams are, in theory, motivated and able to make decisions about how they will manage themselves and their workload. See Chapters 18, 19, 21 and 22 for information about managing the development process.

CHAPTER 4
An introduction to Agile principles

Get them done and check them off! Chapter 4 challenges:

- ☐ Spend time getting to know your customers and confirming that your idea is viable *before* you consider hiring technical staff. Revisit Chapters 2 and 3, get your avatar(s), customer profile(s) and customer interview plan together and get as much clarity as you can first.
- ☐ If you're interested in learning more about Agile frameworks, you can find more resources here:

    - The Agile Manifesto. http://agilemanifesto.org/
    - Scrum Alliance. https://www.scrumalliance.org/
    - Agile Alliance. https://www.agilealliance.org/

Download the entire set of chapter challenges for this book, collated into a work book with an activity log to help you keep track of important tasks:

http://www.mylanderpages.com/donthireasoftwaredeveloperuntilyoureadthisbook/Free-resource-1

CHAPTER 5
How to identify the skill gaps in your team...and what to do about them

In this chapter:
- The roles that exist in software delivery teams
- Skills shortage assessment
- Project pitfalls

A few months ago, I heard about a woman without a technical background who had created a SaaS product (see Chapter 7 for more information about SaaS applications.) However, it had some quality problems. After listening to the story of how she got started and how the project had been set up, I wasn't surprised. She had one developer and had been hoping that he would direct her, rather than leading the project and knowing for herself what should be done (quite a challenge, I agree, as she had never done anything similar before.) She had also made limited provisions for technical testing. Creating code and manually testing software are two different job roles, using different sets of skills. Developers do not generally do manual testing as a key part of their work and there are very good reasons why code should *not* be tested by the person who created it! She had achieved an amazing feat, but was now playing catch up.

If you're not aware of the range of skills and expertise that go into creating a professional software product, you won't be able to cover all your bases. How will you know what activities should be happening on your project, why they should be happening and when?
You might manage for a while - until something that you weren't even aware you needed to do, or pay attention to, comes along and causes a problem.

In Chapter 4 we looked at Agile practices, the *software development cycle* and a lot of terms that will become useful. Now, let's look at the anatomy of a *software delivery team*. Who's involved? What specialist skills do they have? What duties do they usually perform which add value to a software project? Once we've done that, we'll review how to plug the gaps that will exist when you don't have the budget to hire a full team of professionals.

CHAPTER 5
How to identify the skill gaps in your team...and what to do about them

Common software delivery team roles

In alphabetical order:

Back-end developer. Back-end developers write code that works at the server or database level, rather than focusing on the user interaction and visual appeal of software or websites, which is the domain of front-end developers. Even if you're building a simple app, most require some form of database skill. A back-end developer's work might include capturing the information entered by a user on a web page and storing it in a database, and the retrieval of that data at a later date.

Business Analyst (BA). (Roles and responsibilities *may* be similar to a *Product Owner* or *Product Manager*). Business Analysts investigate business problems and assess the pros and cons of business activities using various techniques, setting out conclusions and recommendations on the best course(s) of action. Business analysts can have very different skill-sets, depending on whether they are wholly business focused, "crunch numbers" or are involved with computer systems.
Technical BA's often act as the "bridge" between the business and development functions of a company and will document *system* or *product requirements* in written and diagrammatic forms using process flows, diagrams, charts or tables and may write the *user stories* for the development team. They work closely with development teams, explaining what needs to be built in order for the project to achieve its goals and in some cases, keeping them supplied with work to do. They may also confirm that functionality is built according to their specifications, and often do a lot of client liaison work.

Content writer / technical copywriter / content editor. These professionals are skilled in producing content that attracts and resonates with customers. They also need to be able to write clear, simple instructions. This content might appear on a website, in the description of your app in an app store or inside the app itself; where any words, links, button text (such as "Back", "Next", "Search"), menu items or labels appear. The content writer is usually the person that writes the *help text* or *error messages* for your app that explain how to perform activities within the app, or warn customers that something has gone wrong or that they haven't entered the correct or required information, politely explaining what the customer should do about it. The copy is then passed to the developers to insert into the relevant places in your app. Content editors may also write the text that appears in the body of email messages intended for customers.

Client. (Dependent on the context, also possibly known as the customer or *sponsor*.) The client may be a sponsor; the person who "fronts the cash" to pay for a development project in an organisation or they may be an eventual user of the product themselves. Some clients ask for products to be built which they will sell on to *end-users*; the people who will actually use the software - this is probably your own situation! In this case, *you* are the client of the software delivery team and the *end-users* (the people who will use the software) will be *your* customers! The client (or a representative), should be available to clarify requirements, answer questions, test the product and provide input as it evolves.

Designer (or Visual designer). Designers are concerned with the visual appeal of the product, making sure it is accessible to all users regardless of disability or individual differences. They also strive for consistency in terms of the "look and feel" of the product, making sure this is in line with company branding. They follow key design principles such as *balance, contrast, emphasis, and unity* and consider design elements such as *lines, shapes, texture and colour*. They are the people responsible for *iconography* - conveying messages to users without words, such as the *hamburger menu icon* that began appearing everywhere a few years ago. A designer's vision is not fulfilled until it has been handed over to the developers, (in particular front-end developers) who will implement the design.

Project pitfall!
Don't waste money on impractical designs for your product.
Conflicts between design "form" and development "function" are common. It is possible that designs can look amazing, but be very challenging to implement because the design has not taken into account important practical or technical considerations.
Before you fall in love with a visual design, check that it can be translated into software by a developer - and let designers know that you will be requesting amendments if this is not the case! It is a good idea to get designers and developers talking where possible. Rather than bouncing back and forth between design and development considerations, if necessary, arrange a meeting for the three of you to hash out any implementation issues and to agree on a way forward.

CHAPTER 5
How to identify the skill gaps in your team...and what to do about them

Fig 21. Iconography example. The hamburger menu item. Chris Messley. Flickr / Thinkstock

Front-end developer. These developers are skilled creating the elements of a website or product that the customer sees and interacts with directly, also taking into consideration the look and feel of the product, the fonts used and the general presentation and styling of the product. They are often the ones that spend the most time implementing the visual designer's vision.

Full-stack developer. Developers proficient in both front and back-end skills are called *full-stack developers.* Hiring one may help you cover your bases, but this comes with advantages and disadvantages. See Chapters 15-17 for more about developer skills and hiring developers.

Information Architect (IA). These skills are useful for projects where there will be a lot of information to organise, such as on large websites. The IA ensures that users are quickly and easily able to find what they are looking for and may carry out user tests to confirm that users understand the way information has been grouped or classified by the client or software team. I'm sure you know of at least a few frustrating websites where you can't find the information that you want, despite searching through numerous menu options! IT folk would probably say that the IA on such sights was not *intuitive.*

Product Manager. (Also known as Proposition Managers, with some cross-over with the *Product Owner* role.) A team will usually include one of these three roles, unless a *business analyst* is able to bridge the gap. Product Managers are usually responsible for setting the product vision and strategy. They will carry out research to confirm the need for a product and will define the problem they are trying to solve, the format the solution needs to take and the features the product must have to make it successful. Their role may also include managing the project's budget, forecasting sales figures and keeping track of profits and losses. The product manager will also need to understand how the project should evolve as customer needs and market conditions change. They may be involved in marketing the product; describing and presenting its features (what it does), and its benefits (the value to the customer), answering the WIIFM; *"What's in it for me?"* question for customers, by explaining how the product will solve a pain or bring about a desired result.

Product Owner (PO). This Scrum specific role may be equivalent to a Product Manager or Propositions manager role in software development environments that do not use Scrum. They may be responsible for writing *user stories*, maintaining the *product backlog* (or product to-do list) which keeps the developers supplied with work, holding the vision for the product, prioritising the work to be done and communicating this to the delivery team.

Project Manager (PM). PM's may also be known as ScrumMasters. A team will generally have one or the other, but not both. There may be some cross-over between these roles, however, they are far from identical. The PM is the person in overall charge of the planning and execution for a particular project. They may also manage budgets, staff and any 3rd party relationships with suppliers that are needed in order to build, maintain or support the product.

Fig 22. Where there's a Project Manager, a Gantt chart is probably not very far away. By Vheilman, [CC-BY-SA-3.0 (www.creativecommons.org/licenses/by-sa/3.0)], via Wikimedia Commons.

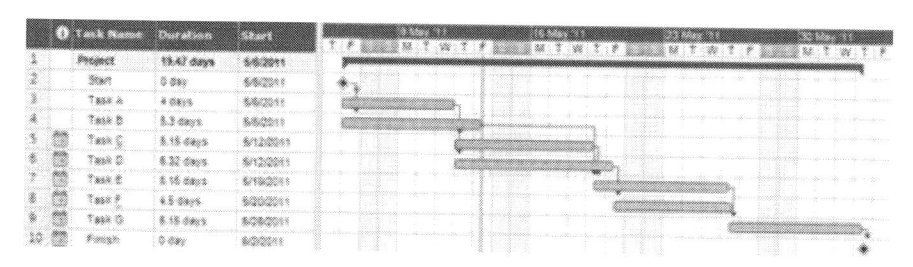

ScrumMaster. (Also see the Project Manager role.) ScrumMasters are often called *servant leaders* because they both serve the team and lead it. They will organise and bring structure to the team, facilitate team decision making and generally support, coach and challenge the team. They have an important role in removing impediments (also known as *blockers*, that prevent the team from making progress or doing their best.) ScrumMasters may perform traditional project management tasks too.

CHAPTER 5
How to identify the skill gaps in your team...and what to do about them

Technical Architect. (TA) These individuals define the architecture or structure of a system, looking at its purpose from a high-level and planning the best way for the system to be constructed. The programming language to be used for the project may also be proposed by the TA. Careful thinking and foresight from a TA at the start of the project *could* make development easier in future, whereas a haphazard approach or a lack of consideration could make development work more complex as your product grows. Technical architects will communicate their plans to the development team in verbal, written and diagrammatic form to ensure that their vision is understood and remains consistent.

Tester, (automation.) Automation testers are skilled at managing the software and tools which can automate the process of testing web browsers, software and systems, reducing the need for *manual testing* by humans. Automated tests can help with maintaining consistency and quality. Tests or *test scripts* first need to be *written* to cover all the bases, but once they exist, these scripts can be *run* repeatedly. Tests can be run to check units of code, specific functionality or even to *simulate* many people performing key activities and important *user journeys* within your product! (You can find out more about user journeys in Chapters 10, 12 and 13.) Some developers have automated testing experience. Developers with experience of *TDD (Test Driven Development)* will write tests for each *user story* based on the requirements of the story *before* they even start to write the code to complete the work.

Tester, (manual.) (Also known as *QA's;* short for *Quality Assurance, software testers, system testers* or *manual testers*). There is no guarantee that a product works correctly until it has been fully tested. Software applications can "break" or malfunction and buggy systems are not popular with customers! Manual testing is the process of testing software for defects by hand and using the naked eye, checking that the work done by developers has been completed, and the way functionality behaves is correct. QA's will test the product in parts, and as a whole, looking for any strange or unexpected behaviour.

Start testing as soon as the first code is released by your developer so you don't fall behind with this important work.

Testing is a strange activity; some people enjoy it; others strongly dislike it. If you dislike it, but are on a tight budget, do your best until you can afford to hire someone to take over from you. Testing will become more time-consuming as your product grows in complexity and the more help you can get with testing, the better. Different people tend to notice different problems, so get as many eyeballs on your product as possible. Target customers should not be used to help find bugs, so don't take a product in poor shape to user testing; you'll need to tidy it up first.

Tester, (performance, security and other specialised testing roles.) Some software testers perform very specific types of software test, including security testing, stress testing or other forms of test. We'll talk more about performance testing and other more specialised forms of testing in Chapters 6 and 23.

User experience designers (are also known by the acronyms UX or UXD). These individuals are the users' champions (although *everyone* in the team should be user focused). They think about what is right for the user and make sure that the user's experience is positive. They are responsible for making sure that the product is *usable*; meaning that it is easy to use and understand, has a sensible and logical work-flow, is *intuitive* and operates in a consistent manner. UX makes sure that products are accessible to all types of users and that they are also *enjoyable* to use!

User experience tester. Also known as *UX Tester* or *Usability tester*, these testers observe people's behaviour to understand how to improve the UX of a product. They are skilled interviewers and translate the results of user tests done on paper or via a desktop or mobile devices into actions that can be used to improve or redesign a product.

Other roles include *User Interface design* (UI) and *User interaction* which considers the interfaces, (or screens) we interact with on our devices and the knowledge and study of human behaviour when interacting with computer systems.

CHAPTER 5
How to identify the skill gaps in your team...and what to do about them

Skill shortage assessment

Now we've covered a range of software delivery roles, you'll need to bridge some of the skill and knowledge gaps that exist. All the roles can be placed into 4 categories and we'll run through each group in turn:

- Essential skills for your developer
- Essential roles to fill, or to be outsourced
- Skills that may be needed from time-to-time
- Skills you can survive without (with adequate planning)

Essential skills for your developer

These should include:

Back-end / full-stack development skills. You will definitely need either a back-end or full-stack developer if you are building an app from scratch. If you can find one with **technical architecture** experience, this may add value at the start of the project in terms of planning the best way for your app to be constructed.

Although not quite essential, **Automated test skills** and Test Driven Development (TDD) experience should be seriously considered for the reasons discussed earlier in this chapter. Discuss these skills with your developer when you hire them. We'll cover interview questions in chapter 17, where there is a script and plenty of interview questions you can use to screen your developer.

Essential roles to fill, or to be outsourced

You could outsource all these roles if you wanted to - a list of freelance sites is provided in chapter 16, if not, you should cover these roles yourself. The first five will need to be performed on a weekly, if not daily basis, whilst the sixth, user testing, can be done on a periodic basis when you have a new batch of functionality you want to get feedback on. Is there anyone you know with the skills or experience to perform any of these roles? Could you partner up, and bring skills or knowledge into your business that you don't have currently?

Business analyst / Product Owner. As a minimum, you'll need someone to: i) manage the backlog of development tasks, ii) supply your developer with work to do and iii) communicate your product requirements as clearly, accurately and in as much detail as possible. *Miscommunication will cost you money if your*

CHAPTER 5
How to identify the skill gaps in your team...and what to do about them

developer builds functionality which isn't what you wanted. Try drawing pictures along with written requirements, even if they are very rough, to increase their understanding. If you're good with process flow charts and can create these to explain the steps in each process, then this will be beneficial. We'll go into more detail about these topics in Chapters 10, 11, 14 and 22.

Client. Please make yourself available to answer questions and provide clarification as your product evolves! If you aren't available to answer questions when they arise, then your developer will need to wait around until you're free, put the task on hold and try working on another one, or guess what you want. If their guess is wrong, there will be a cost to re-do the work in terms of time, money or both. None of these scenarios are good for your project or your budget. Don't disrupt your developer's flow by not having the necessary information ready when they need it!

Project Manager / ScrumMaster. You will need to communicate with your developer, have them report to you and have a method of tracking their progress. You will also need to manage your budget, so you know how much you have spent, what it was spent on, how much money you need to keep the project running each month (your *burn rate*) and how much you have left. Dealing with issues (and actively trying to avoid them in the first place) all falls within the PM's domain. See Chapters 18 and 19 for more about project management and what is involved in performing PM duties.

Product Manager. When wearing the Product Manager's "hat" you'll be focused on gathering evidence and data to confirm your theories and will take the lead with managing the product and steering it in the right direction.

Tester (Manual testing / QA). Testing is essential. If product testing is not up to scratch, your whole product can become unusable, unstable and of poor quality.

You have the option to ask your developer to help with testing, but this is a not necessarily a good idea - some will be able to do it well and some may prefer not to because this is not their area of interest or expertise. Others may not spot errors in the work done *because* it is their own work. This is why a fresh pair of eyes is so important.

If you only have one developer, you'll also be distracting them from writing code if you give them a range of tasks to do. Asking them to perform multiple roles will slow down development output. This seems obvious, but it happens quite often. Coding is intense work and requires focus.

Usability or user testing / user experience testing. You can do the tests for usability and experience yourself if on a budget - often the simplest, most minimally designed products are the most usable, so keep your product simple to start with! It may be a good idea to do a few practice user tests with those closest to you first, to get used to the process. Websites like the Government's usability site; https://www.usability.gov/how-to-and-tools/methods/index.html and *Steve Krug*'s book *Don't make me think,* are good places to gather additional information. Run tests whenever there is a decent chunk of new functionality available to test, or when you need customer input to help you make the right product decision.

Skills that may be needed from time-to-time
All these roles could be outsourced to experts. The content writing and UX could be done by you if you're happy to fulfil these roles.

Content writing. You could create the copy for your website or app. Get your developer's input or assistance from anyone else that you trust to check your work for spelling, grammatical mistakes and readability. Don't leave content writing until the last minute. It is not a daily task, but start thinking about, and experimenting with the language you want to use in your app. Not having the content ready for your developer at the right time will cause delays and rework because it is "cheaper" to insert content at the time when the developer is building the functionality.

Design / UX. You may wish to hire a visual designer at some point during the project, or you can purchase a visual design that a developer can apply for you. If you want to give UX a try, the quickest thing to do is to look at the popular software and apps you use every day for inspiration. Think about which ones you can use almost without thinking (these tick the ease of use and intuitiveness boxes) and take note of button sizes, links, layout and on-screen instructions. Don't try and come up with totally unique layouts if you're new to UX - use simple screen layouts with icons and text labels that will be *familiar* rather than foreign to your audience. Familiarity is often what makes products easy to use. Chapter 11 covers more design and UX considerations and lots of examples are provided!

CHAPTER 5
How to identify the skill gaps in your team...and what to do about them

Front-end development skills. Whether you require a front-end developer or not will depend on the type of app you wish, to build and the range of skills that your back-end, or full-stack developer has. Choosing a generalist will bring both advantages and disadvantages. We'll discuss those in Chapter 15 when we review the specific programming languages, technologies and skills that your developer might need to build your app.

Tester, (performance, security and other specialised testing roles.) These types of tests are usually done towards the end of the project, when your app will be tested as a *whole system*, rather than as a number of small units. Therefore, having your developer do this type of work, (if they have the skills to do it), will be less of a day-to-day distraction.

You will need to decide whether you want to hold out for a developer with these skills, or will hire a good developer to do your development work, who may not have this experience. In that case, you can "draft in" specialist testers to do specific jobs for you. Chapter 23 describes different types of technical test in more detail.

Skills you can survive without (with adequate planning and workarounds)

Information architecture. Occasionally you will need to user test with your target market to check that they know how to find the information in your app if they need it. This can be rolled up as part of the general user testing that you will be doing on a semi-regular basis.

User interaction expert. Get your developer's input and continue to user test the product, so you know where problems exist.

In the next chapter, we'll be talking through some of the less well-known elements to building software applications. These are known as NFR's and they will be essential to the success of your app in many ways!

CHAPTER 6
The insider secrets of the IT industry

In this chapter:
- What are NFR's?
- Data protection
- Hacks, attacks and security considerations
- Software application "health"
- Legal compliance
- Free resources
- Disaster recovery, and more

NFR's are trade secrets. They are rarely acknowledged by people outside of the IT industry, but they must be taken into consideration when building software.

Anyone who prefers software that is secure, reliable, responds rapidly to commands and does not crash, knows the value of NFR's. Your customers will expect these things to happen by default, but the truth is that significant up-front planning and effort goes into crafting a reliable, high-performance app.

Working on NFR's will not necessarily add any extra functionality to your app in terms of things that your customers will be able to *do*, but they *will* make your customers' lives (and therefore your own life) easier. Please set aside budget for non-functional requirements, and other technical tasks, because they are an important, even essential investment. NFR related failures are the nightmare events that can anger or disappoint your customers, disrupt their activities and create PR disasters.

So, what exactly are these NFR's anyway?
Requirements are usually defined as being either *functional* or *non-functional*:

- *Functional requirements* define how a system, or parts of a system works. They are focused on its features; what the system will do, who for and its *behaviours.*
- *Non-functional requirements* (NFRs) define constraints, control mechanisms or boundaries and set out criteria that can be used to judge the operation of your system.

Say what?! Constraints? Control mechanisms? Boundaries? Ah, the joys of geek-speak! This is close to a textbook definition, but it's still pretty vague, isn't it? How about some descriptions and examples to explain what non-functional requirements are?
Here are some of the major NFR's, listed in A-Z order:

Accessibility. Software should be easy to use for everyone, including those with disabilities including deafness, impaired vision, blindness, colour blindness, epilepsy, dyslexia or any combination of these. Not only will you want your app to be accessible to as many people as possible within your target market, but you'll also want to make sure that you don't unintentionally break any disability and equality laws, including the *Equality Act 2010* because your website cannot be used by certain groups of people. The W3C, the World Wide Web Consortium, (the main international standards organisation for the Internet) has a set of accessibility tests you can look at, here:
https://www.w3.org/WAI/eval/preliminary.html

Auditing and logging. What sorts of records does your app need to keep? Will the date and time at which activities in your app take place be important to you, or to your customers?
The downside to logging every activity is the development (and testing) work required to program the app to record them all, and the extra data storage that will be needed to keep the required records; possibly for years into the future.

Availability. Let's consider the *availability* of your service. When you need to do routine maintenance work on your app, what time of day or night would be best? *Usually, this is done at the quietest times for your business.* If you deal with consumers, then weekends might be a bad time to shut down for maintenance, but if you serve other businesses, then the weekend might be your "quiet period." If you understand how and when your customers will be using your app, you can avoid disturbing them at peak usage times.

Capacity. Apps need to be robust. Your app should be able to handle sudden or unexpected spikes in traffic without crashing or slowing to a snail's pace. When your developer comes on board, ask them to estimate the number of transactions per minute and per hour (the *traffic volumes*) that your app should be able to deal with, without breaking into a metaphorical sweat! They should also make sure the infrastructure that supports your app can not only handle the expected activity, but a significant percentage more, so it is always protected by a decent safety margin.

Data storage, back-up and recovery. If you're going to be holding a lot of customer data, make sure your database can handle this. You need to consider how much data is going to be created every day, week and month - from there you can calculate the expected growth of your database on an annual basis. Discuss where your customers' data will be held and how it will be backed up, so that data cannot be permanently lost. *If you're going to use a 3rd party company for data storage, make sure you know where the servers that will hold sensitive customer data are located.* For example, to comply with the *UK data protection laws* regarding the collection, storage and safeguarding of customer data, UK companies should look to hold their customers' data on servers located in the UK, or with a UK owned company. Non-UK companies may not be subject to UK rules and therefore by allowing them to hold your data, you could be breaking the laws of your own country.

Read the terms and conditions of service carefully when you work with 3rd parties, so you know where their servers are based and which country's rules they follow.

You can find more information about the Data Protection Act on the Gov.UK website: https://www.gov.uk/data-protection/the-data-protection-act and there is a Data Protection Self-Assessment located here: https://ico.org.uk/for-organisations/improve-your-practices/data-protection-toolkit/index.html.

GDPR applies to *any* businesses that processes EU resident's data. Non-compliance carries penalties of up to **4% of a company's global turnover.** The law comes into force from 25th May 2018. *The Information Commissioner's Office, (ICO)* set up to uphold information rights in the UK provides comprehensive information about the GDPR. The ICO's GDPR overview can be found here:
https://ico.org.uk/for-organisations/data-protection-reform/overview-of-the-gdpr/

You can find guidance about servers and sending personal data outside the European Economic Area here: https://ico.org.uk/for-organisations/guide-to-data-protection/principle-8-international/, and a guidance document that deals with privacy issues for app developers to consider, here:
https://ico.org.uk/media/for-organisations/documents/1596/privacy-in-mobile-apps-dp-guidance.pdf.

If you're based in the US, you can take a look at the CDT's (Centre for Democracy and Technology) guide here: https://www.cdt.org/files/pdfs/Best-Practices-Mobile-App-Developers.pdf

Disaster recovery. You should have a disaster recovery plan in place which lays out what should happen in the event of a disaster - digital, natural or otherwise and how your app will be made usable again as quickly as possible (with all your data and standard services recovered). In most cases, you will be relying on 3rd parties and in that case, you should check whether they have plans in place that will help them restore services quickly if a serious issue occurs. We'll talk more about vetting and managing 3rd parties in Chapter 19.

Documentation. If you want or need your developer to create technical documentation for you, then this should be budgeted for. Try to avoid burning developer time on writing documents instead of writing code. However, if you do require documentation, Chapter 18 contains a section which explains what to ask for.

Error handling. In the event of unexpected problems when customers access your app, error handling is standard practice. If your app does fail, make sure it provides useful information to users in the process. This might include explaining what has gone wrong, who to contact or what the user might do to resolve the problem. Avoid the "system does not compute, error 117467699787" style of error message! Don't allow this kind of messaging in your app - they are eyesores and provide a terrible customer experience! When testing, if you see this kind of error message, write a human-friendly replacement and ask your developer to add this to the app for you.

Handling unexpected issues with your app – HTTP response codes. Most people know about the infamous 404 page; which means that you've tried to access a web page that can't be found. A 404 is one of over 50 codes known as *HTTP status codes* (or *HTTP response codes*.) *Hypertext Transfer Protocol* messages provide information, about the ability of the *client* or the *server* to deliver the web page that a customer has asked for.

Keep your app professional by asking your developer to provide basic ways to cater for the most common status code errors which arise. This is usually achieved via a customer friendly web page which indicates the type of error found and provides advice to the customer about what to do next – usually along

CHAPTER 6
The insider secrets of the IT industry

with a link back to your Homepage so the customer can continue with their activities.

Here are some common HTTP status codes:

Fig 23. HTTP status codes table

Status code	What it means
400	**Bad request.** An error has occurred because there has been a miscommunication between the front and back-ends of the app.
401	**Unauthorised request.** You have come across a page that you do not have permission to access, such as a page that requires you to log in, or one used by administrators of the app, or other technical staff.
403	**Forbidden.** The page exists, but the database is denying the user access. This could mean the user does not have the right level of "clearance" to access the page.
404	**Page not found.** The user has found a page which either never existed, or does not exist at the current time – this could be a temporary problem (when the page no longer exists at all, it should become a 410, which means that the page is "gone" permanently.)
410	**Gone.** See 404 above.
500	**Internal server error.** An unexpected error was encountered by the server and it was unable to display the web page that was requested.

CHAPTER 6
The insider secrets of the IT industry

Fig 24. A "500" internal server error page

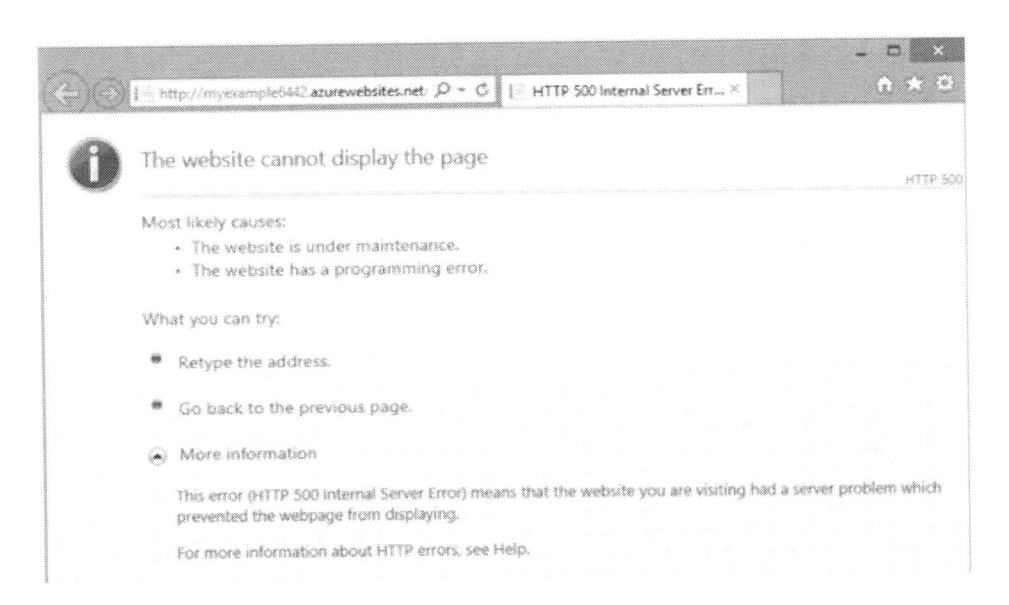

This 500 page is quite plain and has not been "styled up", to look more attractive, but it does *tell* us the basics about what has gone wrong and what to do next.

The next example is of a more appealing and user-friendly "styled up" 404 page, created by *Blue Fountain Media*. There are icons below the Pacman game which allow the user to select other useful destinations - after they've finished their game, of course!

CHAPTER 6
The insider secrets of the IT industry

Fig 25. A 404-page created by Blue Fountain Media. https://www.bluefountainmedia.com/

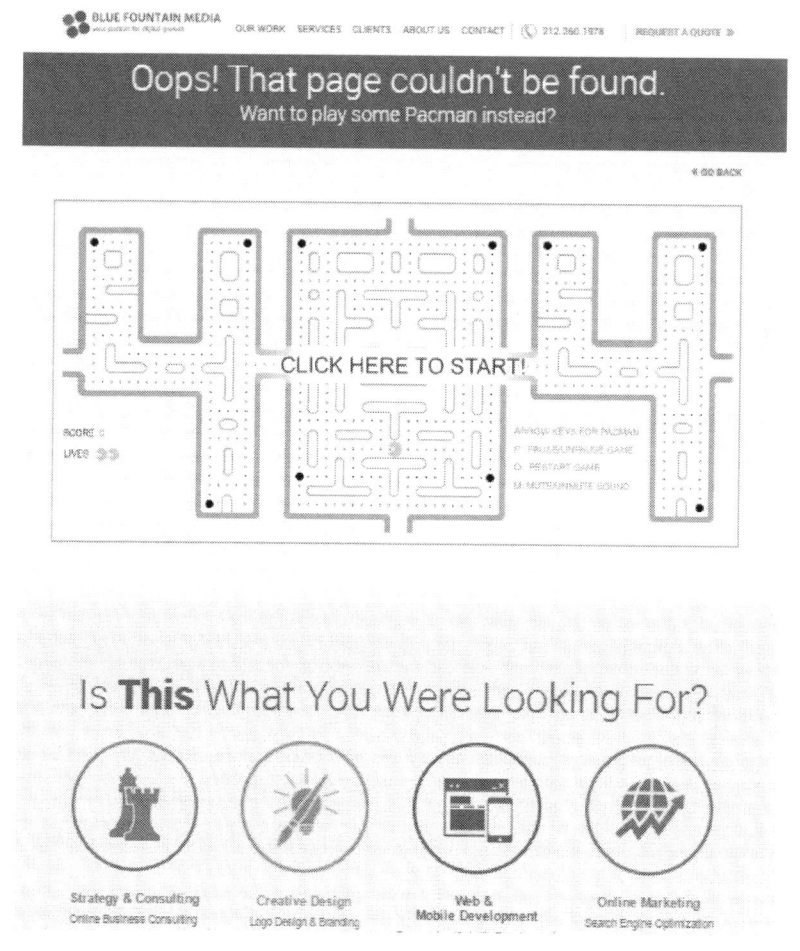

This is an entertaining example of what *could* be done (this is often where developers have a little creative fun) but keep it simple to help keep your budget under control.

Integration. What other systems, tools or software will your product rely on?

However many you're using, your product should feel like one unified product to your customers. Making sure that any 3rd party software, systems, services or suppliers work alongside your own product in an efficient and reliable manner will be very important if you and your customers are relying on these services. You'll find more about this in Chapter 23.

Legal and compliance related requirements. *Confirm the national or international laws that you need to comply with.* The *US CAN-SPAM act* sets out rules for the sending of commercial email and is a form of anti-spam legislation, whilst The EU's *Privacy and Electronic Communications (e-Privacy) Directive*; also known as the "EU cookie laws", state that UK businesses must request permission from website visitors to "drop" non-essential cookies (little data files) on a visitor's device if they are not essential to the operation of their website. Businesses should also explain what their cookies do.
The Information Commissioner's Office, (ICO) upholds information rights in the UK and offers advice about cookies to businesses:
https://ico.org.uk/for-organisations/guide-to-pecr/cookies-and-similar-technologies/

Registered companies (i.e. those registered at Companies House) must provide their company information on their website - business name, company registered number, their registered office address (the address provided on registration, which can also be your accountant's address or a virtual office address.) This information usually lives in the *website footer* section at the bottom of a web page.
Your website's *Terms of usage* and *Privacy policies* are also classed as "legal matters" and should be provided on your website. If you have a web app, your terms of usage will cover a wide range of topics, including details of how customers may or may not use your software.
TermsFeed, https://termsfeed.com provides documents including Privacy Policies, Terms & Conditions, EULA's (End User Licensing Agreements) and Cookie Policies, whilst Iubenda.com provides privacy policies, https://www.iubenda.com/en.

EULAs form an agreement between anyone who *installs, downloads or purchases* software and the person or organisation that provides the software. Apple provides a sample EULA here:
http://www.apple.com/legal/internetservices/itunes/appstore/dev/stdeula/

The Google Play store does not have a sample EULA, although they do provide a *Developer Distribution Agreement (DDA)*:
https://play.google.com/about/developer-distribution-agreement.html#showlanguages.

You will have to decide whether these will provide you with adequate cover in the event of losses, or the theft of your idea through software piracy or other methods. Consider what sort of losses could be claimed against you as a result of an issue caused by your app. If in doubt, discuss these issues with a lawyer and with your business insurance provider.

Monitoring, and monitoring tools. I'm a big advocate of asking developers to set up early warning detection systems when new products are built. They can provide a vital heads-up that all is not well *before* your app lets you down, giving you time to react and prevent negative or disruptive events.

The monitoring you do will depend on the type of app you're building. Examples of alerts you could set up include asking for you and your developer to be warned by email, SMS or other methods if:
- There are errors occurring within your app.
- The app is failing to process user requests.
- You are approaching a memory, processing or data storage limit.
- Your app or the services that support it have gone down or are struggling for some reason.
- Page load speeds rise above a certain number of seconds. (Waiting even 3 seconds for a page to load is slow.)
- Server "*pings*" fail to get any response. (Server pings are like little pokes to the server asking it, *"Are you there?"* If the server doesn't respond, then there is cause for investigation.)

Here are some monitoring tools that can be used for web and / or mobile apps: *Uptrends* covers websites, web apps, mobile apps and server monitoring; https://www.uptrends.com. Their uptime and availability checker will tell you the availability and page download speed for any web page, from almost anywhere in the world; https://www.uptrends.com/tools/uptime.

Montis specialises in websites, networks, servers and app monitoring; http://www.monitis.com/product.
Site24x7 monitors web apps, mobile apps, servers and more, https://www.site24x7.com/ and *Paessler* is a network monitoring company, https://www.paessler.com/tools.
Sentry's calling card is that it provides real-time crash reporting for mobile apps, web apps and games, https://getsentry.com/welcome/.

You could also ask your developer if there are any tools that they would recommend.

CHAPTER 6
The insider secrets of the IT industry

Fig 26. Example of the Uptrends monitoring console. You can see an anomaly has been identified and the date and time at which the "spike" occurred. Gathering data like this helps developers to investigate problems.

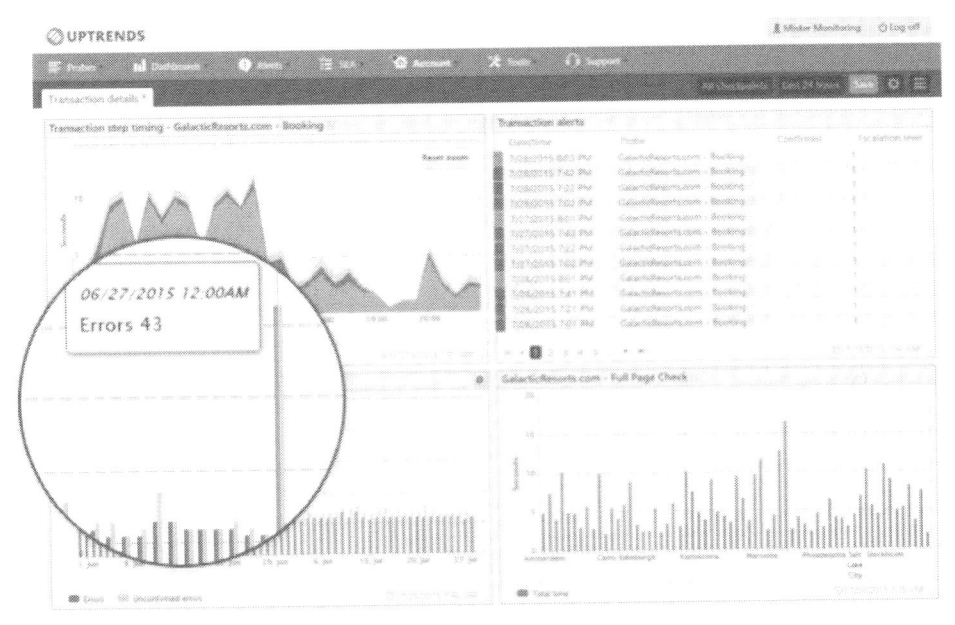

Mobile app health monitoring and app crash alert tools. App crashes are a real nuisance. You should be aware of how often your app is crashing (and ideally) how many customers were affected by the crash. Here are a few other tools that provide mobile app monitoring:

Fabric, which includes a service called *Crashlytics* (owned by Twitter), currently serves over 2 billion devices. It includes daily alerts, anomaly detection (so you are alerted to any unusual activity within the app), plus additional stability alerts. This is currently a free service: https://answers.io/pricing

Apteligent, https://www.apteligent.com/ provides app health dashboards which monitor the "vital signs" of your app and alert you to issues. They also provide crash reporting among other services.

Performance. *Every* customer expects your app to load and work quickly! When people click buttons, run searches or try to use your app to perform a task, they will expect these things to happen in a matter of seconds. When your app is built, consider scheduling some performance tests to see where improvements in speed and responsiveness are needed. An experienced developer will be able to do this and should report back to you with their findings, so you can decide which actions(s) you want to take. Back-end developers can performance "tune" your app to make it faster, and there also front-end tasks that can improve the perceived speed of an app. Some clever tricks are reviewed in Chapter 11!

Reliability. In an ideal world, your app should only go down when you take it down. All apps experience failures from time-to-time, the important thing is to reduce the frequency and duration of these events as far as possible. *Unplanned downtime,* as it is known, can lead to complaints, reputational damage and general annoyance. Unfortunately, you won't know *when* this downtime will occur - it's unplanned! Uptime of 99.9 to 99.99% means that you can expect unplanned downtime to be between 8.8 hours and 50 minutes per year. Unplanned downtime can be influenced by the suppliers you use for your services, servers and web hosting, so if this is not acceptable, consider looking for 99.999% reliability, however, this will cost more and there will be less suppliers able to guarantee it.

Reporting. There are data analytics tools you can set up for mobile apps which will tell you how many downloads you are getting, along with other stats that will indicate how and when your app is being used. If you have a website or web app, you should ask your developer to add *Google Analytics,* https://www.google.com/analytics/ to your site to provide you with data that will tell you what people do when they visit your website or web app, such as which pages customers are visiting, how long they stay, and their geographical location.

Security. This will include considering your app's vulnerability to some of the common security threats and forms of cyber-attack. If you have a website, you may want to increase security and apply for an *SSL* (Secure Sockets Layer) *certificate*. SSL is the certificate that will enable you to get the green padlock symbol on your web pages. This can increase trust that your site is both genuine and secure, and ensure that the data entered into your app cannot be read or intercepted by a 3rd party.

Fig 27. A website with an SSL certificate.

CHAPTER 6
The insider secrets of the IT industry

PCI DSS (Payment Card Industry Data Security Standard,) is a worldwide standard that was set up to help businesses process online card payments securely and reduce card fraud. To comply you would need to adhere to tight controls of the storage, transmission and processing of card holder data. *The PCI Security Standards Council,* which includes the major card payment companies including Visa, MasterCard and American Express have a guidance document. The importance of the standards is explained on page 4 of the document and an overview of how to comply starts on page 5: https://www.pcisecuritystandards.org/documents/SAQ_InstrGuidelines_v3-1.pdf

Hacks and attacks. There are a number of ways that software applications can be attacked. When you interview developers to work on your product, I suggest asking what they recommend in terms the most important security measures that are relevant for your app. (Information on how to do this in provided in Chapter 17.) If they understand these threats, then you will have a better chance of preventing them.

Here are some common ones:

- **Brute force attacks (or brute force cracking).** These attacks are the digital equivalent of systematically trying every combination on a safe until you crack the combination. Unfortunately, a hacker will create a program that will guess a huge range of combinations (often using lists of commonly used passwords) at break-neck speed to do this. When you build your app, help customers to construct passwords which are harder to guess, to help them protect their accounts from unauthorised use. A longer password of at least 8 characters, containing a combination of upper and lowercase letters and non-alphanumeric characters is best.
- **DoS (Denial of Service) attacks** usually originate from one machine and one Internet connection. They make websites or apps unavailable by bringing them down - usually by requesting a large number of URLs in a short period of time. This is the equivalent of a huge number of people visiting your app *all at the same time*. If this is activity is more than a system can handle, then it will be brought down.
- **DDoS (Distributed Denial of Service) attacks** originate from multiple computers and multiple Internet connections, rather than just one as with DoS attacks.
- **SQLi (SQL injections)** can happen when SQL (database code) is used to "trick" a database into giving the hacker the data that they request. Other

CHAPTER 6
The insider secrets of the IT industry

types of code can also be "injected" into the website or app to gain access to it or to gather data without authorisation.
- **XSS attacks (Cross site scripting)** cause a user's session ID (the unique number assigned to your "visit" to an app) to be sent to the hacker's website, which allows the user's session to be hijacked. It is then under the hacker's control.
- **Reverse engineering** involves using information gathered from looking at the code in your app and engineering a way to steal the source code or data from the app, or to exploit any vulnerabilities discovered. Mobile apps can be reverse engineered so that the hacker has the elements needed to create a counterfeit version.
- **Exploitation of loopholes.** *Loopholes* that exist in apps can make them vulnerable. Authentication and session management flaws occur where these processes are broken, or deficient. Hackers can exploit flaws in the checks that confirm that a user has the right to log in to a website, or the process that should verify that a user's active session is secure, as a way to take control of an account.
- **Cross-Site Request Forgery (**also known as *CSRF,* or *one click attacks***)** involves malicious links, web pages or software tricking a web browser into performing actions, often without the user being aware of it. In this scenario, the web page believes that the user is requesting the actions.

The Open Web Application Security Project (OWASP) is a community that provides a range of resources to support web application security. They have several cheat sheets available, organised by programming language:
- Ruby cheat sheet,
  https://www.owasp.org/index.php/Ruby_on_Rails_Cheatsheet
- PHP cheat sheet,
  https://www.owasp.org/index.php/PHP_Security_Cheat_Sheet
- There was no cheat sheet available for the Python programming language at the time of writing.

SEO (known as ASO for mobile apps). *Search Engine Optimisation* is also classed as a non-functional requirement, and like most of the items discussed in this chapter is a huge topic in its own right. SEO is achieved over the short, medium and long term through a range of activities that improve your visibility and *ranking* for particular keywords in SERPs (Search Engine Results Pages, the pages of results you see in Google, Bing or other search engines when you run a search.)

The objective of SEO work is to attract more visitors to your website or app. We'll explore SEO, ASO and marketing in more detail in Chapter 9.

You can download a checklist version of this list of NFRs to help you keep track of the work you might need to do on your app:

http://www.mylanderpages.com/donthireasoftwaredeveloperuntilyoureadthisbook/free-resource-4-nfr-checklist

In Chapter 14 we'll talk about task and project management tools to help you store and prioritise your product related tasks, whether functional, non-functional or technical, but before that, let's look at the different types of software application that you could build, along with their merits and drawbacks.

CHAPTER 7
What type of app should you build?

In this chapter:
- The different types of mobile app
- The different types of web app
- Building a mobile app using "app maker" tools
- Desktop apps and desktop app builder tools
- Choosing the right marketplace to sell your mobile app – and some shocking statistics!

Between Chapters 10 and 13, you'll be creating and testing a simple representation of your product. However, before we get to that, you may want a little more clarity about what you want to prototype. If you'd also like to find out more about the range of mobile and web applications that exist and which one(s) would be the best option for your business, this is the chapter for you, so let's talk about all things "app!"

There are many types of app, or "application." All apps are types of software, the difference is that they run on different browsers or devices, are built using different technologies and have different advantages and disadvantages. We'll start with mobile apps first, and then move on to web applications.

Mobile apps

There are four main types of mobile app:

Native mobile apps are apps designed specifically to run on mobile devices. They require device storage space and you may, or may not need Wi-Fi in order to use them.

Apps that don't require Wi-Fi and can be used "offline," or in dual mode may be more convenient for users.

These apps are downloaded through the *app stores* (also known generically as *app marketplaces*), the largest of which are: *Google Play* (Android), Apple's *App Store* (iOS) and the *Windows* and *Amazon* app stores.

CHAPTER 7
What type of app should you build?

Mobile web apps are software applications that are accessible via the *web browser* on a mobile device. They are simply web pages that have been *mobile-optimised* for smaller devices, (we'll talk more about this later.) Wi-Fi is generally required to use them.

Hybrid apps display characteristics common to both native apps and web apps.

They are web apps and were not created to run on iOS or Android, but they *can* be used as mobile apps and downloaded via the app marketplaces*[1]. They aren't as flexible as native mobile apps; the interactions and gestures that can be performed are more restricted and they *may* also be more dependent on Wi-Fi than native apps.

There is often some form of synchronisation between the mobile app and the web app, which keeps the data across the apps consistent, but this can vary depending on the app. Hybrid apps are generally cheaper and quicker to build than native apps.

HTML5 apps. HTML5 is the latest version of H*ypertext Markup Language (HTML)*, used to control the layout and presentation of content on the web. These apps are built using HTML5, JavaScript and CSS. As with hybrid apps, they are resource efficient; relatively quick to develop and once built, can be used on the web *and* submitted to the app marketplaces*[2]. They lack the benefits of native apps in terms of speed and the range of gestures available, and may not be as secure as native apps, being susceptible to *cross-site scripting attacks* - a type of cyber-attack discussed in chapter 6.

*[1 & 2]Please note that not all hybrid or HTML5 apps are accepted by the app marketplaces, especially if they are not "complex" or "interactive" enough - actual reasons that have been given for apps being rejected by Google Play and Apple's App Store.

A money saving tip!

The purpose of a *mobile app* is to solve a *specific problem* and to solve it well. Your app doesn't have to have a huge amount of functionality, but the functionality it does have should be of significant value to your customer. More is not necessarily better. Focus on building an app with features that customers really love and want to use rather than cramming it with lots of

CHAPTER 7
What type of app should you build?

> extras which are mediocre, cost you extra to build and are of low value to your target market.
>
> When building any kind of software, this is worth bearing in mind. It makes good business sense!

Mobile websites, for example, https://m.facebook.com are a *copy* of your website with its own mobile domain specifically for mobile devices. They are now regarded as being quite old-fashioned and they create an extra maintenance overhead; you would be required to maintain your website and its domain, *plus* the version of the site which is presented on mobile devices and the mobile domain. *Responsive design* is now the gold standard and using this approach, *one URL* (i.e. web address) can be used to access your website, no matter which device is being used. The main reason to mention m. sites is to make sure that you're aware that it is probably best to *reject* a proposal to set up your domains in this way! We'll talk more about *responsive design* later in this chapter.

Fig 28. "m." websites, an old-school approach requiring two different URLs, one for the web and one for mobile. Source. Google Webmasters, mobile friendly website advice.

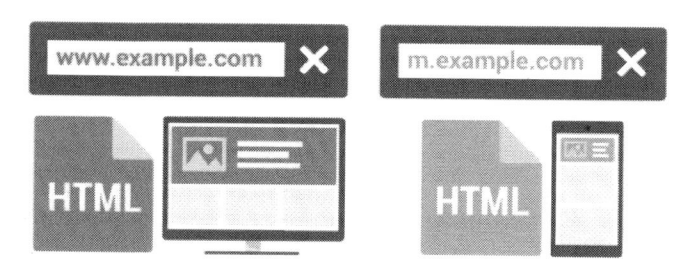

Separate mobile URLs serve different code to desktop and mobile devices (and perhaps even tablets), and on different URLs.

CHAPTER 7
What type of app should you build?

Web apps

Any software that can be accessed via a *web browser,* for example, Chrome, Firefox, Safari or Internet Explorer (I.E). is known as a *web app.* Types of web app include:

SaaS *(Software as a Service)* products. SaaS apps, (also known as *Cloud Computing* or *on-demand software*), are not yours for life, but are "rented" via a subscription service. Microsoft Office 365 and Salesforce.com are examples of popular SaaS products which are available "in the cloud."

Websites also work within a browser and are therefore a form of web app too.

Web apps accessed via mobile device. When you use a smartphone or tablet device to access a website or other services available from a web browser, you are *still* using a web app.

***Browser extensions* (also known as *add-ons*) and plug-ins** also belong to the web app family. Each web browser has its own set of extensions that only work with that specific browser and work by extending the browser's functionality. Browser extensions have their own marketplaces, called *web stores.* You can access the web stores via these links:

Firefox add-ons, https://addons.mozilla.org/en-US/firefox/

Google Chrome, https://chrome.google.com/webstore

Microsoft Store, https://www.microsoftstore.com/store/msusa/en_US/home

Safari extensions, https://extensions.apple.com/

Responsive design

Responsive web design ensures that your website or web app looks attractive and is easy to use, regardless of the device you are viewing it from. A few years back, software teams would consider a design for desktop and a design for mobile as separate work items, but nowadays they will treat these as one and the same thing. The philosophy is now to have a single website, with a single URL which must be usable on all devices. Responsive sites automatically adjust based on the width of your device, resizing and readjusting content on the page as the screen width decreases from desktop, to tablet, to smartphone sizes.

CHAPTER 7
What type of app should you build?

Taking this approach when you have a website or web app is part of having a *mobile first strategy*. By considering what will work on the *smallest devices first,* you will be making choices that will work across *all* devices.

Fig 29. How content should "respond" when displayed on different device sizes. Diseño web adaptativo http://www.dobuss.es/ JOSE LUIS DOBUSS

Fig 30. "Why make a website mobile friendly?" by Google,

https://developers.google.com/webmasters/mobile-sites/

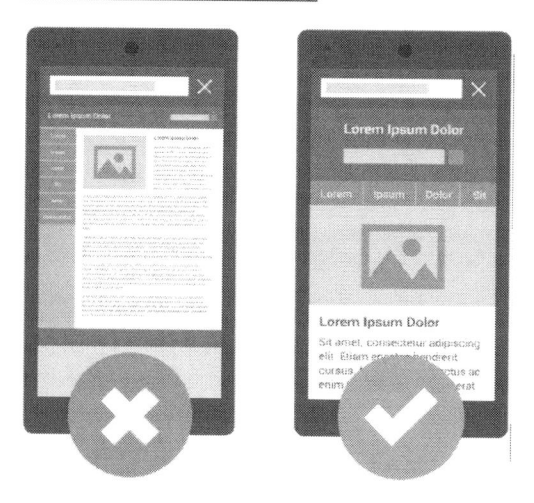

Mobile friendly web design is focused on making design tweaks and adjustments to an *existing* website, making it easier to use on a mobile device. Here is a free Google resource for checking the "mobile-friendliness" of your website: https://www.google.co.uk/webmasters/tools/mobile-friendly/.

App maker services

App maker companies work by transforming *web apps* into *mobile apps* of the hybrid or HTML 5 variety. Unfortunately, the full range of functionality and gestures available with native mobile apps may not be possible, but they are a quick way to increase your reach across platforms, if you like the idea of having a presence online *and* in the app marketplaces:

- http://buildfire.com/
- http://www.goodbarber.com/
- https://www.appmakr.com/
- https://www.biznessapps.com/
- http://www.appypie.com/

If you're interested in this option, in most cases you will need to create a web app / website first and then create your mobile app using services like these.

Phonegap, http://phonegap.com/about/faq/ requires some technical expertise. HTML, CSS and JavaScript skills are needed, rather than programming languages such as Objective C, Swift and Java needed to build native mobile apps. We'll review the technical skills needed to build web and mobile apps in chapter 15.

Other types of app...

Desktop apps run on a PC or laptop and *generally,* a web browser or an Internet connection is not required to use them. However, you may have noticed that you can now connect to the web through Microsoft Office products that were launched from your desktop, so even that constant has started to change!

Once upon a time, desktop apps not already installed on your PC or laptop used to make it onto your desktop via CD-ROM or USB, but nowadays apps for desktop use can also be downloaded from the web. If you like the idea of building a desktop app, here are some things to consider as positives:

- If your app does not require Wi-Fi to work, that could be an advantage, as it removes worries about unreliable connections or being unable to operate the software without a connection and

concerns about the safety of public Wi-Fi if being used in a public place.
- Having your app icon on people's desktops is a constant reminder of your product.

Whilst on the downside:

- Not everyone likes to download software from the Internet, so you'd need to consider whether this would deter more cautious users afraid of viruses or even of using up storage space on their machines. Downloading software from the web can also be time-consuming and the process is not always smooth or reliable.
- If you have a download once / pay once revenue generation model, this is unlikely to be as lucrative as the SaaS monthly recurring revenue model.
- Desktop apps come with compatibility challenges. Your app would need to be compatible with all the popular operating systems for Windows (Windows 8.1, Windows 10 etc.) and Mac machines (including recent OS X versions). You'd want to make sure that as many of your target market as possible could download and use your app, so you'd need to know which operating systems are most popular with your target market to avoid building a lot of versions of your app. Once built, they'd need to be maintained and updated, not once like a web app or mobile app, but across all the different operating systems... so software updates, (and the testing of these updates) would be a more complex affair. This isn't to say that there aren't technical tests to be done for other types of app. Native mobile apps need to be tested on different devices, and web apps need to be checked across different web browsers and devices. We'll talk about how to do this in chapter 23.

Creating desktop apps from web apps

There are tools which will enable you to create a desktop app here:

Electron, http://electron.atom.io/

Fluid app for Mac users, http://fluidapp.com/ will help you turn a web app into a Mac desktop app.

CHAPTER 7
What type of app should you build?

Choosing the right app marketplace

Which app marketplace should you choose? This is the 6-billion-dollar question! Let's do a little digging and data analysis to help you decide:

In this book, we're going to focus exclusively on the Google Play and App Store marketplaces, let me show you why. The graph to follow shows the number of apps available in the four largest app stores as of June, 2016.

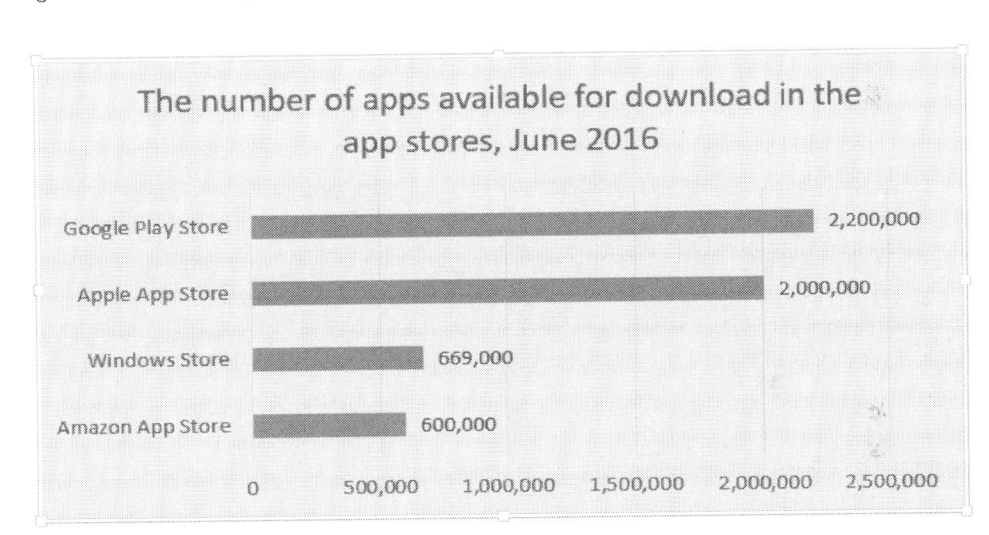

Fig 31. The number of apps in the top 4 app marketplaces in June 2016. Source of data, Statista.com.

The number of apps available for download in the app stores, June 2016

App Store	Number of apps
Google Play Store	2,200,000
Apple App Store	2,000,000
Windows Store	669,000
Amazon App Store	600,000

You can see that Google Play is the marketplace with the most apps available, followed closely by Apple, with the other two stores lagging behind by a large margin.

Now you have this information, you may be wondering which smartphones are more popular - those powered by the Android operating system or by iOS?

The International Data Corporation, (IDC), providers of market intelligence for the IT, telecommunications and consumer technology markets, has published data which shows the market share of smartphone devices by operating system, measured in *device shipments*. The results may surprise you!
According to the IDC in 2016, **Android devices hold over 85% of the market share**, whilst **Apple's market share stands at just under 14%**. Based on current projections, these figures will remain almost static until 2020. CAGR stands for

CHAPTER 7
What type of app should you build?

Compound Annual Growth Rate, the mean annual growth rate of a commodity over a specified period of time.

Fig 32. Worldwide Smartphone Shipments by OS, Market Share, and Annual Growth, Source: IDC Worldwide Quarterly Mobile Phone Tracker, March 2017.

http://www.idc.com/getdoc.jsp?containerId=prUS42334717

Worldwide Smartphone Platform Shipments, Market Share, and 5-Year CAGR, 2017 and 2021 (shipments in millions)

Platform	2017 Shipment Volume*	2017 Market Share*	2017 Year-over-Year Growth*	2021 Shipment Volume*	2021 Market Share*	2021 Year-over-Year Growth*	2016-2021 CAGR*
Android	1,305.0	85.0%	4.6%	1,513.4	85.3%	3.3%	3.9%
iOS	226.0	14.7%	4.9%	258.8	14.6%	1.9%	3.7%
Windows Phone	1.8	0.1%	-69.5%	0.8	0.0%	-8.4%	-33.8%
Others	2.0	0.1%	-56.0%	1.1	0.1%	-5.4%	-24.7%
Total	1,534.8	100.0%	4.2%	1,774.1	100.0%	3.1%	3.8%

Source: IDC Worldwide Quarterly Mobile Phone Tracker, March 1, 2017

* Table Note: All figures are forecast projections.

What does this tell us?

Well, there are many apps available in the Google Play Store and there are many Android devices in circulation from which to download those apps. In contrast, there are almost as many apps in Apple's App Store, with far fewer iOS devices in circulation. iPhone users have a huge range of apps to choose from. Based on current figures, any gains in the market share of iOS devices are going to be *very* marginal for the short to medium-term at least, so this situation is unlikely to change anytime soon!

Based on the information we've just examined, it would be logical to conclude that Google Play / Android is the way forward, wouldn't it? That is, until you consider that Apple users are more *conditioned* towards paying for their apps!

CHAPTER 7
What type of app should you build?

Allow me to explain.

i) It's true there are less iOS smartphones in circulation than those with the Android operating system.

ii) It's also the case that iOS users have more apps to choose from *per head* than their Android counterparts.

However, the Quarter 2 report for 2016 published by App Annie, a US business intelligence company, confirms that the Apple App store's revenue was **double** that of Google Play in the first few months of 2016. Unbelievable, isn't it?!

You can see a few articles on the topic here:

http://www.telegraph.co.uk/technology/2016/04/20/apple-app-store-makes-twice-the-money-googles-play-store-does/

http://appleinsider.com/articles/16/07/19/apples-ios-app-store-now-generating-4x-revenues-per-app-vs-android-google-play

This is at least in part because the App store has positioned itself as a store where people *expect to pay* for the services they enjoy. It's the same with the Apple devices too - premium quality, premium price. That's the culture that exists around Apple and how they are *positioned* in their markets. Despite predictions of an almost static market share into 2020, the App Store is still the place to find paying customers, whilst the Google Play culture leans more towards access to free apps.

If you want to get your app in front of more people, then the Android app store looks like the way to go - *but those people may not be keen to pay you.*

For now, you might find the phrase: *"Cash in the App Store, people in the Play Store"* useful – please refer to chapter 8 for monetisation strategies to use, including those which work when you're *not* charging your customers directly. Of course, you can launch in both marketplaces, but there is work and expense involved in getting an app built and launched in each marketplace, and the app stores have their own ways of doing things, so start with your "lead" app store based on the revenue generation model you have in mind. We'll talk about this in the next chapter.

> **Tip**
>
> **Work smart using industry reports**
>
> Websites such as http://www.statista.com/ and https://www.appannie.com/ provide reports and data on device, web and app marketplace trends. They can save you time and help you stay on top of latest news and developments in the digital world. Revisit chapter 2 if you'd like a reminder of how to set up *Google Alerts* - it will let you know when companies on your "watch list" have published a new report.

App marketplace commission fees

Let's talk about app store commission charges before we move on.

Both the App store and Google Play stores take a 30% cut of the amount a customer has paid to download your app, whilst you keep the remaining 70% less any taxes due. Make sure you factor in all deductions and taxes when you do any projections on your expected earnings!

How might this information affect your plans?

Now you know more about the kind of apps available and have an idea of the relative popularity of the app marketplaces, can you say for sure which type of app you should build?

You may find it a bit maddening that there is rarely a straightforward answer in technology.

The "right" answer frequently depends on making choices based on what you're trying to achieve.

You need to know your target customer group and understand which platform and type of app will suit them best. Seek out their opinions and try to understand the usage patterns of your target group. How tech savvy are they? Are they Android fans or Apple devotees? Are they Mac or PC users? Do they love to use mobile apps, or would they prefer to use a desktop app that doesn't depend on an Internet connection? Would a hybrid app be best?

Depending on your product and its functionality, it might be better suited to one type of app than others. You can come up with some theories about what you think will work best and then review the pros and cons of the different options based on:

- Functionality - how can you best showcase your app's functionality?
- Your target customers and their preferences.
- The technical challenges of creating each of the different types of app.
- What you might be able to charge for your app. (We'll review models for generating revenue in chapter 8.)
- Feedback from prototype testing. (Chapter 12.)

You will be much more likely to create the right product for your target market if you consider all the options. You could certainly create prototypes in desktop, mobile or web app formats to discuss with a developer and target customers to get more detailed feedback.

Don't spread yourself too thinly

Whatever decisions you make, start with one type of app first, and then move on to others. Don't try to build an app for Android, one for iOS and try and create a web app all at the same time! Each app marketplace has its own distinct sets of users, rules and requirements for getting set up, submitting your app and getting accepted into the store (chapters 23 and 24), so keep it simple. The different marketplaces also require different programming languages for creating an app (which we will discuss in chapter 15).

Even if you choose to build a hybrid app, select your initial marketplace first, based on the strategy you have in mind for building your business. There'll be plenty for you to consider in terms of pricing strategies in the next chapter!

SECTION 3
MONETISATION AND MARKETING

CHAPTER 8
Generating revenue from your software

In this chapter:
- The freemium model
- Free forever models
- The free trial model
- Pro tip
- The one-off fee model
- The recurring revenue model
- A few more complex models...

In this chapter, we'll consider some of the models that could be used to help you generate income from your app.

Let's review some of the options available, and look at some companies that have used these tactics.

The freemium model

The word freemium is a *mash-up* of the words *free* and *premium.*

This model can be used by those developing mobile or web apps for the B2C (business-to-consumer) market or B2B (business-to-business) markets.

Here, the *app vendor* (i.e. you) offers a range of functionality or services, some free, some requiring payment. The basic service is offered totally free of charge, with *extras* bundled up and offered for sale as upgrade "packages" with different price points. Customers are usually charged a *subscription fee* on a monthly, quarterly or annual basis. The paid upgrades may be linked to extra functionality or higher usage limits.

When considering consumer behaviour, there are some psychological factors to consider:

Customer loyalty. As customers outgrow the boundaries of the free, entry-level plan, the app vendor hopes they will remain loyal to the brand and transition over to the paid service.

CHAPTER 8
Generating revenue from your software

Customer inertia. After using a product for a while, a customer may consider it to be too much hassle to go shopping for a new supplier.

Reciprocity. The customer may feel a sense of gratitude for getting "something for nothing" for a time, which may make them more amenable to paying for the service in future.

You may have come across the term *in-app purchases*. The term relates to purchases of extras within a *mobile app*. Examples include the "health" and "currency" important to gamers, payments to have ads or branding removed from content, or other services or conveniences that you might decide to sell to customers whilst they are "in" your app. Upgrading to a paid subscription in exchange for more services, also qualifies as an in-app purchase.

Here are some pricing table "plug-in" examples that can be set up to run on a website. If you have a hybrid app, you could sell subscriptions for your services online and then give customers access to your web app *and* mobile app. If you have a mobile app, you could make sales *in-app*, or take payments online.

You will find information about website builders and plugins in chapter 9.

Fig 33. Pricing table plugins compatible with websites built using WordPress.

https://wordpress.org/plugins/pricing-table/

Free	Pro	Business	Dev
$Free	$11	$35	$75
for free	single	webmaster	devs
1 Domain	1 Domain	5 Domain	60 Domain
1 GB Storage	1 GB Storage	5 GB Storage	60 GB Storage
1 FTP Account	2 FTP Account	3 FTP Account	5 FTP Account
[n] Add-on domain	[y] Add-on domain	[y] Add-on domain	[y] Add-on domain
Sign Up	Buy	Buy	Buy

CHAPTER 8
Generating revenue from your software

Fig 34. Responsive pricing tables for WordPress, screenshot.

https://wordpress.org/plugins/dk-pricr-responsive-pricing-table/screenshots/

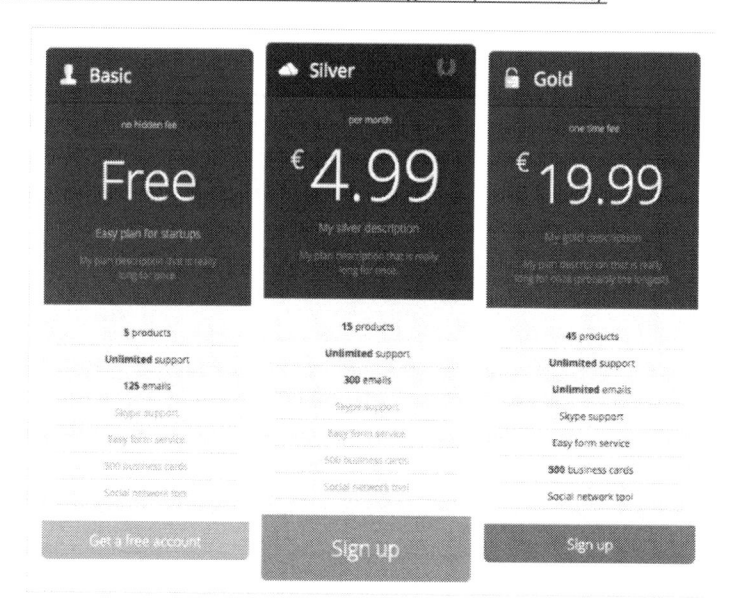

Things to consider

If you are interested in this model, feedback from carrying out *customer interviews* and *user testing* will help you identify the functionality that your customer base will be most willing to pay for.

Customers who prefer to use free apps will download your mobile app, or sign up for your web app if they like the look of it. However, some entrepreneurs debate whether users drawn to the free version of an app will *ever* turn into paying customers. Conversion, enticing users to transition to becoming paying customers will be the challenge.

Frequently used mobile or web apps will not only be less easily forgotten than others, but regular use may help users to justify the cost associated with purchasing an upgrade. Is there any functionality that you could include within your app that would encourage people to come back to it more regularly?

Who uses this model?

Survey Monkey, https://www.surveymonkey.co.uk is an online survey creation SaaS product. Its basic free plan allows up to 10 survey questions to be asked. Exceed that limit, and you will be bumped up to a paid plan. This approach is very

CHAPTER 8
Generating revenue from your software

common in the SaaS market where two, three, four or more service packages are offered to clients via pricing tables like the ones we have just reviewed.

Evernote, stores ideas and information. It is a mobile app and SaaS product (a hybrid app, actually), https://www.evernote.com/. The mobile app can be downloaded for free, however, additional services attract a fee. There are two packages, Plus and Premium. Evernote allows access across 2 devices with their free plan and across all your devices if a paid plan is selected. Paying customers also get more storage. The limit is 60 MB for the free plan and up to 10 GB for the Premium plan.

It's possible to go online and use the Evernote web app, or download the mobile app from the Google Play or App Store. The mobile app will regularly "tease" and remind users of the added benefits available if they upgrade to a paid plan. The data entered in the app is synchronised so it's consistent whether customers use the mobile app or the web app.

The free forever model, #1 - "ad-supported"

Both Facebook and Google grew their businesses by offering a product totally free, building massive customer engagement and then charging advertisers and marketers for the privilege of reaching out to their colossal user bases.

This model can be observed in action everywhere, from mobile apps to web / SaaS apps available online. What many of them have in common is advertising, so let's review a range of advertising options next.

Google advertising for web apps

If you would like to go down the ad-supported route and are thinking about building a web app, you have the option to use *Google AdSense,* which will display ads on your website. Just place the AdSense code on the pages where you want the ads to appear. You'll need to apply to AdSense to do this, which can take several days. After that, you'll be paid based on the number of clicks the ads receive. You can find Google's AdSense tips here:

https://www.google.com/adsense/start/#?modal_active=none

CHAPTER 8
Generating revenue from your software

Fig 35. AdSense ads by Google

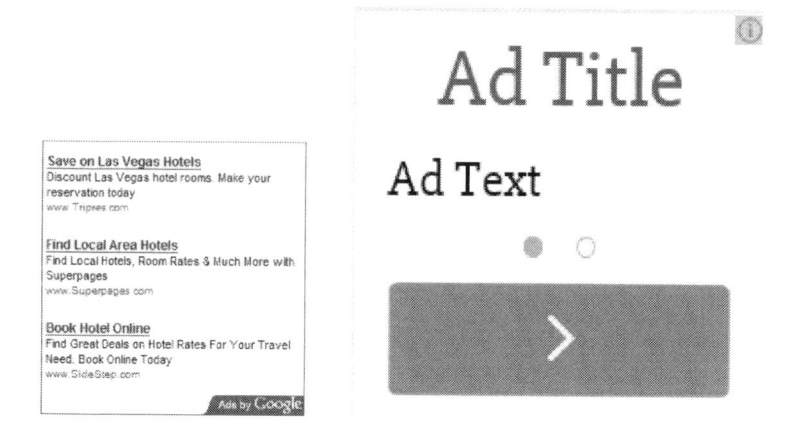

Google advertising for mobile apps

Google ads can also be displayed within mobile apps and there are independent advertising networks that you can work with too. Here are a few options.

Google's *AdMob* for mobile apps

When advertising within mobile apps, *AdMob* by Google will let you "Show ads from millions of Google advertisers in real time." It can be used for both iOS and Android devices. https://firebase.google.com/docs/admob/

Mobile advertising networks

There are many different types of ad. Their size, location, format and the degree of interactivity possible are just some of the variables that exist. Finding the types of ads that your customer base is most attracted to will require data analysis and fine-tuning. Keep track of your advertising statistics, including *click-through rates (CTR)*, and build up your understanding of what does and doesn't work. Use advertisers and tools that provide high-quality statistics, as this will help you understand what is happening (and how to influence it) much more easily.

CTR is defined as the number of clicks on an ad, divided by the number of *impressions* (the number of times that the ad is shown). The Internet Advertising Bureau (IAB), have a comprehensive jargon buster A-Z reference tool of advertising and marketing terms, which you can find here:

https://www.iabuk.net/resources/jargon-buster

CHAPTER 8
Generating revenue from your software

You can find a mobile app monetisation directory here;

http://appindex.com/app-monetization/. It contains a large network of advertisers who can produce *rich media ads* such as audio, video ads and other more interactive styles of ad, which entice users to listen, watch or click.

Sponsorship deals for web or mobile apps

If a *sponsorship deal with advertisers or larger companies,* sounds attractive, be prepared for them to ask about your app's *performance metrics.*

For online advertising, they may ask for details about your website traffic; the number of *unique monthly visitors* you receive, dwell time and user demographics including age, gender, geographical location etc.

For mobile apps, active users (the number of people using your app every day or month) and average session length (average time spent using your app) are important KPIs (Key Performance Indicators) that data-driven businesses will monitor to see how their app is doing. Make sure you have Google Analytics https://www.google.com/analytics/ or the Google equivalent for mobile apps, Firebase, https://firebase.google.com/docs/admob/ enabled as a minimum. They are both free and will give you data that can be presented as evidence. Think about industries and services that complement your own when seeking out sponsors. If there is a natural synergy between your sponsor and your customers' needs and interests, the arrangement is more likely to be successful.

Things to consider

- Monetisation via ads, instead of charging a fee to use your app means more downloads and sign-ups. You'll be able to build a user base more easily and at a faster pace when cost is taken out of the equation.
- The more active users you have, the higher the chances that some of them will click on the ads, which will generate more revenue for you. The percentage that click will vary, depending on the characteristics of your customer base and other factors including the relevance, location and appeal of the ads.
- Ads do not always look very pretty and can "clash" with your app's aesthetic. Make a commercial decision about whether to display them based on the income you can generate vs. possible conflicts with your company's brand image. Be prepared to experiment with different types of ad to find those that are a good fit.

CHAPTER 8
Generating revenue from your software

- Ads may be irrelevant to your customer base if they are not targeted, and poorly targeted ads mean less clicks.
- Ads can be intrusive and annoying for users.
- "Ad blindness"; where people simply ignore or fail to notice ads, is becoming more common.
- To generate consistent income, you'll need to have a large number of users returning to your app and to increase it, you'll need to hold on to your existing user base and attract new customers too, or increase the number of clicks per user.

The free forever model, #2 - source of revenue, TBC

In this example, an app is completely free for consumers to use, whilst the source of revenue is... to be confirmed! To go down this route, you will need a strong conviction that your idea has huge potential, the patience to take a long-term view and enough financial backing from investors, loans or from your own personal reserves to keep you going. There are a few ways this might work:

- You could continue to build your user base whilst you consider your options and attempt to find the optimum way to monetise your app via third parties. Which companies would be most interested in (or have something of value to offer) your customer base?
- You could build up your user base, with the end goal of putting yourself in a strong position to "exit" from the business with a payoff in future. There *are* businesses that are bought and sold that have large user bases, but where the seller has not been willing (or able) to monetise their service for some reason.

Once you promise that the app will be free forever, you'll need to stick with this, so make sure you're certain that this is the right approach to take!

Who uses this model?

Clue, a period and mood tracking app is still pre-revenue, (no revenue has been generated yet.) They are backed by investors and have a user base across the Android (Google Play) and iOS (Apple App store) marketplaces. The company was founded by Ida Tin and her partner, who identified a gap in the market for managing and tracking data relating to women's health. They launched the app in 2013 and now have over *100,000 reviews* in the Google Play store: https://play.google.com/store/apps/details?id=com.clue.android&hl=en_GB

WhatsApp is the world's most popular mobile messaging app, with over 1 billion users. It was founded by Brian Acton and Jan Koum, former employees of Yahoo! Koum was introduced to a Russian iPhone developer found by a friend on RentACoder.com (now Freelancer.com), and hired him to build the app. (Please see Chapter 16 for information about Freelancer.com and other places to hire developers.)

WhatsApp have fluctuated between offering their app totally free and charging a $1 annual subscription fee for the service. They have shied away from having ads in their product and the service became completely free to use again in January 2016 under the free forever model.

How will WhatsApp generate income without the subscription fee?

In January 2016, WhatsApp announced that they will be testing tools that will allow their users to communicate with businesses and organisations, so watch this space! https://www.whatsapp.com/

The free trial model

To use this "try before you buy" model, you will need to make a particular service plan, (or all your plans) available for free for a short period of time. Seven, fourteen and thirty day free trials are used most frequently.

This model can be used for mobile and web apps.

Things to consider

If this model interests you, then consider: i) how you will ensure that trial users get the maximum benefit during the trial period and ii) how to convert users into paying customers after the trial ends:

- Try to make the trial period long enough to whet people's appetites. Bear in mind that after 7 days some people may not even have tried the product yet and you will have "lost" them unless you contact them and try to recover the situation.
- Contact your trial users by email and ask them how they're getting on. Do they like the product? Have they had any issues? Do they have any

concerns or questions? People won't convert if they have unaddressed issues with your app.
- It would be useful if you could track which customers have logged in to use their free trial and which ones have not, so you can follow up with both groups, but with a different message. You'll need to ask a developer to set up rules within your app so you can track important events.
Setting up different messages for different types of customer can be handled via *marketing automation*. This information from MailChimp provides a good overview; https://mailchimp.com/resources/guides/working-with-automation/html/ and here are some popular tools; http://blog.capterra.com/most-popular-marketing-automation-software-solutions/
- Why not remind users that their trial will soon be coming to an end via email? You have an opportunity to gather feedback - if they're not interested in upgrading, I'm sure you'd like to know why!
- Will you ask customers to provide a payment card in order to sign up for the free trial, or allow customers to try your product without any form of commitment? Be aware that some customers will be deterred if you ask for a payment card up-front. To overcome that barrier, some companies very openly state that customers can sign up for a free trial with no credit card required.
- What should happen when a trial period ends? Whatever the rules are, they should be included in your *terms and conditions of use*. You will need to have a developer build your app so that access to it is revoked, unless a valid form of payment is received. Decide how this should work and let your developer know what you want them to do.

Who uses this model?

This model is very common, but to give you a specific example, Salesforce, the giants of the CRM (Customer Relationship Management) software market offer free trials on their products. They have a product sign up page where customers can elect to have a free trial with one of their packages,

https://www.salesforce.com/uk/editions-pricing/sales-cloud/,
https://app.salesforceiq.com/start?d=undefined&nc=70130000000fIHO.

CHAPTER 8
Generating revenue from your software

> *Pro tip!*
> **Configuration settings can be used to make your product more flexible.**
> Parts of your mobile or web app can be made *configurable,* by putting *settings*, also known as *logic or rules* in place behind-the-scenes of your app. *Config* can be adjusted to suit your needs and can be set up by developers to control who can do what within your app, when they can do it and to impose limits and restrictions on users based on *user roles*, or according to the package, or payment plan they have signed up for.
> Let's look at an example that's relevant to this chapter.
> You could have a free product trial set to last for 30 days, but in reality, the free trial might be set to last for N number of days. In your case, N is equal to 30, but N can be any number you want; 7 days, 14 days, 30 days or even 100 or 1000 days if that's what you want. In this case, the number of days that the free product trial lasts is *configurable.*
> Configuration settings can cost extra to build and add complexity to your system, but they may be necessary - especially if you want functionality to be restricted or revoked after a time limit has expired or if you want your app to be more "intelligent", or flexible.
>
> What is N? It is the mathematical notation for "natural numbers," which are simply positive whole numbers. Note that zero is a natural number too, so if you set N to zero, you would effectively cancel your customers' free trials!

Charging a one-off fee for your app

In this scenario, your app must be paid for before it can be downloaded and used.

This pricing model can be used for desktop apps, web apps (some charge a one-off fee for lifetime access to their products), and mobile apps.

Which well-known apps have used this model?

The UK's top 5 selling apps in the Google Play Store at the time of writing are shown below.

CHAPTER 8
Generating revenue from your software

Fig 36. The UK's top 5 selling apps in the Google Play store at the time of writing. https://play.google.com.

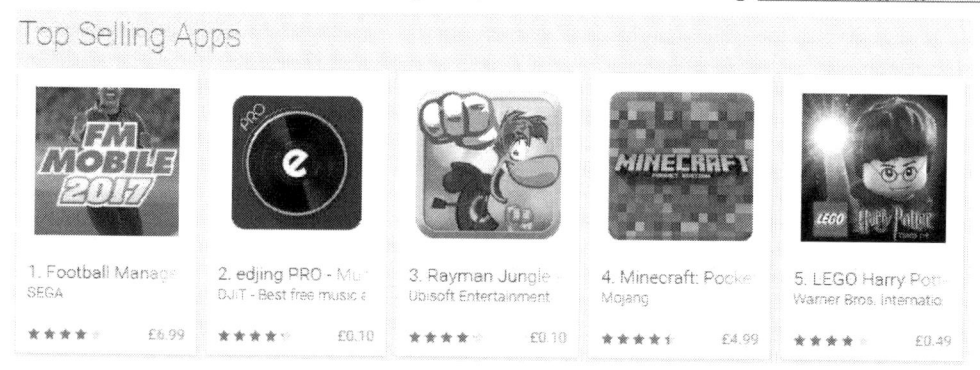

You can check for the latest data using *AppAnnie*. There's a menu option that will allow you to switch between countries, so you can check for the top iOS or Android apps, both for sale and free, in more than 15 different countries.

https://www.appannie.com/apps/google-play/top/united-kingdom/overall/

https://www.appannie.com/apps/ios/top/united-kingdom/overall/iphone/

Things to consider:

- Many users are not keen on paying for apps, so you will need to be clear on what functionality people *would* pay you for.
- Assess other ways to monetise your app, such as the free trial or freemium models and charging for in-app purchases. This will remove the initial hurdle of getting people to pay for the app up-front and will increase the chances of it being downloaded.
- There is no "try before you buy" with this option. Some people may worry that they may not like the app and this could stop them going ahead with the purchase. The freemium model deals with this issue - people can use your functionality and then decide whether they want to pay for it.
- *Check the small print for your app marketplace of choice regarding the amounts they might claim from you if customers who have purchased your app wish to return it and get a refund.* If you had any lingering doubts about the importance of understanding your users, focusing on their needs and user testing your product, I hope this will convince you!

The recurring revenue model

The recurring revenue model involves charging customers a subscription fee on a recurring cycle, for example, monthly (known as MRR; meaning monthly recurring revenue) quarterly, six-monthly, annually or longer, in return for "rented" access to the service. These models have existed for years in other markets in the form of cable TV subscriptions and gym memberships, to name a few examples.

This is a departure from the traditional software license-fee model where business customers in particular, may pay thousands for software licenses, plus support, maintenance and upgrade costs. The recurring revenue model is commonly used for B2B web apps (especially SaaS products). However, it can be used for B2C and for web and mobile apps too – you may have noticed that this model is starting to become more common in the app marketplaces.

I'm sure it will become the norm in future as the recurring revenue model can be very lucrative, can increase the stability of your business and makes forecasting revenue much easier!

Apple now have a page explaining the subscription related services that can be set up for App Store customers;

https://developer.apple.com/app-store/subscriptions/.

Things to consider:

- Subscription fees usually range from a few dollars a month to several hundred pounds, dollars or Euros a month, more at the very top end.
- Recurring payments generate more income in the medium to long term and make it easy for you to budget and forecast earnings. If you have 100 customers paying £50 per month, you know *exactly* what your monthly takings will be and if you don't lose subscribers (or manage to replace leavers with new subscribers), this income will be stable. You can easily project forward to see what your revenue might be if you had 500 customers, or 1000.
- Once you know how much it costs to run your business on a monthly basis, you'll know how many subscribers you need as a minimum to cover your costs - your threshold between breaking-even and profitability.

CHAPTER 8
Generating revenue from your software

Which well-known apps have used this model?

Microsoft has adopted it in recent years, since starting to offer SaaS, as well as desktop versions of their products.

Consider the cost of buying Microsoft Office 365. Currently, you can purchase the PC version, Microsoft Office Home, for around £110. However, you will pay £79.99 per year or £7.99 per month for Office 365 via the Microsoft store. Based on these costs, early in the second year of "renting" Microsoft Office 365, Microsoft will have received more revenue than that taken for the one-off fee for the PC Office Home edition.

Why do people agree to pay more?

- There's less money to pay up-front and the relatively low monthly cost to get started is attractive.
- Access to updates - the PC version will become outdated over time, whilst the online version will receive updates and new functionality when it becomes available.
- Flexibility. The Office 365 subscription can be cancelled, but once you pay for the PC version, you're stuck with it for life. (Conversely, the benefit is also that it's yours for life!)
- It's a hassle-free approach - no software to download, which saves time and energy.
- Convenience. Office 365 is available "everywhere," because it can be used across multiple devices.

How long do most people intend to use MS Office for? This monthly expense could run and run. It could be a monthly bill for decades and how much will Microsoft have earned by then? That isn't the end of it either. There's also the matter of inflation. Microsoft will no doubt increase prices in future to cover increased expenses (and to maintain or increase profit margins.) Rather nice for them, don't you agree?

Examples of some more complex models....

Bluehost.com, one of the world's largest web hosting companies present their prices as the monthly equivalent, but request that accounts are paid upfront and in full when customers sign up: https://www.bluehost.com/shared Does this deter some people? I'm sure it does. The question is whether getting 12 month's

CHAPTER 8
Generating revenue from your software

commitment from a smaller number of customers works for Bluehost from a financial perspective.

Next, let's look at *Zendesk,* a customer service SaaS product that helps companies keep track of their customers' queries and issues – their recurring pricing model is probably one of the more complex that you will see.

Zendesk was "born" in a loft in Copenhagen, Denmark in 2006 and was launched in 2007. The company charges a recurring fee to access their services, which are split across 4 packages. In addition to the 4 service plans, Zendesk charge *per head* for access to each package, according to *the number of customer service agents* using the software. The price advertised for each level of service needs to be multiplied by the *number of agents* that will be using it to get the true monthly cost. The cost of the service also increases depending on whether the service is *paid for up-front for the year or on a monthly rolling basis*. There's a free trial available for each price package too.
https://www.zendesk.com/product/pricing/#faqs

Now we've talked about the types of apps available, the characteristics of the app marketplaces, and a range of pricing models, in the next chapter we'll be discussing some important marketing activities you can put into action once your app is built.

CHAPTER 9
App marketing basics

"The aim of marketing is to know and understand the customer so well the product or service fits him and sells itself."
- Peter Drucker

In this chapter:
- ASO: Marketing and optimisation for your mobile app
- Basic SEO: getting your product found online
- Why your website or web app must be mobile friendly and how to test whether it is
- Using Push Notifications to drive and monitor customer engagement
- Create an online presence fast using website or landing page builders

We'll start this chapter with the essentials for getting your mobile app found in the app marketplaces, and then we'll move on to SEO basics for the web.

The information you present to the world via your *Store Listing Page* in Google Play, or your *App Store Product Page* in the App Store, will play a big part in marketing your app and in making sure it can easily be found when people are browsing the marketplaces for new apps to use.

Marketing your app using your marketplace store listing

ASO (App Store Optimisation) is a similar principle to SEO, Search Engine Optimisation; but in this case, you are optimising in order to be found in an *app store*, rather than a *search engine* like Google, or Bing.

The "sales information" you provide in the app marketplace will help people decide whether they want to download your app. Choose some screens from your app that showcase it well so your *store listing page* or *app product page* is attractive to potential customers. You can do this by using images that a designer has created for you, or you could take screenshots of the different parts of your app, once it's built.

Let's break down the various sections of the store listing / product page and run through some tips you can use for each one.

CHAPTER 9
App marketing basics

Fig 37. WhatsApp Inc's store listing page.

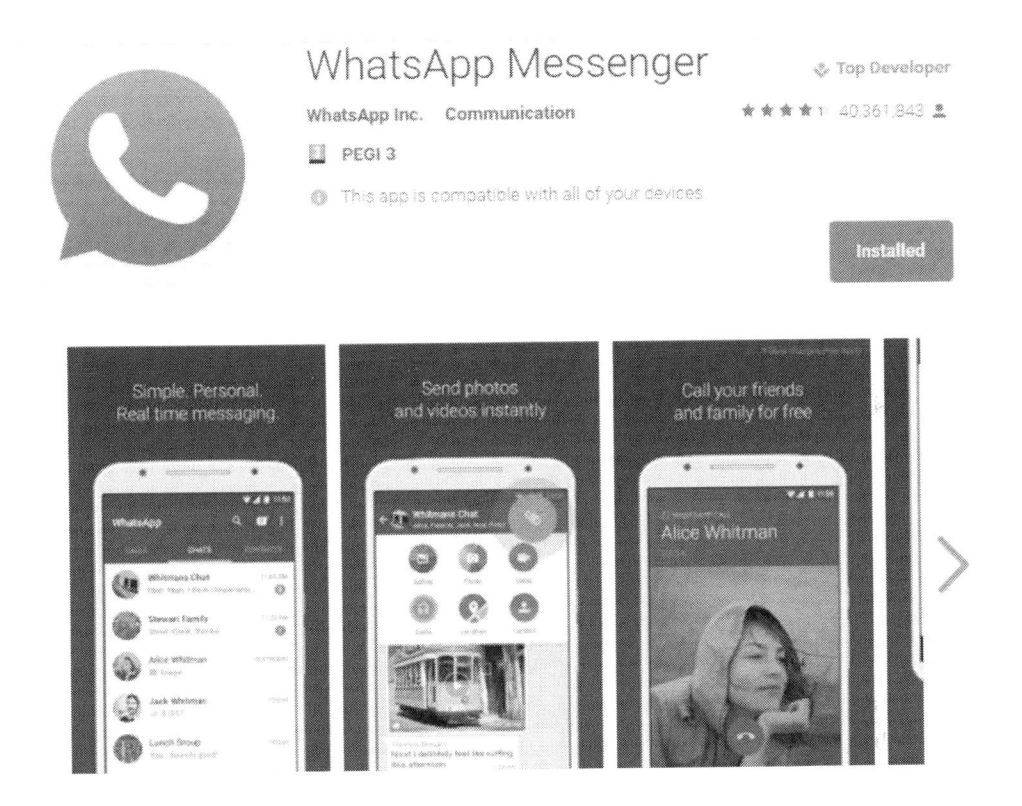

Titles and keywords are searchable within the app marketplaces. Use them to increase the *discoverability* of your app so it can be found and downloaded. Prepare a title and description for your app which clearly explains:
- What it does and clearly outlines its features.
- The problems your app will solve and / or the benefits that customers will receive when they use it.

Your title and description should contain the keywords that your target market would use when searching for an app like yours, so consider how they might describe your functionality and services. Refer to your customer interviews for information and inspiration on what to say and how to say it in order to "sell" your product!

Market research data will helpful here too. Revisit the keyword tools from Chapter 2 for ideas. People search for information about apps on the web too, so you could pick up some good ideas from doing this. Look at the listing pages of apps similar to yours and see what keywords they use to market their apps. Have you missed any important ones?

At the time of writing, *WhatsApp* uses a number of *keywords* in their store listing, including: *free, messaging, call, SMS, photos, videos, documents, 4G, 3G, 2G, Edge, Wi-Fi, voice, send* and *receive*.

https://play.google.com/store/apps/details?id=com.whatsapp&hl=en_GB

Include some enticing images or a video of your app "in action". Both Google Play and the App Store provide space for several images or videos within your listing to showcase your app. Knowing your target market well will help you select images and create video(s) that will appeal to them.

Provide positive feedback and quotes to convince people browsing the app stores to go ahead and download it. We'll be talking about creating and testing prototypes over the course of the next few chapters. This will be a brilliant opportunity to collect positive feedback from customer interviews and user testing sessions and to include them in your app store listing and in other promotional materials.

Ask people to download your app and leave you a review. Reviews are important in the app marketplaces, so ask previous user testers, and as many people as possible to download your app and leave you a review. Continue to ask for reviews after your app is launched.

Here's some more information to help you maximise your marketplace listing from Apple; https://developer.apple.com/app-store/product-page and the Google Play Store (scroll down to the "Set up your Store Listing" section); https://support.google.com/googleplay/android-developer/answer/113469?hl=en-GB and guidelines; https://developer.apple.com/app-store/guidelines/

If you're wondering what the App Store equivalent looks like for WhatsApp, that's a good question! It's not very easy to display here, but here's a link to the *App Store Product Page* for WhatsApp:
https://itunes.apple.com/gb/app/whatsapp-messenger/id310633997?mt=8

CHAPTER 9
App marketing basics

Creating icons for your app

Icons for mobile apps

If you haven't yet done so, you'll also need to create your own *mobile app icon* (or *app launcher icon*.) It's well worth coming up with several different designs and showing them to your target customers, as well as friends and family to get opinions about which are the most visually appealing and why. If your app icon is more eye-catching than others in its category, you just might beat the competition and entice more people to download it! Take a look at the app icons displayed here. Which one draws your attention the most and why?

Fig 38. App launcher icons.

Here are the guidelines for app icons provided by Google Play and Apple, including the icon sizes you'll need.

Google Play:
https://developer.android.com/guide/practices/ui_guidelines/icon_design_launcher.html
Apple:
https://developer.apple.com/tvos/human-interface-guidelines/icons-and-images/

If you'd like to see some more examples of app launcher icons without having to search the app marketplaces, try Homescreen.is, http://homescreen.is/

Icons for web apps

Even if you're not going to build a mobile app, you will probably want a logo that you can display within your web app, on your website and for marketing and branding purposes, both on and offline. If that is the case, you can follow the tips for mobile apps in the previous section.

Favicons

If you're developing a web app, or creating a website, then ideally, you should also have a set of favicons. *Favicons* (short for *favourites icons*) are tiny icons that make your website easier to identify (especially when you have multiple browser windows open, like I do in the example below!) They too are part of your online branding. Can you see the two browser tabs that are missing them?

When working for a client I would expect to get all these elements taken care of *before* launch, but nothing will break without them, so put dealing with favicons on your to-do list and remind your developer to upload them when they have time.

Different web browsers require favicons in different sizes and formats for websites, smartphones and tablets, so speak to your developer about the specific file formats required.

If you're stuck, there are favicon generator tools available online, like this one: http://www.favicon-generator.org/.

This sort of task is well-suited to designers or front-end developers, but a back-end developer should know had to add the favicon files to your app. See chapter 16 for places to find a designer to create your logo, icon and favicon in the correct formats and dimensions.

Please note that if you use a landing page builder, it may not be possible to have a favicon - the functionality to add them to your landing page is not always provided. We'll talk about website and landing page builders later in this chapter.

CHAPTER 9
App marketing basics

Getting your product found online

Whether you're building a web app or a mobile app, a website will give you a marketing presence online.
Good SEO (Search Engine Optimisation) will ensure that you rank highly in search results when people search for keywords relevant to your business or product. There are several hundred factors that can improve (or damage) SEO and the current stats for Google search results are terrifying - 98% of people searching only look at the first page of results on Google and just 2% of people click through to page two.

Google is the dominant search engine in the UK and US, so if you focus on SEO work to improve your ranking on Google, that will be the most efficient use of your time, however, SEO work can also be done on Bing and other search engines, if you wish to cover every base. Statista.com has rankings for many countries available, so you can see which browsers people use to find content on the web in a range of countries.

Fig 39. Market share held by the leading search engines in the United Kingdom (UK) as of June 2016, Source Statista.com, https://www.statista.com/statistics/280269/market-share-held-by-search-engines-in-the-united-kingdom/.

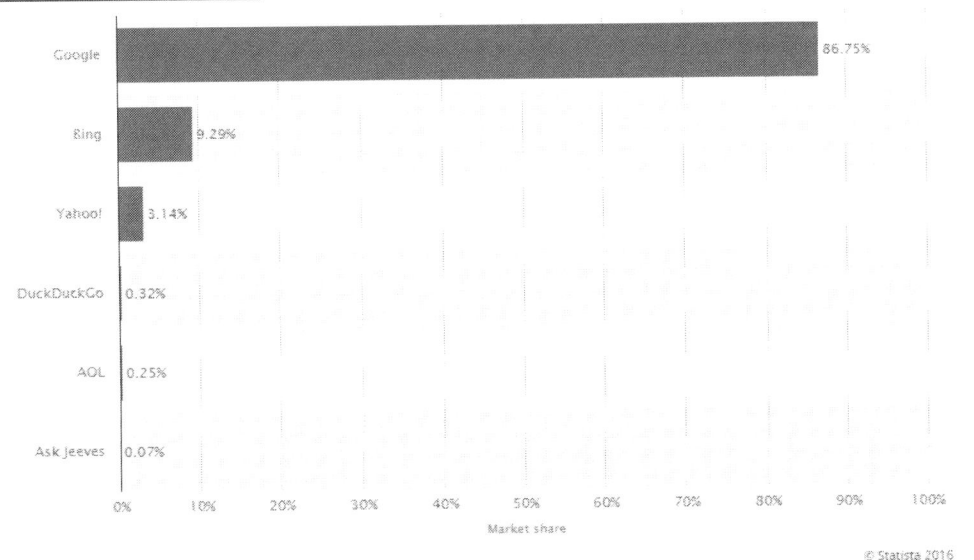

Search Engine	Market Share
Google	86.75%
Bing	9.29%
Yahoo!	3.14%
DuckDuckGo	0.32%
AOL	0.25%
Ask Jeeves	0.07%

© Statista 2016

CHAPTER 9
App marketing basics

SEO and driving traffic to your website to convert into users and revenue is an ongoing activity more like running a marathon than a sprint! Creating a *blog* (web log) gives you an opportunity to attract target customers interested in the topics that you are writing about. However, this is more likely to produce results in the medium to long term.

So how can you make an impact in the short term? When you create a new website, there are some immediate actions you can take to help boost SEO:

Write page title and **meta-description tags** for each one of your web pages. The page title is the title of your page and the meta description is a summary of the content on your page, which is displayed in search results. Make sure they are both "keyword rich" and contain the words or phrases your target customers might look for.

Fig 40. Page titles and meta descriptions, plus image and video search rankings.

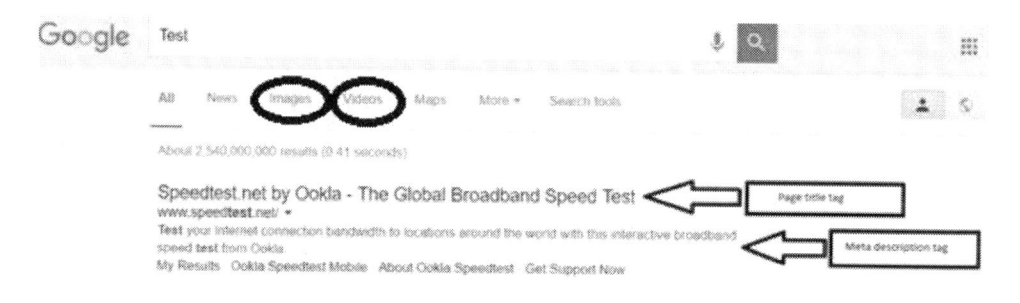

Set the headings for each of your web pages. Search engines rely on the headings used on websites and web apps to make sense of the structure of your web pages. H1 defines the most important heading on your page (usually your product, brand name or business benefits) whilst h6 defines the least important heading, with headings 2-5 in between. Your developer can set the relevant page headings for you. You don't have to define all 6 headings, h1 and h2 are most important.

CHAPTER 9
App marketing basics

Fig 41. Page headings are used to structure your content and to indicate the relevant importance of each heading and section of content.

h1. Heading 1

h2. Heading 2

h3. Heading 3

h4. Heading 4

h5. Heading 5

h6. Heading 6

Write SEO friendly "body text". The main body of content on each page should contain important and relevant keywords.

Write image and video descriptions. Images and videos should have descriptions and *alt (or alternative) tags,* which explain what they are. If your videos are tagged i.e. labelled with relevant keywords, you will have the chance of ranking in Google's Image and Video search results, as well as making non-text content meaningful for blind people and those with other disabilities. Some disabled users rely on screen readers that "speak" aloud the labels on your images and videos in order to understand what this content is. This improves the *accessibility* of your website, which is a legal requirement we discussed back in chapter 6.

Register your website with Google (log in to a Gmail account first): https://www.google.com/webmasters/tools/submit-url?continue=/addurl&pli=1

Submit your website's sitemap to Google. This invites Google's *bots* or *spiders* to "crawl" your website or web app, so your pages show up in Google search results. See the SEO starter guide below for details. You may need help from a

CHAPTER 9
App marketing basics

developer to do this, although you can do all the other tasks yourself if you have access to the "back-end" of your website where all the administrator controls are located.

A word of warning, don't *keyword stuff*, (repeat the same keywords over and over to try and boost search rankings.) You could be penalised by Google for trying to game the system. They have ways of detecting overuse of the same words and phrases, so make sure your content flows naturally.

Only Google knows *exactly* how many criteria go into an SEO ranking and how websites are scored and they can change the algorithm that determines the search rankings whenever they please. I believe that it's best to get SEO advice straight from the source, so here are some guidance documents from Google:

- Create descriptive page titles and good meta-descriptions:
  https://support.google.com/webmasters/answer/35624?hl=en - 1
- SEO starter guide:
  https://static.googleusercontent.com/media/www.google.com/en//webmasters/docs/search-engine-optimization-starter-guide.pdf

---

Pro tip!

Allow Google to promote your *mobile app* on the *web* using *Firebase*.

As soon as you launch your app, get it *indexed* by Google, so that it's registered on Google's servers. Once Google "knows" about your app, it can be launched or installed if it comes up in Google's search results, https://firebase.google.com/docs/app-indexing/

Page speed is important, both for SEO (as Google can penalise "slow" websites) and because anyone coming to your site will expect your pages to load quickly. Google has some web page speed analysis tools here. Check periodically to see how your web pages perform:

https://developers.google.com/speed/pagespeed/insights/?hl=en

CHAPTER 9
App marketing basics

Making sure your website or web app is mobile-friendly

More people now access the web via mobile than by any other method and as a result, Google has begun penalising websites that are not mobile-friendly. The reasoning behind this is that your content is of less use to customers if they can't read it properly or are unable to use your website's functionality on their phone. Dropdown menus and pop-up boxes are not phone friendly, nor are websites with lots of tabs.

Since close to 90% of the UK's population use Google (the figures are only slightly lower in the US at the time of writing), there isn't much of an alternative. Your site will need to be mobile friendly or else you will have to rely on paid searches and other indirect methods in order to be found online.

Improving customer engagement

Now that your mobile or web app can be found and has been optimised for search and for the app stores and you've done your best to encourage customers to sign-up for your app or download it, what happens next?

Not everyone who downloads an app, or signs-up to access one takes the next step and actually uses it. Therefore, encouraging them to use it - and *to continue* using it, will become your next priority.

It would be misleading to focus on measuring the number of downloads you have, if only a small proportion of those who download your app then *activate;* and start using it. If 10 people activate for every 100 that download or sign up, that's a 10% conversion rate. Could you find out why people didn't start using your app? How might you increase the number of activations you get and in doing so, increase your conversion rate?

You may also wish to consider monthly *uninstalls* of your app and the numbers of people cancelling their web or mobile app subscriptions. Why is this happening? You may not be able to keep every customer, but what can you do to reduce this number as much as possible?

You will be seeking to:

- Increase the number of *downloads* or product sign-ups that happen each month.
- Increase the number of *activations* per month, and as a total percentage of all downloads, so that your conversion rate increases.
- Decrease the number of *uninstalls* and subscription cancellations.

Push Notifications - a low-cost engagement tool for mobile and web apps

Push Notifications are short messages that can be sent to mobile devices or displayed via websites and web apps. Push Notifications are marketing tools used to increase activation and conversion rates. They can help businesses to maintain or increase their visibility, communicate with customers and remind them about their services. Unlike email communications, which are not always delivered and can go into junk, spam or promotional folders, these notifications are displayed directly on customers' web browsers or in the *message*, or *notification tray* of their mobile device, *even when they aren't using your app!*

Fig 42. A mobile app requesting permission to send push notifications to a customers' mobile device.

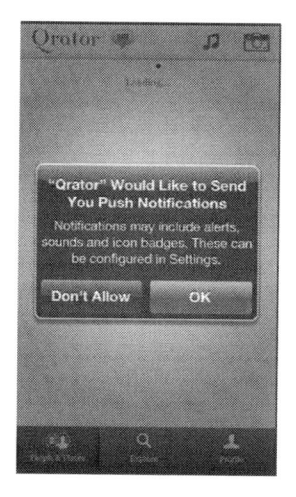

Push notifications for mobile apps are economical to send. Via Amazon Web Services, (AWS), the cost is $0.50 USD per million notifications: https://aws.amazon.com/sns/pricing/.

Analytics tools such as *Mixpanel* https://mixpanel.com/notifications/ and *Parse* http://parse.com/ can be used to monitor the effectiveness of the push notifications that you send.

Push notifications for web browsers. Websites and web apps can request permission to send notifications to customers. If the customer agrees to receive the notifications (and therefore becomes a notification subscriber), then these will appear as small notices in the corner of their browser window. The notifications can be sent in real-time and may contain links which will open a

CHAPTER 9
App marketing basics

specific web page if clicked. Google provides advice for developers on how to make these notifications available in Chrome browsers here:

https://developers.google.com/web/fundamentals/getting-started/push-notifications/step-06?hl=en.

Fig 43. Example of a web browser requesting permission to send push notifications to a customer.

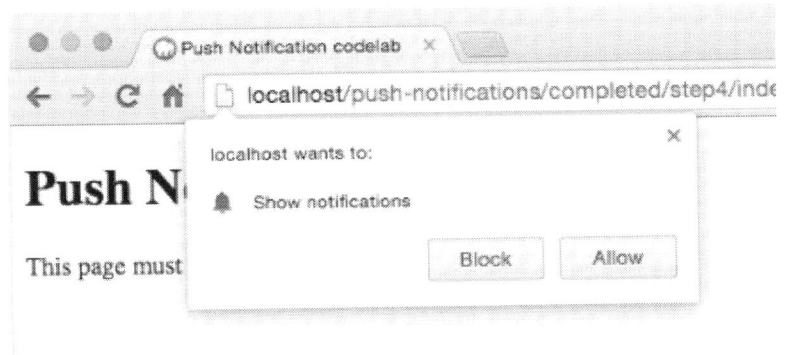

Create an online presence using a website builder

If you would rather not pay to have a website built from scratch, there are many website builder tools that you can use that do not require any code to be written.

This might be useful if you wish to build a mobile app and do not also want to hire someone to build you a website.

You could use the website to demonstrate the benefits of your app, to showcase video demonstrations or screen shots of it, or to tell people about your beta launch, (see chapter 24 to find out more about running a beta launch once an early version of your product is built.)

If you'd like to see how businesses that sell *mobile apps* promote themselves *online*, take a look at these sites:
Toshl Finance (iOS, Android, Windows, Blackberry and more), https://toshl.com/
The Headspace app (Android and iOS), https://www.headspace.com/headspace-meditation-app.

The following are all well-established players in the website builder market:
Wix, http://www.wix.com/
Weebly, http://www.weebly.com/
1and1, https://www.1and1.co.uk/

Squarespace, https://www.squarespace.com
WordPress, www.wordpress.com/
Moonfruit, http://www.moonfruit.com/
Zohosites, https://www.zoho.com/sites/website-builder.html

They all offer a large selection of website templates and the majority have plug-ins available which will add extra functionality to your site. Plug-in examples include online review plug-ins, the ability to add PayPal buttons to the site to transform it into an e-commerce store and price plan comparison widgets (see the links and examples in chapter 8), which are used to display the service and pricing options available to customers. Double check that the template you select is *responsive* and will re-size for mobile.

Give your chosen site(s) my 30-minute test. If you can't make progress quickly and without getting too frustrated within that period, it's time to switch!

Landing page apps

Landing pages are 1-page websites used to perform a specific purpose such as promoting or selling a product or service, or to collect sales leads.

Launchrock http://launchrock.com/ and *Kickoff labs* https://kickofflabs.com/ focus on providing services for startups. Other landing page tools include:

Instapage, https://instapage.com

Landingi, https://landingi.com/

Leadpages, https://www.leadpages.net

ActiveTrail, https://www.activetrail.com/

Mailerlite, https://www.mailerlite.com/full-feature-list

Ontraport, https://ontraport.com/

Landerapp, https://landerapp.com/

All the tools offer a free trial, and prices start from around $29 per month, apart from ActiveTrail which starts from a budget-friendly price of $7 per month and supports email and SMS marketing and Mailerlite which offers a freemium package. Most of these apps will let you create *as many landing pages as you like* under the same account, and as a rule, most will allow you to connect domains you have already purchased to a limited number of landing pages.

CHAPTER 9
App marketing basics

Some also offer A/B testing functionality, which lets you compare two different versions of a landing page by displaying them both to customers on rotation. A page showing the effectiveness of each one will be available for you to review within the app.

My tip would be to sign up for 2 or 3 tools on a trial basis with the functionality you want. (Most will give you between 14 and 30 days for free.) See how much you can achieve with each one in a set period of time, then decide which product is right for you.

Fig 44. Inside the *Landerapp* landing page builder.

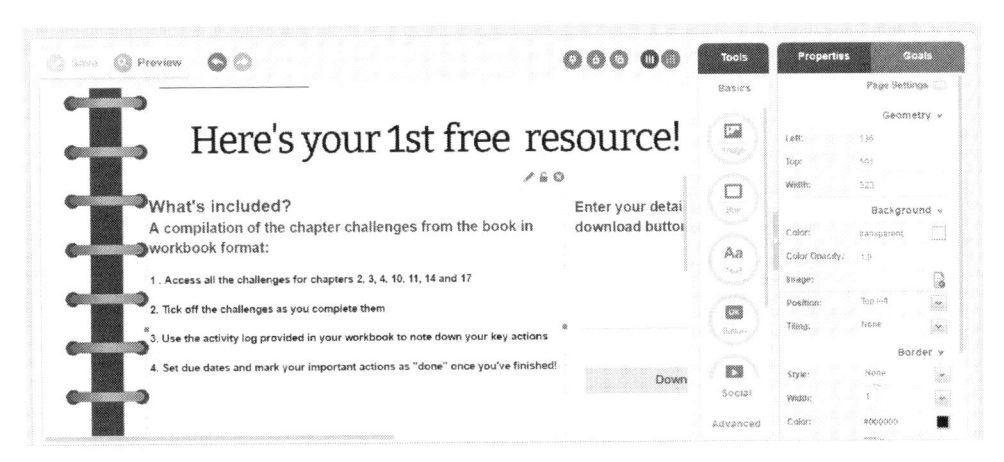

This marks the end of section 3! In section 4 we'll be looking at user experience and how to create a clean, easy to use app for your customers. I'll be showing you some tools and techniques for creating a prototype from scratch and explaining how to test the prototype with members of your target customer group.

SECTION 4

PROTOTYPING, USER EXPERIENCE AND CHOOSING YOUR MVP

CHAPTER 10
Prepare to prototype!

"A lot of times, people don't know what they want until you show it to them."

- Steve Jobs

In this chapter:
- The benefits of prototyping
- Pro tips and Project pitfalls
- Creating user journeys and capturing processes
- A worked example using the avatar resources from chapter 3
- Save money using the Pareto Principle!
- Chapter challenges

Do you sigh, roll your eyes, or get annoyed when a computer program takes too long to load?
Have you heard friends or colleagues complaining bitterly about terrible software that no-one understands how to use properly?
You already know how frustrating it feels when software is clunky, disjointed, difficult to use or requires too many clicks, or steps to operate, so give your customers a break! Have these common bugbears in mind *before* you even start to build your software. Placing emphasis on a positive customer experience can begin right now – at the prototyping stage of the project.

Shortly we'll cover information that could save you hundreds if not thousands of pounds in development costs and will bring you closer to having the blueprint for a killer product.

The quote from Steve Jobs at the start of this chapter refers to the confidence he had in his vision for the first version of the iPhone - something the world had never seen before. Mr. Jobs had his own blend of genius, but this book is about helping you manage risk and safeguard your interests, so we're not going to take any chances!

CHAPTER 10
Prepare to prototype!

Let's recap on some key points from section 1:

- The first version of your idea won't be perfect and doesn't have to be.
- Your idea will evolve as you speak to more people about it.
- At the concept, or idea stage of a project, focus your energies on research – learn about the market and your competitors and speak to as many target customers as possible to understand their problems and to test that your assumptions and theories are correct.
- Investing money, time, and effort in a product *before* you know the level of demand for it is a major risk.
- You don't need to have all the answers - your target market will give them to you both directly and indirectly. *You just need to start the ball rolling by asking the right questions, listening carefully and staying observant.*

The power of prototyping

According to The Oxford Dictionary, a prototype is defined as "a first or preliminary version of a device or vehicle from which other forms are developed."

Therefore, a prototype is not intended to be a finished product, but a starting point.

The definition does not refer to how the prototype will evolve into other forms, but this will happen naturally as the prototype is used to gather feedback – *if* you act on the best of it, of course!

Had you considered using a prototype to test out your idea? Either way, I'll outline the benefits:

- A prototype provides a low-cost way of testing out your theories.
- Prototypes can help you save money by increasing the amount of *clarity* you have about what you should build *before* you spend money on building "the real thing."
- Prototypes reduce the risk that you'll pay a developer to build something that your target customers aren't interested in.
- Creating a prototype speeds up the rate at which you can refine your idea and work through any challenges.

CHAPTER 10
Prepare to prototype!

- Prototypes give people something real to look at and interact with – this will give you a better quality of feedback than trying to describe your idea in words.
- *Prototyping also weeds out "half-baked" ideas.*

To be successful, your idea *must* work in practice as well as in theory. Usually when we have an idea, we imagine the bright and shining end-result, and everything comes together perfectly and works just like magic! But, as you know, your idea is only the beginning of the story.

I'd like to demonstrate exactly what I mean, but I'll need your help! I'd like you to imagine a red car.

Now, hold that image for me please, this will all make sense very soon…

Project pitfall!

Don't hire a developer too soon.
I've seen costs mount on projects when teams have been hired or assembled without there being a clear idea of what we actually needed to build. This is a bit like calling a taxi and then having it wait for weeks with the meter running because you know you need to go *somewhere*, but you're not sure exactly where!

Why does this happen? Often, it's because under the surface of an idea there is a HUGE amount of detail that needs to be worked through – sometimes the effort of doing that takes much more time than anyone imagined. It can be hard to see where the complexity lies in tasks until you dig much deeper and therefore it is easy to underestimate the work involved.

If you haven't hired anyone to work for you yet, then now is the best (and cheapest) time to rectify any issues or challenges that exist in relation to your product idea. You can rip up a sheet of paper or create a new mock-up in minutes - amending software can take far longer and the cost of changes will erode your budget.

Once you hire a developer, you will also be under more pressure - you'll have someone relying on you to supply them with a steady stream of accurate information so they can do their job and you'll need to be available to answer their questions.

CHAPTER 10
Prepare to prototype!

> *Make sure you're ready and able to do this!* We'll talk about hiring developers in chapters 16 and 17.

Please think back to your red car and now take a look at this image.

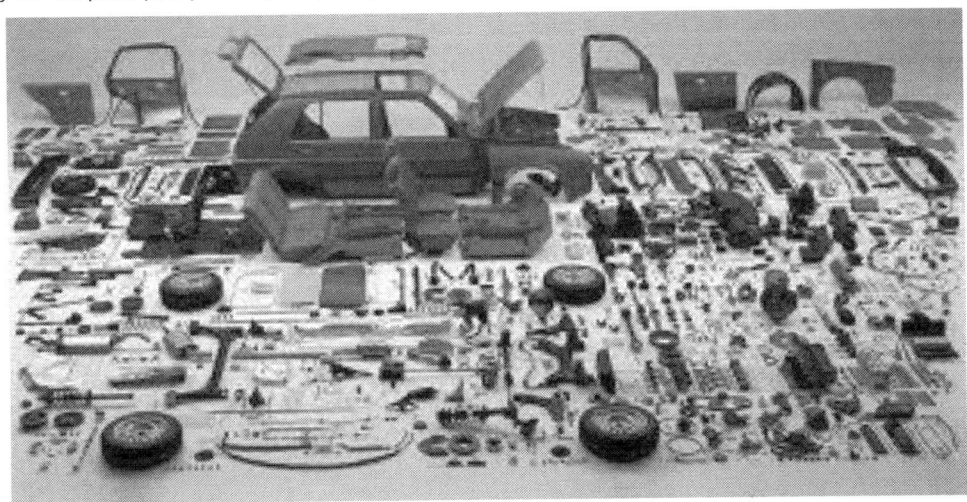

Fig 45. The parts (and parts of parts) of a product.

Was this the car that you visualised? I doubt it was!

The car you imagined a few minutes ago, represents your "bright and shining" idea and what you visualise as being *your end result*. However, the image in fig 45 is much closer to the reality of what you'll have *before* you receive your finished car; a collection of parts to arrange in a logical (and commercially viable) order so that you can serve your customers and make money from it.

You and your developer will be working together to make sure you have all the right parts, and to get them assembled.

You'll need to give them explicit requirements (even if they seem obvious, this is no place for assumptions) for instance; "I need to be able to open and close the car doors", "I need to be able to sit down in it and drive forwards", "I need to be able to drive in reverse", "I need to be able to drive up to 70 miles per hour in it" etc.

Now your developer needs to wave their magic wand (or rather, do a lot of thinking, coding and head scratching) to make this happen!

CHAPTER 10
Prepare to prototype!

Mapping out user journeys will help you create useful prototypes

A user journey covers the steps or interactions required to complete a specific goal or activity whilst using your app. User journeys can help you explain what needs to happen step-by-step using drawings or diagrams.

You could have any number of user journeys within your app and you will need to capture all the journeys that exist, plus the steps that are involved in getting from start to finish within each journey. As part of this, you will need to consider how users will move from one screen, web page or activity to another. Some products will also have different user journeys for different users. I'm going to explain using the Freepik avatars from chapter 3, so you can see how to put them to practical use.

Creating user journeys and capturing processes

This example is relevant for all types of app, but for those of you not wanting to create a *B2B* app, please stay with me and follow along - a user journey is still a user journey whether it's based on business activities or consumer ones. This is about understanding the *thought process* behind getting your user journeys mapped out.

When you're creating your user journeys, don't forget to use the customer profiles that you put together in chapter 3 to remind yourself of the key problems that you are trying to solve.

Let's imagine that we intend to create a software product for Human Resource Managers.

In this example, our first avatar, Sam Morris, is an **office junior.** He does all the **admin** work at his company. His boss, Robert Harris an **HR Manager,** wouldn't normally do admin roles, he's too busy. They don't share the same user journeys because these users have *roles* which are different. They don't want, or need to perform the same activities in the application.

One of Sam's activities is simple.

He checks that new employees have been registered into the HR Database with the correct start date.

CHAPTER 10
Prepare to prototype!

He logs in (step 1) checks the relevant employees' start dates, (step 2) and then logs out (step 3.)

This is just one user journey and each step needs to be investigated:

- How does an administrator like Sam log into the app?
- How will they log out?
- What about passwords and security?
- Where does the data Sam is checking come from?
- How do Sam and Robert want to see their company's data presented on-screen?

You can give each user journey a name that describes what it is about and what the key activity is - Sam's user journey might be named **View employee information**. That name could be improved upon really, it's a bit vague, so this might become **View employee start and end dates**, for instance.

Pro tip!
Gather all ideas and feedback, but manage expectations.
When user testing, you might learn that potential customers would like specific functionality or wish to perform an activity in a certain way. Note down all requests, and if you speak to a range of customers who ask for the same thing(s), then you will have discovered a trend.

You may find it helpful to ask a developer about the practicalities of building certain functionality *before* you promise that this can be done! If you commit yourself to doing work that you later discover is very complex or expensive, you could find yourself in a difficult, or embarrassing situation if you need to change your plans. In chapter 14 we'll talk about different strategies to help you decide what you will and won't build for your first *product release.*

CHAPTER 10
Prepare to prototype!

Fig 46. User journeys for an office administrator and an HR Manager.

Sam Morris, Office junior

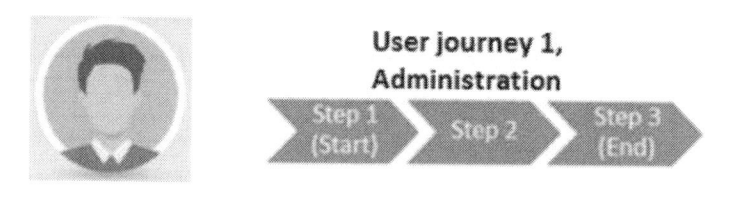

User journey 1, Administration
Step 1 (Start) > Step 2 > Step 3 (End)

Robert Harris, HR Manager

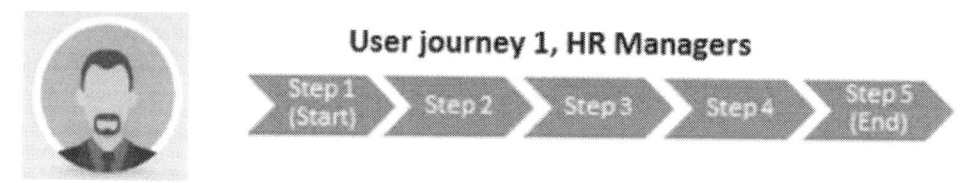

User journey 1, HR Managers
Step 1 (Start) > Step 2 > Step 3 > Step 4 > Step 5 (End)

Rob's first user journey is more complex, but in both cases, once you've laid out what you *think* the user journeys are, based on your current level of knowledge. Next, you can create a prototype that represents them in the form of screens or web pages, that you can demonstrate to your target customers.

You might discover that you have Rob's steps in the wrong order, or that there are steps missing or that not all the steps are necessary. If you'd just gone ahead and done what you thought was right, you may have gone off track - that's the power of prototyping and user testing!

If you're interested in B2B software development, always consider the hierarchy within an organisation and seek agreement from all the decision makers and influencers. We ask both Sam *and* Robert for their opinion about how the functionality should work, because it is important to consult both those who will use the software (who may know the details of day-to-day processes) and the management that they report to - who are likely to be paying for it and will have a deeper understanding of the strategic objectives of the company.

CHAPTER 10
Prepare to prototype!

Other ways to map out your user journeys

There are some simple ways to capture an overview of the steps in your user journeys:

Use a numbered list

These have been written in *the voice of the customer,* by stating each activity with the words, "I can" and describing what they are able to do using the app. For instance:

A user journey for a customer amending their profile details in an app.

- From the starting point: https://www.mywebapp.com
- Step 1. I can log into the app
- Step 2. I can view my profile details
- Step 3. I can log out

Use a simple diagram

Fig 47. Using a simple diagram to represent each step, or process in your user journey.

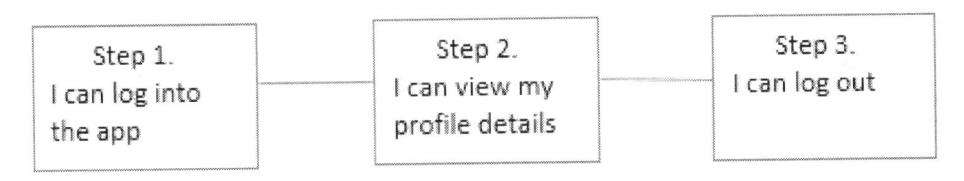

```
[Step 1.              [Step 2.              [Step 3.
 I can log into   —    I can view my    —    I can log out]
 the app]              profile details]
```

Create a process flow diagram

For more complex journeys, a *process flow diagram* could be used to capture each step and indicate any decision points along the journey. You can access a range of process flow templates at the link below. To create a more complex process diagram which includes user or system decisions, you can use the symbols in the chart below.

CHAPTER 10
Prepare to prototype!

Fig 48. Flowchart symbols. *Braille ATM.*

Symbol	Name	Function
(oval)	Start/end	An oval represents a start or end point
(arrow)	Arrows	A line is a connector that shows relationships between the representative shapes
(parallelogram)	Input/Output	A parallelogram represents input or output
(rectangle)	Process	A rectangle represents a process
(diamond)	Decision	A diamond indicates a decision

You can also use an app like *Lucidchart* to create your diagrams. There is a plan available that will allow you to create a small number of diagrams free of charge. https://www.lucidchart.com/

Fig 49. Lucidchart template.

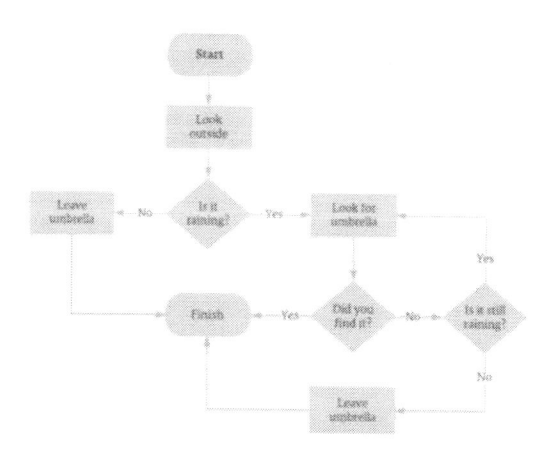

CHAPTER 10
Prepare to prototype!

If you're familiar with process flow diagrams, you should use them – most developers will find them easy to follow. If not, then capturing the steps in writing and clearly stating what happens at each point along the journey is good enough for now.

If flowcharts don't appeal, a mind map will do the job too. The important thing is to do some planning! Try Bubble.us https://bubbl.us or Coggle, https://coggle.it/ for free mind mapping tools. These mind maps can be printed and downloaded, so they're pretty flexible.

Your developer is going to want all this information in future, (and will be very grateful for it) so if you can start capturing what these steps are right now, you'll be making great progress!

The Pareto Principle and software

I claimed at the beginning of this chapter that it could save you a lot of money.

Making sure you are ready before you hire your developer, and avoiding building too much functionality will both help you to reduce your costs.

Feel free to explore and consider the wide range of tasks that you *could* do, but use the feedback from prototyping to *narrow down* tasks to what you *must* do, rather than trying to build "everything" and increasing your expenses in the process.

If you're familiar with the Pareto Principle (also known as the 80/20 rule), you may be aware of how it applies to software: we use approximately **20% of the same functionality, 80%** of the time. Think of the software you use and the proportion of the available functionality you actually bother with and you'll see what I mean! Here's a link to an interesting business article on the topic: http://www.forbes.com/sites/davelavinsky/2014/01/20/pareto-principle-how-to-use-it-to-dramatically-grow-your-business/ - 53bb678a1259

Why not save time and money and focus on that magic 20%?

To find out what your 20% is, listen carefully to what your target customers say about their essential and favourite features - *before* you pay to have any functionality built! The only way to truly know what functionality people will use is to build it and track what functionality is used, but the more people you ask and the more insight you can draw from their feedback, the closer you'll get to the right answers.

Whatever functionality you *do* decide to build, make it very obvious so that customers know it exists and can get the maximum benefit from your app. If people can't or don't use the functionality you've provided, you will have wasted time, energy and money unnecessarily.

> *Project Pitfall!*
> **Don't forget the additional functionality needed to <u>manage</u> your app!**
> It's a common rookie mistake to forget about the functionality that is needed "behind-the-scenes" of your app, and we talked about NFRs in Chapter 6.
>
> I want to emphasise the importance of allowing budget for these items: for example, tools such as *administration screens*, that will allow you, or anyone who supports your app to log in as a customer in order to *see what they see* and to troubleshoot issues.
>
> There will be some tough decisions to make, because you will have to decide which ones will be most valuable when your app launches.
>
> It can be useful to brainstorm different ways to achieve your goals which are "cheaper" and require less development time.

CHAPTER 10
Prepare to prototype!

Get them done and check them off! Chapter 10 challenges:

- ☐ Think about all the activities that users will need to perform using your app.
- ☐ Draw out all the user journeys for each activity on paper. You may also wish to organise them using a mind mapping tool or process flow diagram. Be sure to capture all the steps in each journey.
- ☐ Repeat this exercise for each *user role* that exists within your app. (You have multiple roles if different people need to perform *completely different tasks* in the app.)
- ☐ Now consider any functionality you will need to support your customers, or to understand how they use your app.
- ☐ Next check that the journeys and the steps within them make sense and "flow" logically from one step to the next. Repeat this until you can't find any more gaps or issues. You can use the most accurate version as a basis for your first prototype! In chapter 13 we'll talk about how to run some user testing sessions so you can gather feedback.
- ☐ Keep all this information somewhere safe. Photograph and upload your drawings, store all your user journeys and keep notes on all the functionality you believe the product should have.

You can download the chapter challenges work book, with an activity log to help you keep track of important tasks by clicking the link below:
http://www.mylanderpages.com/donthireasoftwaredeveloperuntilyoureadthisbook/Free-resource-1

CHAPTER 11
Creating a positive "user experience" for your customers

In this chapter:
- The fundamentals of UX (user experience)
- Standards and conventions for web and mobile apps
- Mobile app gestures and interaction design
- Adding colour to your app
- Mascots and mind-tricks
- Chapter challenges

In chapter 5, we reviewed the importance of a number of technical roles, including UX and Design, and in the previous chapter, we looked at how to map out the journeys within your app and the high-level steps involved in each journey.

Now we're going to look in more detail at how that translates into a user interface for your app. We'll be talking about what customers will see, how they will interact with your app, and how you will create a positive, and uncomplicated experience for them!

These important UX and user interface pointers will give you the basics you'll need to create your prototype, which we'll do in chapter 12.

User orientation and navigation

"Don't buy that product. It will drive you crazy!"
There is a particular landing page product that bloggers and Internet marketers have been criticising online and on business webinars over the last year or so. Don't worry, I didn't include it in the list of landing pages I provided! The quote above is a real one from a customer of the company. Others have even made up unflattering nicknames for it because of the frustrating experiences that they have had.

When people start advising others *not* to buy your product, you have serious user experience - and business issues!

Let's talk about a few ways to help your users and make your product easier, and more pleasant to use.

CHAPTER 11
Creating a positive "user experience" for your customers

User orientation helps users answers the question - "where am I?" as they navigate their way around your app. If there are 5 steps to go through to perform a task, how would your users know how much progress they'd made and how many steps were left? Unfortunately, they won't - unless you tell them!

When you invite guests into your home, would you:

Welcome them in and escort them around?
Let them in and at least point out where the basic conveniences are?
Or, open the door, walk away leave them to fend for themselves?

I'm sure very few people do the latter, yet with software this behaviour is so common!

Your customers will appreciate clear *signposting* which confirms:

- How to start a process.
- How to continue with that process and what is going to happen next.
- Where they are *right now* in the process. (Users should know where they are within your app at all times.)

Have you ever used software that reminds you of being trapped in a maze? Feeling "lost" when using an app is a negative experience for customers.

Fig 50. Feeling lost? https://upload.wikimedia.org/wikipedia/commons/7/78/Traquair_House_Maze.jpg by marsroverdriver

Here's a tool that does a good job with user orientation and addresses many of the points that we've just covered.

CHAPTER 11
Creating a positive "user experience" for your customers

Now redesigned and rebranded to *Mailshake*, https://mailshake.com/ it's a SaaS web app that can be used to send out emails.

Fig 51. A simple, user-friendly interface. https://mailshake.com/

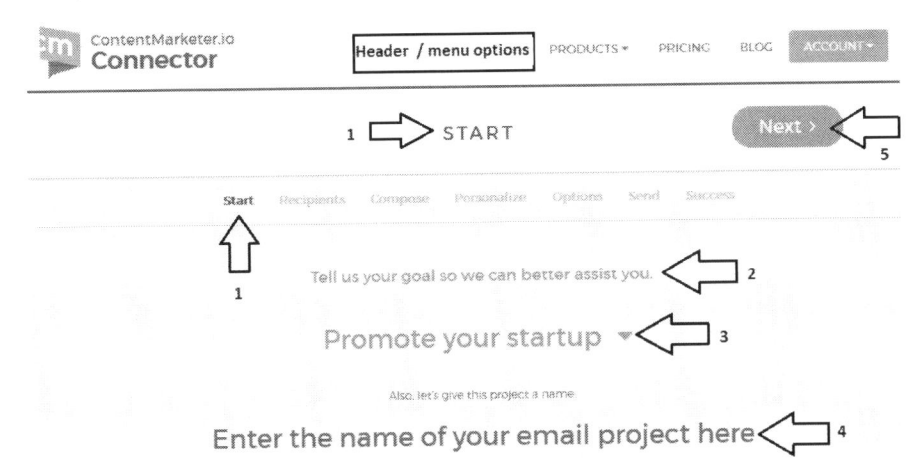

At the top of the screen, you can see the big START text. **Arrow 1** also makes it clear that I'm at the start of the process and shows me that there are seven stages that I need to pass through, beginning with "Start" and ending with "Success."

There is some on-screen copy that encourages me to tell the app my goal, indicated by **arrow 2** and although we can't see the options, the little upside-down triangle that **arrow 3** points to, tells me that there are some choices available to me in a *dropdown menu*.

Arrow 4 points to a prompt to give my project a name, whilst **arrow 5** encourages me to go to the next step. Before I even get there, I already know that the next step is going to be about "Recipients." The process is clear and transparent.

With Connector, I feel comfortable that I know exactly where in the process I am. In fact, I'm being "escorted" through the entire user journey. *This is a nice, guided experience with no guesswork required. The menu options* in the app are clearly named and the interface is quite minimalist - this is far better than cluttering the user interface with too much functionality.

I've worked with people in the IT industry who think being subtle and using lots of icons rather than text is better, but my experience is that people want to know *where they are, what options are available* and *what to do next*. How you fulfil those requirements is up to you, although I think it's possible to be a bit too cool when it comes to design. When people don't understand what icons mean, this approach becomes a problem.

Your functionality also needs to be presented to users in a way that is *intuitive* and meaningful to *them*. Don't just "slot" information, buttons or other widgets onto a part of the screen where there's free space, think about *where* people would *naturally* look for it when they need it. Try and retain a critical eye when it comes to this. If this was *someone else's app*, would you like the way the app is presented? Try to see the product through your customers' eyes, and not your own.

Make your best assessment of what you believe will be a good experience for your customers, based on all you've learned about them so far, and test those theories!

Error scenarios and feedback messages

The way your app communicates with users is also part of the overall user experience. Some apps can be quite painful to use because they don't consider what would be best for their users. Let's look at an example:

A customer enters something other than an email address in email address field.

Email addresses have a specific format and in this case, the information entered contains a blank space (these are not allowed in email addresses), or the @ sign, or end of the email address the .co.uk or .com is missing.

If your app encounters any of these 3 scenarios, then it should *reject* the data in the email address field and display an error to the user who entered it.

This could be handled in several ways:

- *Inline help text* might be provided by some applications. This is a preventative measure, rather than a reactive approach to a user error. Inline text remains on screen permanently in specific parts of an app to provide guidance and information to users. This particular inline text might include information about the acceptable formats of email addresses.

- Some apps will *explicitly* tell the user what the problem is using an *error message*. The message might be something like; "Blank spaces are not permitted in email addresses."
- Others will highlight the email address field in red and display some text which says that there is a problem with the email address field and ask the user to review the field.
- Other apps will display their error messages *right next to the issue* so it is easy to spot. (Very helpful.) Or they may display the error messages at the *top of the screen.* (Not so helpful. What if I've scrolled down to the bottom of the page and I can't see the message at the top? In that case I *still* might not realise what the problem is!)
- Highlighting the field *and* providing a very specific error message is another option. This might take more development effort, but is very helpful.

You can see that there are lots of options. Bear in mind that it's frustrating for users if an app tells them that they've broken a rule, but doesn't clearly explain what the problem is, or places information in unhelpful positions.

Be as specific as you can and save your customers' time by providing consistent, user friendly on-screen information that doesn't leave them guessing.

Standards and conventions for web and mobile apps

Using common conventions and familiar reference points will reduce the likelihood of users becoming confused when using your app. We'll review some of the standards and iconography that you may wish to use, along with some examples of hand-drawn wireframes.

Gestures and interactions for mobile apps

If you're building a mobile app, you'll need to consider the mobile app *interactions* (also known as *motion gestures, gestures* or *events*) you want your developer to set up for you.

Some may really enhance your users' experience if you decide to cater for them. On the other hand, some will be overkill! They will eat into your budget and offer little benefit in return, so make sure each gesture really adds value to your app. Speak to a developer about the cost vs. the benefit of implementing less common gestures before you commit to doing the work.

CHAPTER 11
Creating a positive "user experience" for your customers

Fig 52. Touch Gesture Reference Guide, by Luke Wroblewski:
http://static.lukew.com/TouchGestureGuide.pdf

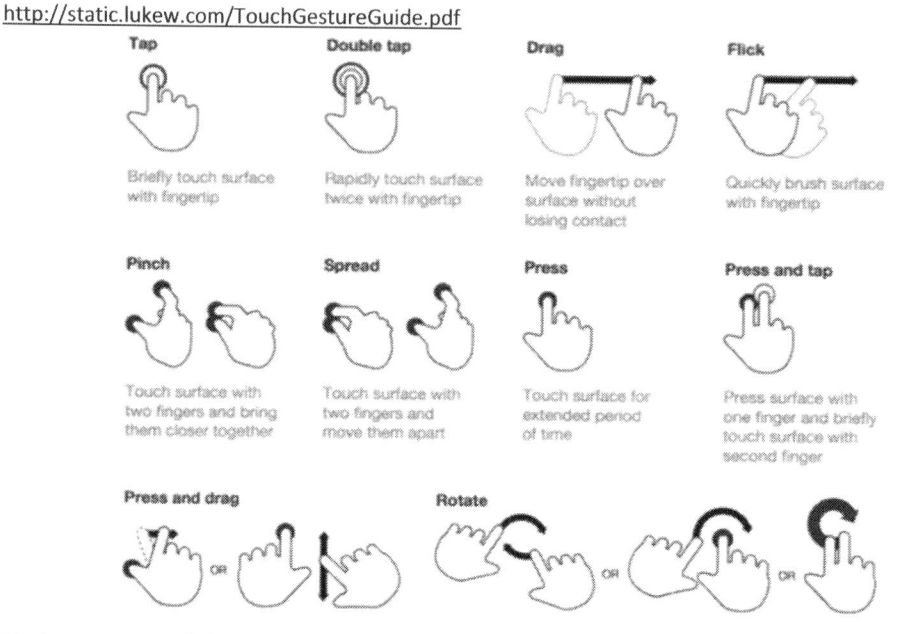

Make a note of the main gestures that you want to cover, and what you expect to happen in each case. Standard gestures and their *use cases,* tech speak for: *"under what circumstances would someone need to do that?"* include:

- **Pulling / dragging down,** to refresh content.
- **Pinching in,** to shrink content and make it smaller.
- **Panning out**, to enlarge content.
- **Tap**, used to confirm, enter, submit or select.
- **Double tap**, to zoom in or out or jump if playing a game.
- **Press and hold**, to drag mobile apps to different locations or to see more information.
- **Flick**, for scrolling quickly or as a gaming command.
- **Slide / swipe,** to move to a new screen or reveal more content.
- **Rotate screen,** to switch from portrait to landscape. If it makes sense to do this, how should your app look and behave in landscape mode? If not, ask for screen rotation to be switched off, so the app looks the same even if the smartphone or tablet device is rotated.
- **Scrolling,** to bring new content (text, images, options etc.) into view.

Creating a log for the gestures in your mobile app

CHAPTER 11
Creating a positive "user experience" for your customers

You may find it useful to create a table containing all the gestures you want, which you can keep for reference and as a guide for your developer to check against, as they work on your app.

I can't emphasise enough how much this sort of preparation will help avoid delays, mistakes and misunderstandings!

Let's create a sample table for an imaginary news app.

Fig 53. A hand drawn wireframe for an imaginary news app.

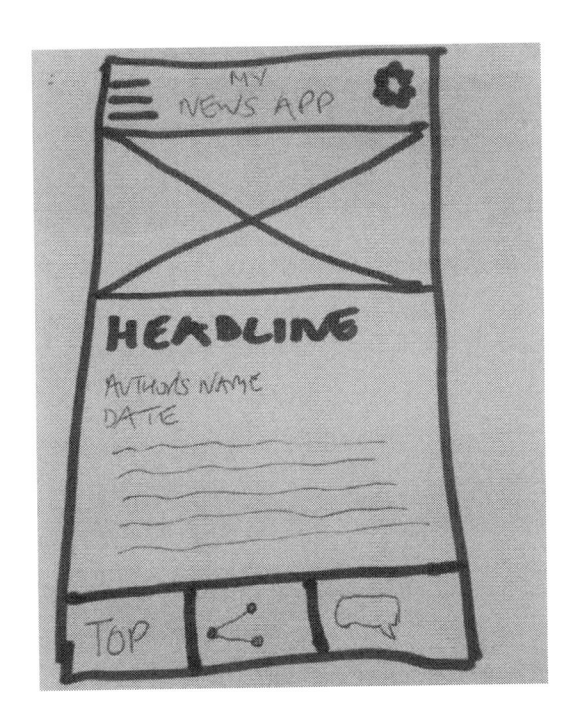

This table is a log of mobile gestures which are relevant to my news app. You could create something similar for your own app. It will help your developer understand which gestures you require and what you expect to happen when the gesture is triggered.

Fig 54. Mobile app gestures log for a news app.

App gesture	Expected result	Where in the app does the gesture need to work?
Pulling / dragging down to refresh content	The app "refreshes" and all content is updated to the most recent version available.	Across the entire app.
Pinching in to shrink content	Text gets smaller	On all article pages.
Panning out to enlarge content	Text gets larger	On all article pages.
Tap	Used to confirm a selection, to click on a link, or the title of a news article	1. On the three line "hamburger" menu (top left of drawing), which should display an options menu when tapped. 2. On the "gear" icon which displays settings when tapped (top right of drawing.) 3. On the TOP, 4. Share and 5. Comment icons at the bottom of the screen.
Press and hold	App opens	Only used to launch app. There are no press and hold gestures within the app.
Rotate screen	None	Disable (i.e. turn off) rotation.
Scroll	Reveal more article text	On every article page.

Interactions for websites and web apps

To avoid confusing your users, your app should follow standard conventions for websites and web apps where possible. This should include actions performed

CHAPTER 11
Creating a positive "user experience" for your customers

using a finger (on touch operated desktop devices) and activities performed using a mouse, keyboard or trackpad / touchpad on laptops, including:

Keyboard controls. When using a website or web app, it should be possible to hit the tab key and see it highlight every option on your page, in order as you tab through them, and to use the enter key to select or submit. This will also help you comply with Accessibility laws, as users with mobility issues may prefer to use a keyboard rather than using a mouse to navigate around your app.

Standard widgets, or functionality for selecting information, such as:

- Radio buttons; used when only one option from a list is applicable to the user
- Check boxes; when one or more of the options presented is applicable to the user (with the options laid out in full view) and
- Drop down menus; where there are several options available and one or more of these is applicable. (All the options are visible only if the user clicks on the menu and expands it.)

Fig 55. Radio buttons.

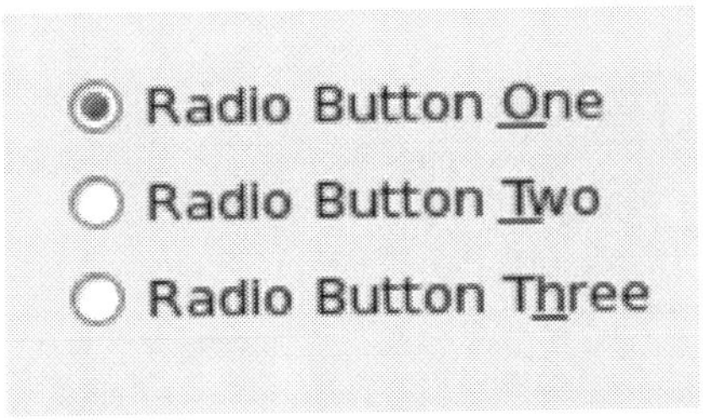

⦿ Radio Button One
◯ Radio Button Two
◯ Radio Button Three

Fig 56. Checkboxes.

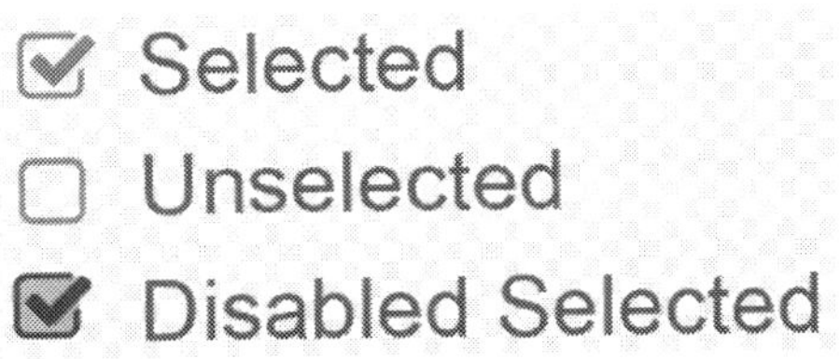

☑ Selected
☐ Unselected
☑ Disabled Selected

CHAPTER 11
Creating a positive "user experience" for your customers

Fig 57 i. Dropdown menu.

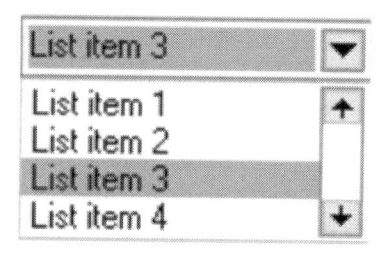

Dropdown menus are difficult to manipulate using a smartphone or tablet, so options that can be tapped on, or scrolled through are often used as an alternative.

Fig 57 ii. Alternative 1. Selecting items (in this example, US States) from a list using a mobile device. http://wiki.processmaker.com/3.0/JavaScript_Functions_and_Methods by ProcessMaker.

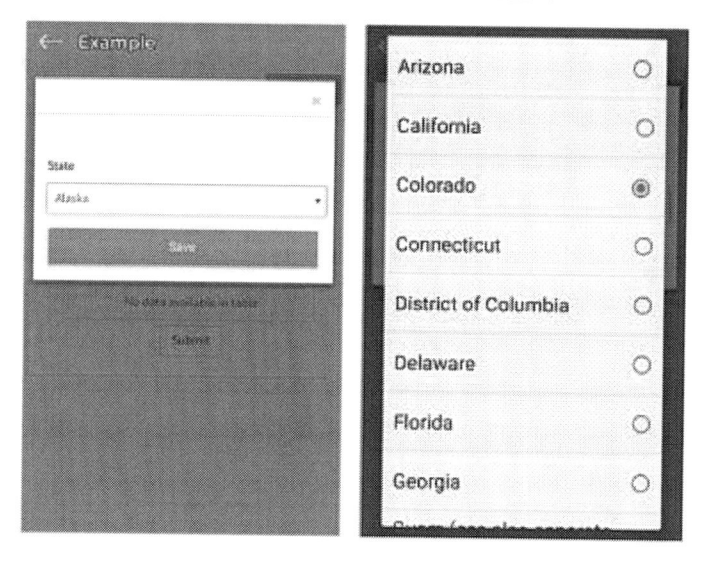

CHAPTER 11
Creating a positive "user experience" for your customers

Fig 57 iii.

Alternative 2. jQuery date picker for mobile devices. (This widget can be adapted to select times too.) http://www.jqueryscript.net/time-clock/Stylish-jQuery-Date-Time-Picker-For-Mobile-Devices-mobiscroll.html

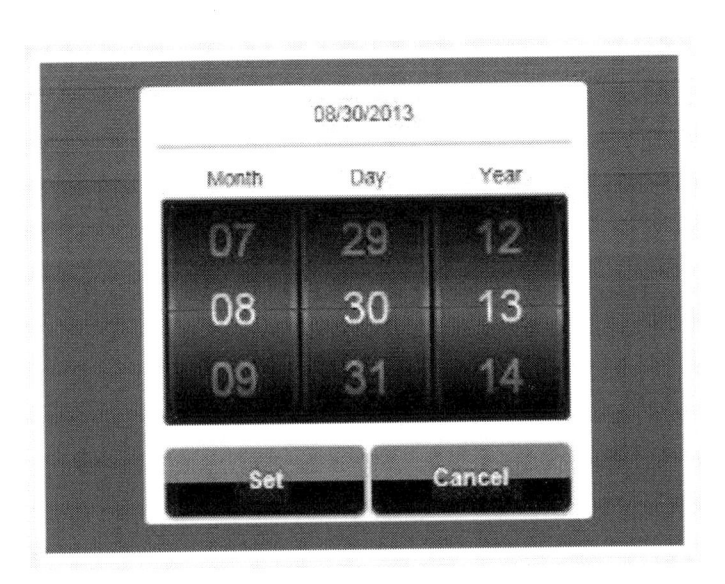

Hover. Hovering over links with your cursor generally "underlines" that link and shows you the web address for the link in the bottom left-hand corner of your web browser, whilst hovering over menu items on a web page may cause their colour to change and change your cursor from a white arrow to a hand. Links should be blue or represented by text; for example, click here. The hover action can also cause information to appear in a *tooltip*, often where an **i** or **?** is displayed.

Fig 58. An example of text appearing in a *tooltip* in response to being "hovered over" by a user.

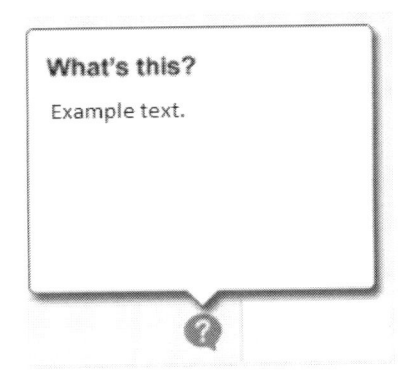

CHAPTER 11
Creating a positive "user experience" for your customers

Clicking. Clicking on the logo of a website should take you back to the Homepage of a website or web app.

Iconography

Which icons will you use when creating your wireframes?

Whether you're building a mobile or web app, the following icons are recognised as standard representations for:

Image, Video, Menu (hamburger), Settings (cog, gear or wrench), Share, Home, Edit, Comment, Search, Buy (shopping cart), Profile, Location (pin /point), Secure (padlock), Information (i).

Add a simple text label along with your icons if user tests show that your target customers do not understand the iconography that you've used.

You can also try Googling: *icons for [insert what you're looking for]*. There are websites that will allow you to use their icons for free.

Remember that familiarity is your friend! Avoid obscure icons – users should feel comfortable using your app as quickly as possible, and giving them a learning curve will *not* help them to get used to using it.

Fig 59. Iconography. Common symbols for web and mobile apps.

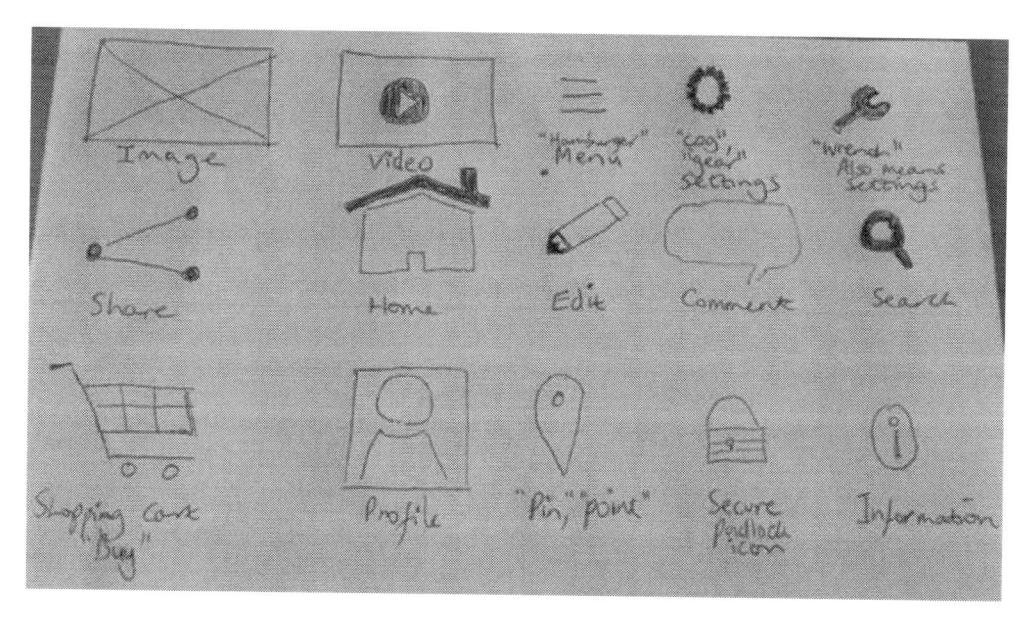

What other functionality will be available within your app and what else will your app allow people to do? *Make sure that all the functionality available to your users is made completely obvious, and easy to access!*

CHAPTER 11
Creating a positive "user experience" for your customers

Adding colour to your app

You'll also need to tell your developer which colours should be part of your app and you can do this by annotating your wireframes to explain where the colour should go and by providing them with the relevant *hex numbers.*

Hex numbers, (short for hexadecimal numbers) are used to represent colours in computers and applications. For example, the shade of green named "Aquamarine 4" has a hex number, #458b74. (You can Google this number and switch to image results to see what colour it is.) You can select a *colour palette* for your app, along with the corresponding hex numbers here:

http://www.color-hex.com/color-palettes/popular.php. Click on a palette to see the specific hex numbers for each colour. If you're not keen on any of these combinations, you can search for other colour palettes online.

The use of colour in apps can be quite subtle, often confined to the *headers* and *footers* (the top and bottom sections) of a website or web app, and to the app's *action buttons (*or *call to action buttons, CTAs)* that direct customers to act, such as "next", "back", "Go", "Buy now" etc. Be aware of colour blindness; green and red, green and brown, blue and purple, and green and blue are some of the worst combinations for colour blind people.

Using Lorem Ipsum

Lorem Ipsum is used by designers worldwide as a standard substitute for written content in an application. If you are creating your mockup / prototype using a tool or software application (rather than drawing it), Lorem Ipsum can be useful for several reasons:

- If you don't yet have any text prepared for your app, Lorem Ipsum acts as placeholder copy.
- During user testing or product demonstrations, Lorem Ipsum helps users focus on the *design or layout* of a mockup and *not the written text in the app.* Including it will distract people because they will start trying to read it! Replace the Lorem Ipsum text when you are ready to receive feedback on the "real" text that is going to appear in the app. Copy is usually tested *after* other visual elements of the app have been reviewed.

CHAPTER 11
Creating a positive "user experience" for your customers

You can find Lorem Ipsum text here; http://loripsum.net. Use the menu options in the left-hand margin of the website to format your Lorem Ipsum text to suit your needs, then copy and paste it into the empty spaces in your mockup or app.

Fig 60. Using Lorem Ipsum to focus attention on graphic elements in a webpage design proposal. https://en.wikipedia.org/wiki/File:Lorem_ipsum_design.svg by Mysid.

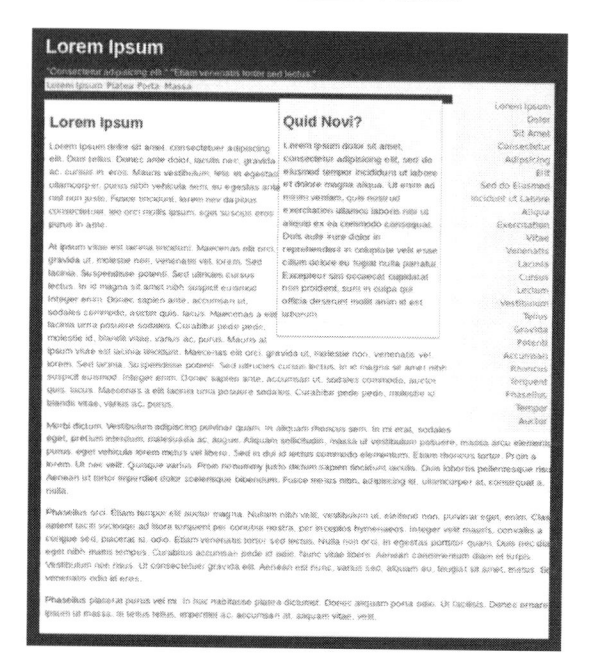

Other UX considerations
Mascots

Tunnelbear have their bear, Trello has Taco the dog, Zendesk has "The Mentor."

These are all relatively young companies with SaaS and mobile apps. Depending on the nature of your business and your preferences, you may wish to hire a designer and front-end developer to create a company or product *mascot*. This is, of course non-essential, but it's an option you may wish to consider.

Mascots are used to increase customer engagement; by humanising your company and as a marketing tool to emphasise an idea or concept. Company mascots can be a distinctive way of branding your company and giving it a personality.

CHAPTER 11
Creating a positive "user experience" for your customers

Fig 61. Taco, the Trello mascot, 62. Zendesk's "The Mentor", 63. The Tunnelbear mascot

Copy

The copy used in your app can also convey your brand's personality. Select the words you use on your website and within your app, (including company information, the copy on your app marketplace page or website, error messages, help information, button text, link text, warnings and calls to action) to communicate whether your company is relaxed, formal, lively or serious, or any other characteristics that you feel are relevant.

Images

If you use images in your app, be sure to use ones that are appropriate for your target customers. Images liven up apps and bring a human element to them, but they are also a strong non-verbal way of communicating about your app and who it is for. When customers look at your images, they should feel that your app is *for them*. Use of the wrong images can actually deter customers, so use business images for a B2B app, and select the kinds of business images that would match your target market's working environment, company culture and dress code. For example, you would have a mismatch if you selected images appropriate for a relaxed media agency if you wanted to sell your product to corporate finance companies.

For B2C customers, make sure the people in your images match the age range of your target market and focus on men, or women if the app is for a specific group, or are socially inclusive to reflect both genders and different races if it is not. To find places to purchase or access low-cost images try Googling "royalty free stock photos." *RF,* or *Royalty Free,* means that you do not have to pay the person or company who owns the photo *for each use* of it, however, the images are not necessarily free.

CHAPTER 11
Creating a positive "user experience" for your customers

Here are a few sites to try. The Adobe and Depositphotos images must be paid for, but the other 2 sites have free images available:

https://stock.adobe.com/uk/

http://depositphotos.com/

https://stocksnap.io

https://pixabay.com/

Visual feedback and software Jedi mind tricks

Make sure that your app provides *visual feedback* that it is responding to customers' requests. Imagine this scenario:

You walk into a cafe and ask for a tea or coffee. The assistant doesn't answer right away, so you make your request again. The assistant still doesn't respond so you ask again. Still no answer. You ask again...

Finally, they respond and bring your order, **but why didn't they just acknowledge you the first time?**

This is what happens with software. When people click, and click...and click again, they do so out of confusion or frustration. *Did the app "get" my request? Is it even working? What's going on...?* In a second scenario, you get multiple orders, one for each time you placed an order with the assistant! Neither is ideal.

Now, with all the extra clicks it has received, your app has *more* processing work to do, which makes it even slower. Extra clicks are totally counterproductive, so if your app is processing a request, say so and if a customer enters data into your app, confirm that it's been received. *Acknowledge your customers' requests!* (Note that it should be possible to code your app in such a way that only the first click is registered.)

Design and UX can be used to distract, inform and entertain.

Let's look at a few ways to use design and UX to show that your app is busy working, and not sleeping on the job!

A commonplace example of this includes clever page loading effects that appear wherever users have to wait for the app to perform an action. Displaying messages such as: "We're working on it," or placing moving images on screen

CHAPTER 11
Creating a positive "user experience" for your customers

whilst the app is processing tasks serves two purposes; they confirm to the user that the system is working *and* help them lose track of how long they've been waiting! The more complex styles may require front-end development skills.

Fig 64. Page loading notifications (or page loading "spinners"). From top, W Brett Wilson, Lazarevic Ivan, http://workshop.rs/2012/12/animated-progress-bar-in-4-lines-of-jquery/ and others.

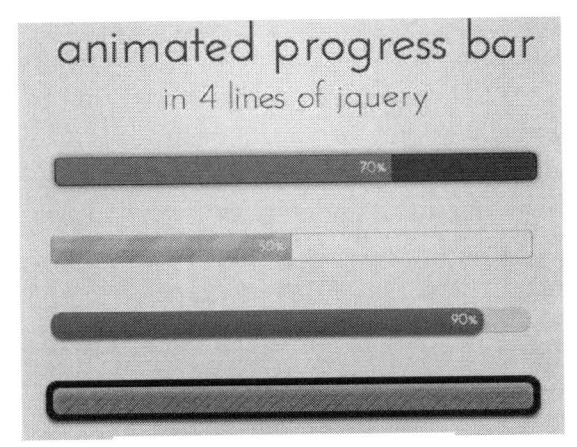

CHAPTER 11
Creating a positive "user experience" for your customers

Working on it...

Loading, please wait...

Bringing all the elements together

When it comes to the practicalities of turning an idea into working software, you may still need to work through any leaps of logic that exist. Check that the steps the user will perform make sense and are as intuitive as possible.

An example of this would be having missing steps in a user journey and "magically" jumping from step 2 to step 4. In this case, you'll need to work out what step 3 is and how to pass from step 2 to step 3 and from step 3 to step 4.

I call this Swiss cheese thinking because it's solid in places, but has holes in others! This happens a lot at the concept stage and just means more thinking is required before you start building your product. In the near future, you may need to explain your idea to a developer and they will find it helpful if you have worked through your idea and identified as many leaps of logic and flaws as possible. These challenges can, of course, be worked through with a developer, but their time will need to be paid for.

Whether you're building a mobile or web app, as you draw out your prototype, consider your audience and the type of interactions needed for the app, and ask yourself the following questions:

- How many user journeys *are* there?
- How many steps are there in this particular journey? Where does the journey begin? (The answer to this is usually after the user has logged in, or signed up to the app, but some mobile apps will automatically start up without the user having to log in at all, or needing to repeatedly log in each time the app is used.)
- What happens next? What triggers that to happen? Then what?

CHAPTER 11
Creating a positive "user experience" for your customers

- What information needs to be provided by the customer at this stage and how will it get into the app?
- Where will the information be stored once the customer provides it?
- Do I need to present the customer with any of their own information at any point(s) in the process and if so, when and what will they expect to see?
- What options will the user have at *this* stage of the process?
- Do I need to provide any on-screen messages for the customer, such as errors, warnings, confirmation messages, or thank you messages? How will these messages be presented?
- If the customer gets stuck or confused at any point, what help, or information will be available?
- Will I need to rely on external (3rd party) tools and systems? What will they need to do and at which stage(s) of the process are they needed? (This question may take some time to resolve, just keep this in mind for now.)
- Where does the process end? What happens then?
- Is this logical? How can I make this journey quicker, easier and more straightforward for users?
- What colours do I want to have in my app?
- Do I want a company mascot?

You can see some examples of how others have managed the design of their web and mobile apps here:

http://nectafy.com/saas-website-design-examples/

http://www.webdesignerdepot.com/2013/07/20-beautifully-designed-smartphone-apps/

There can be a lot to do when building an app, so don't worry if this feels a little overwhelming. Allocate time every day to thinking about all the screens and functionality you need and keep going until you've covered all the things you believe are important.

In the next chapter, we'll start working on your prototype!

CHAPTER 11
Creating a positive "user experience" for your customers

Get them done and check them off! Chapter 11 challenges:

- ☐ Which gestures will users need to perform activities using your mobile app? Review the mobile gestures diagram and the options, and opportunities available.
- ☐ What choices might your customers need to make as they use your web app? What buttons, widgets, links, options or icons will they be clicking, hovering over or tabbing through? Start drawing out your screens, and include annotations wherever additional information is needed.
- ☐ Answer all the relevant questions in the *Bringing all the elements together* section and keep a note of the answers. You'll use these to build your prototype and you can use them as a starting point for the requirements that should be given to your developer to help them build your app. Review chapter 10 for a reminder of how to record all the user journeys that you will need for your app.

Download the entire set of chapter challenges compiled into a work book, with an activity log to help you keep track of important tasks:

http://www.mylanderpages.com/donthireasoftwaredeveloperuntilyoureadthisbook/Free-resource-1

CHAPTER 12
Your prototyping options

"All things are created twice; first mentally, then physically. The key to creativity is to begin with the end in mind, with a vision and a blueprint of the desired result."

– Stephen Covey

In this chapter:
- Paper prototypes
- Hand drawn examples
- Clickable prototypes
- Creating prototypes with help from a developer
- Prototyping tool-kit

Now that you know the important elements that should be considered when planning your product, let's run through the options available for creating your prototype, including simple, hand-drawn prototypes, those you can "mock-up" yourself using apps or online tools, and more complex prototypes that will require development assistance to build. This will give you something tangible to use when you start the user testing process.

Types of prototype

1. Paper / lo-fi prototypes

If you can make time and would like to save money early in the process, then you will find paper prototyping a valuable, yet cheap way of making progress with your idea.

A flat, black and white sketch will usually be referred to as a "lo-fi" or "low-fidelity" prototype. A hand drawn prototype or simple *wireframe* (a basic "skeleton" of a product, used for planning the layout and elements of screens or web pages) can take a matter of minutes to create and can be easily be improved, and amended.

CHAPTER 12
Your prototyping options

When doing a "show and tell" using a paper prototype, explain that you are at the planning stage of your project, show the person the prototype and talk them through it. Try and build up a picture in their minds of the product, and ask them to comment on any points that spring to mind.

It's worth noting that most people will be more attracted to bright and colourful representations than black and white drawings. A colour version may create more interest and engagement with the user and you could try out brand colour combinations too, but the downside is that *this will distract people from the functional elements of the prototype.* Therefore, it is best to review the user journeys and key features of the product *first,* then ask people to comment on branding at a later date. User testing is an ongoing process, so you should try to get feedback regularly as your product becomes more advanced.

When should you use a paper prototype?

This basic form of prototype can be used to:

- Test your concept.
- Identify any gaps or inconsistencies relating to the product and how it should work.
- Review how realistic and logical the user journeys you have come up with are to someone other than yourself! Is the way you have visualised a user journey the way it should work in reality?
- Gauge initial reactions and to encourage comments, suggestions and feedback.

How about a few examples?

The basic wireframes in this section were hand drawn in under 10 minutes. They are definitely not works of art, but are included here to show you real examples of what can be achieved in a short time with a pen and paper. The numbers and commentary you will see on them are *annotations* used to explain all the interactions that the user will have with the app, screen by screen.
They explain what the app can do, and the *rules* that determine what data is displayed and how it is displayed. (This information will be *very* useful to a developer.)
Example 1: A wireframe of a mobile app with some simple annotations.
Title of wireframe: An article screen within My News App.

CHAPTER 12
Your prototyping options

Description of wireframe: This wireframe shows what the app looks like when a specific news article has been selected.

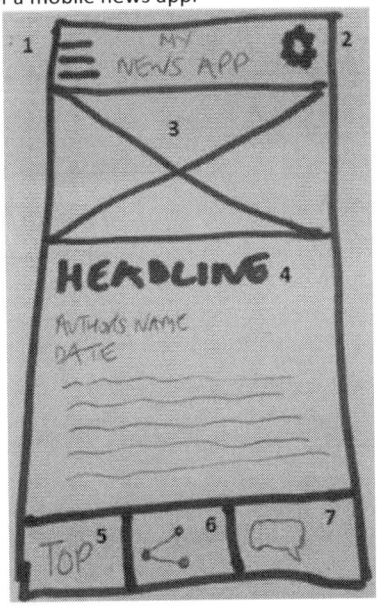

Fig 65. A hand drawn wireframe of a mobile news app.

1. & 2. *The menu and settings icon appear fixed at the top of every screen to give customers constant access to a range of functionality within the app.*
[You will need other drawings to show what these are, so people can see the options which exist when they tap the menu or settings icons on their mobile device, and what happens when they interact with each of those options.]

3. *Each article will contain a landscape image that will need to resize to fit the mobile device being used.*
[Your developer will need to set this up for you and advise you on the best approach, either cropping and / or resizing each image so it works on a range of devices and adjusts correctly between portrait and landscape mode if the device is rotated (and this option is activated).]

4. *The article sits underneath the image. An article must always have a headline, display the author or journalist's name and the date the article was written.*
[I have used wavy lines to represent the article text because this is a hand-drawn wireframe, otherwise, I would have used Lorem Ipsum text instead.]

The annotations should continue by referring to 5, 6 and 7 in turn, The TOP rated article functionality, share functionality and the commenting functionality.

Should the content look different on a tablet?

Tablets have more *screen real-estate* available and because more information can be included on-screen, there are often extra menu and navigation options displayed in the left or right margins on tablet devices. Here are some varied examples of menu options for tablets:

Example 1:

https://s3.amazonaws.com/media.nngroup.com/media/editor/2015/09/22/sephora-swipe.png

Example 2:

http://seanrice.net/media/2013/09/burtonmenuUX.png

Example 3:

https://s-media-cache-ak0.pinimg.com/736x/28/83/e7/2883e72ac3ebc705549eadc00011da04.jpg

Example 4:

https://scdn.androidcommunity.com/wp-content/uploads/2012/04/Screen-Shot-2012-04-18-at-10.36.58-PM-540x448.png

Create a tablet version of your wireframe as a guide for your developer, so they know how the tablet version of your app should look, and operate. Here are a few tips:

- Start with some research. If you don't own a tablet, consider getting one, choosing 4 or 5 apps and using those same apps on a smartphone and a tablet to see what the main differences are and which extra features you like that are available with the tablet versions. Try doing this exercise using competitors' mobile apps rated 4* or above in the app marketplaces, as well as looking at some of the more "famous" apps.
- Look to see how apps in the same category as yours make use of the extra space available on a tablet.
- Don't forget to rotate the tablet to see how the app behaves in landscape mode!

The next example shows a landing page, (or entry point), for a web app, with annotations.

CHAPTER 12
Your prototyping options

Fig 66 i. A hand drawn wireframe of a landing page for a web app. I'm no Picasso, but a picture is worth 1000 words!

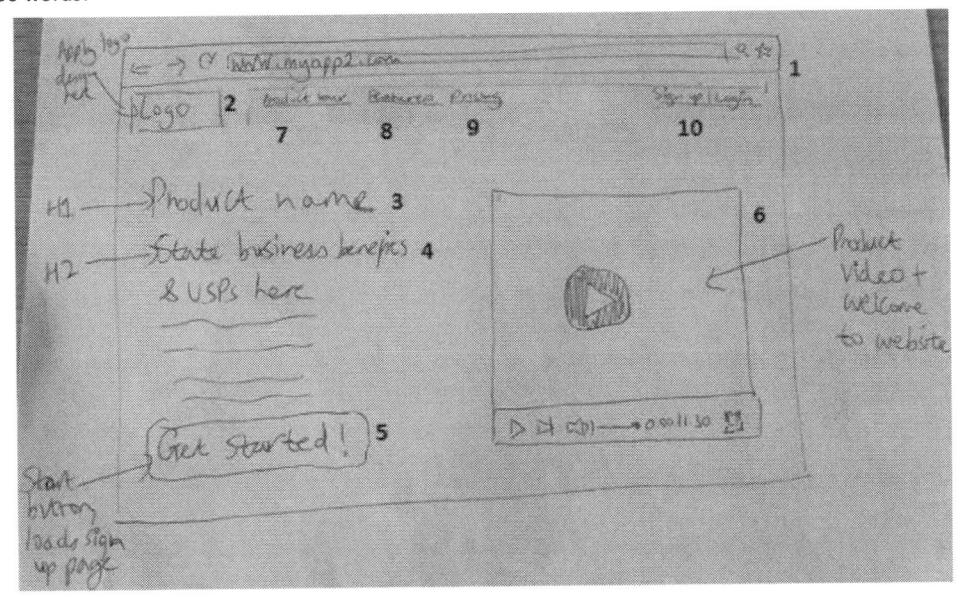

1. *The web app sits within a web browser.*

2. *The app's logo will sit in the top left-hand corner of the browser window.*

3 & 4. *The product name and its consumer (or business) benefits sit beneath the logo. The Product name / page title should have an H1 title tag and the benefits and unique selling points (USPs) should have an H2 title tag.*

[These title tags are also useful for SEO.]

5. *The page includes a button, "Get started", which will initiate the sign-up process when clicked.*

[This is your main call to action, (CTA) - so make it big, bold and enticing!]

6. There is a video player on the page which will provide a brief welcome to the website. This video could be hosted in a number of ways:

- Via YouTube; https://support.google.com/youtube/answer/161805?hl=en-GB
- Wistia; https://wistia.com/pricing
- Vimeo; https://vimeo.com/join
- Or via a service like AWS; https://aws.amazon.com/media-sharing/

7, 8 and **9.** *There are also links which will open new web pages to give a tour of the product, product features and pricing information.*

Additional wireframes will be needed to show what happens after a user clicks on any buttons or links. These should show which pages the user will be taken to, and what they will be able to see and do.

10. *There is a sign/up login link, which does the same thing as the "Get started" button.*

[It's normal to have several ways to perform the same action. The text may be different, but the destination, or end result will be the same - they are just different ways to encourage people to go ahead and click.]

Explainer videos are good ways to showcase what your product can do, to provide help to users or to give a product tour or demonstration. An image could also be used in this position; however, short videos less than 5 minutes long show higher rates of engagement.

Don't worry about your drawings being perfect. The most important thing is to start sketching. Use the first few versions for practice and to get things looking as you want them. You can take your time and sketch a neat and tidy version later, or take your sketch and recreate it using a prototyping tool instead. Let's talk about that next.

2. Clickable demos / high-fidelity prototypes

"Clickable demos" (or demonstrations), will help you test how appealing and easy to understand your *UI* (user interface) is. This includes your navigation; how users can move through the product in order to achieve their goal(s) and what users think of the transition between screens or web pages as they move through the stages in each user journey. If you can set the clickable demo up on a laptop, or even on a smartphone, you can give this to target customers to use. Any costs incurred will depend on whether or not you use free tools. There's a selection of tools you can use in the tool-kit towards the end of the chapter.

When should you use a hi-fidelity prototype?

- You should use one to create a basic, but *interactive* representation of your idea.

- You'll still be testing your concept, observing people's reactions and noting all comments, feedback and suggestions and you'll want to find out *how* and *where* your initial idea can be improved and *which elements* of your idea are most (and least) appealing to people.
- You'll also be doing more work on the logical "flow" of your user journeys. *You may find that some people do not like the order in which the activities happen*. Where necessary, reorder your user journeys and adjust your prototype ready for the next time you show it to anyone. If people follow the steps in your user journey easily or do not comment (or complain), then you have probably resolved the issue. If not, ask people what seems "wrong" about the processes, then decide what to do next based on what you've seen and heard.

3. High-fidelity prototyping with development assistance

You can hire a developer to build a more complex prototype or *"clickable mockup"* for you. This prototype will probably look and behave very much like a real app or web page. The relevant links or buttons on each screen should work and take the user to the next stage in the journey or correct place within the app. You could have a design applied to it to make it look more appealing. Techies often call this "applying a skin." This can become a fun but easy way to burn money. The prototype should be created only as a tool for planning and obtaining feedback, so you'll have to draw the line on how far you go with this. A simple compromise would be to add some colour to the app in key places and have coloured on-screen buttons and maybe some images or icons depending on the type of app you wish to build.

You may find it useful to have a few key objectives for the prototype.

It should be substantial enough to include some of your key user journeys and screens, or those that you have the most questions about, for example: "Does this journey work?" or "Will people like the way this functionality is presented?" Focus on having these built and get some initial feedback to help you decide what to do next.

Ask your developer if they can make the prototype available at a web address that is not open to the rest of the world so it is not found by accident, (although if you don't submit your URL to Google and have the site indexed, this is unlikely to happen. There are also ways to proactively ask Google NOT to index your site. This is done using files called *robots.txt*.) You could also password protect the website and change the password as needed so access is restricted.

There are some important things to note if you have your prototype built for you:

Prototypes are not usually coded or tested as rigorously as a "real" product. The work is usually rushed though as quickly as possible, so once the prototype is built, it would be incorrect to assume that the product is "almost finished." In fact, the code from prototypes is often thrown away. They are a tool for learning, for both you and your developer. Even if the code is thrown away, the lessons learned during the process will be preserved - your developer should keep these front of mind as they build the "real" product.

Remember to timebox the work. Set a time limit and stick to it. Explain what you want and ask your developer how long (realistically) it would take for the work to be done. Agree on a fixed price or hourly fee for the work and consider this as an extra on top of the main development work that will come later. Once you agree a time limit, confirm this verbally and in writing. A couple of days to a week for a clickable demo is normal, depending on its complexity. To keep the process under control, *select the most important user journeys to be covered first,* get those built by your developer as the priority and see where you are in terms of time and budget after that.

Project pitfall!

Provide the right information and keep track of progress.
Take the time to write out the requirements for the prototype, covering what the prototype should and should not do. Give the developer an idea of the most important elements that you want to user test. (They may come up with some points you hadn't thought of, which is a benefit of paying to have a prototype created for you.)
An easy way to waste money is to provide a loose set of instructions to a developer that you don't know very well and then to leave them to their own devices, assuming that everything will be o.k. You could be in for an unpleasant surprise!
Ask for a daily progress update and ask them to notify you if they have any questions.
This will minimise delays and stop your developer going too far along the wrong track before checking in with you.

Test it *before* you put it in front of a user. You'll need to test the prototype to make sure that it works as you expect before showing it to people from your target market. Factor in some time for checks and amendments before your user testing sessions are due to start.

There is a lot of testing and checking and retesting in software development, but that is the nature of the beast, I'm afraid!

You will dodge a *lot* of bullets if you remember: i) to never assume things are fine unless you've *checked* that they are and ii) to always confirm what has been discussed or agreed, to make sure that your plans do not go awry!

Think about NDAs. Decide whether or not you want to ask the developer to sign a non-disclosure agreement. (Review chapter 1 for more details.) If you send information by email, consider marking the email private and confidential and emphasising that the content is not to be shared (unless you want it to be.)

Creating a site map

How might you capture the "big picture" view of your web or mobile app?

This can be done via a *site map*, a visual representation of your web pages, or web app screens showing their layout and how they connect to each other.

Site maps can be used for different purposes and may look like process flow charts, lists of links, or they may be technical items that a developer might create and provide to Google to help it index your web pages for SEO purposes.

Site maps are also connected to your *IA, Information Architecture,* as discussed in chapter 5, because your site map shows how the information within your app is organised.

Let's briefly review the role of site maps, user journeys and wireframes before we move on:

The site map is an overview of all your pages or screens, whilst your user journeys capture the steps involved in completing a specific activity within your app, and your wireframes show the detail of what each screen looks like, how users can interact with the screens, and the functionality on them.

I've mocked up a few examples so you can see what a site map might look like, and the different tools you can use to create one.

CHAPTER 12
Your prototyping options

This is a "quick and dirty" site map I created using the Bubbl.us mind mapping tool. http://www.bubbl.us/. The site map is based on my hand drawn wireframe, as seen in figure 66.

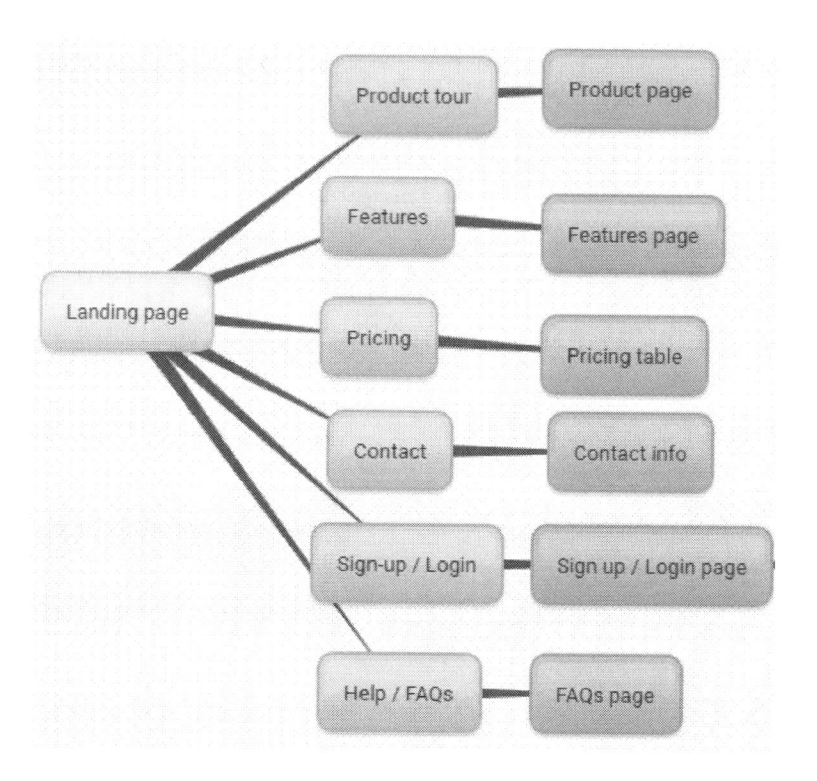

The first level of blocks in light green are the links you can see at the top of the wireframe. I've now *iterated over* this original drawing, having remembered that I also need a *Contact* page and a place that users can go for *Help or FAQs (Frequently Asked Questions.)* The second level of blocks in darker green, represent the pages you would see when you click the links at the top of my wireframe. If there were a third level, this level would represent the pages seen when a link in a level two page was clicked.

Here's an alternative and more formal style of site map created using PowerPoint. This site map also has two levels, but a third, or fourth level could also be added if needed; you could use a different colour for each additional level added to the site map.

CHAPTER 12
Your prototyping options

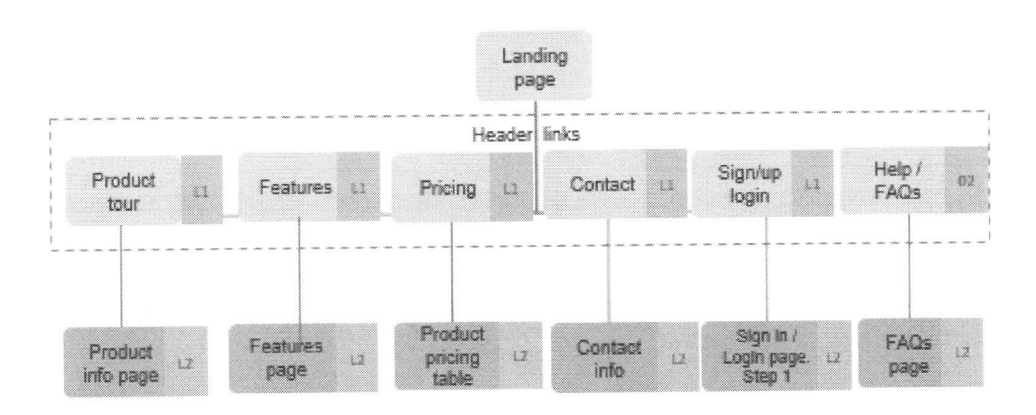

You can do something similar for a mobile app, by mapping out the screens people will pass through as they tap on the menu, settings and other options within the app.

In chapter 14 we'll look at how to select your MVP from all the screens and ideas you've gathered together and I'll show you how to narrow your focus so your resources are channelled on the most important work to be done.

Prototyping tool-kit

Prototyping templates

You can draw straight onto paper, or use *templates* in the relevant device and browser "shapes." These can be downloaded and used in Word, PowerPoint or Paint format, or printed, and sketched on. You can find templates on these sites:

- *Interfacesketch*, www.interfacesketch.com. Scroll down to the section marked: "Create your own template."
- *Interactive logic*, http://interactivelogic.net/wp/2009/09/iphone-wireframe-templates/ offers a range of templates that you can use.
- You can also use Word or PowerPoint to create your mockups, with or without using the templates.

Add the text, buttons, features and functionality you require, take screenshots or photos of your work and use an app like POP, (see below) to turn them into a clickable demo.

CHAPTER 12
Your prototyping options

Fig 67. Device and web browser templates. http://www.interfacesketch.com/

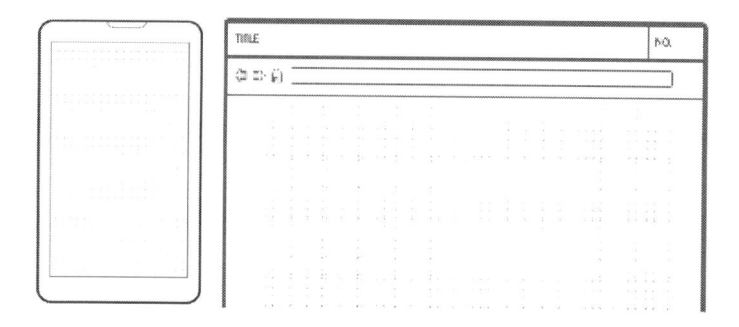

In this example, I've taken the 3-step user journey for Sam Morris from chapter 10 and laid the journey out, so that each web template displays one step in the journey.

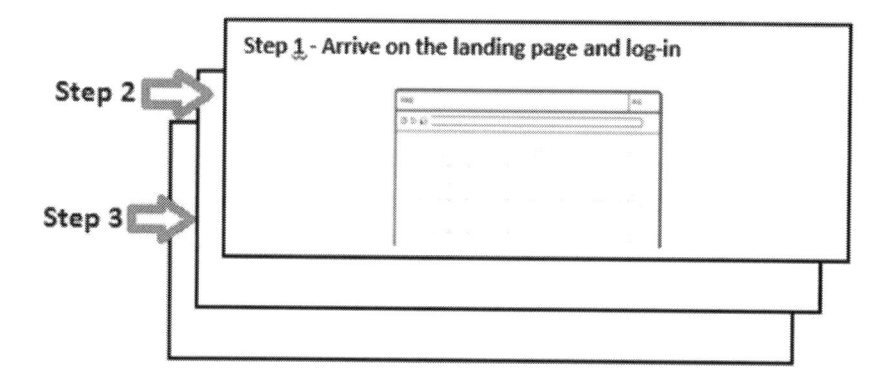

Prototyping tools

These tools are all quite different, see which ones you like and find easiest to use:

- The *POP (Prototyping On Paper)* mobile app. Available from the Google Play, Windows and Apple stores. Take photos of your screens, mark the clickable areas and your prototype is ready! https://popapp.in/.
- *AppyPie* provides mobile app building and prototyping software for iPhone and Android, with no coding required,

http://www.appypie.com/app-prototype-builder.
- *Mockupbuilder* offers prototype creator software, http://mockupbuilder.com/Gallery.
- *Cacoo's* services include mind maps, process flow charts, and wireframes for web or mobile apps, https://cacoo.com/lang/en/sample.
- *Mockingbird i*s a tool for creating clickable wireframes that can also be shared, https://gomockingbird.com/.
- *UX Pin* can help you build wireframes, mockups and interactive prototypes for web or mobile apps, https://www.uxpin.com/examples.html.
- *Balsamiq* is a well-known wireframing and mockup tool, which supports prototyping for web and mobile apps, https://balsamiq.com/.
- *Proto.io*, https://proto.io/en/new-features/ will allow you to build interactive prototypes for web or mobile devices without development assistance. You can choose to *moderate,* and run and observe the user testing sessions yourself, or share the prototype using links or QR codes so users can test the app remotely. Proto.io also contains integrated mobile screen recording too, so you the testing sessions are recorded for you!

Fig 68. An example using the POP app.

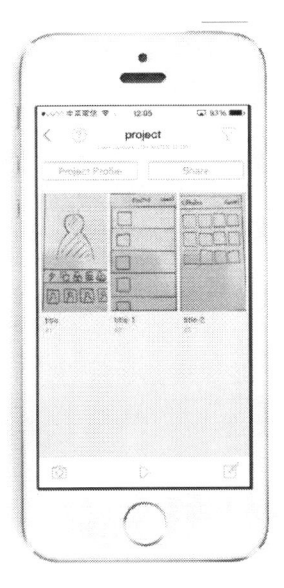

Presenting your prototype

If you want to give a demonstration or present to a group, screen-mirroring tools like *Reflector 2* will allow you to share a *web or mobile app* from your iPad, iPhone or Android device wirelessly to other devices, or to a common access point like YouTube, so people will be able to see whatever is visible on your device. http://www.airsquirrels.com/reflector/in-action/development/

Proto.io, https://proto.io/ also supports demonstrations, by enabling you to record and display your screen whilst you talk through the events happening on your device.

In the next chapter, I'll be showing you how to carry out user testing on the prototype(s) that you have created!

CHAPTER 13
How to test your prototype

"When I started... I thought we'd spend months under wraps and release the perfect product. I discovered it's most important to get your product above the noise so that people can encounter it. There are a very small number of complete product geniuses that can labor in the dark for years and... pull off the sheets and say "ta-da!" and it's the right thing and everybody uses it."

- Reid Hoffman, co-founder and executive chairman of LinkedIn (at the time of writing to be acquired by Microsoft for $26 billion)

In this chapter
- Types of user test
- How to run a user testing session
- User testing session example
- Running tests with an interactive prototype
- Running tests with a paper prototype
- Project pitfalls

Fresh eyes bring fresh insights, so it's time to find out whether your target market understands your product, likes the functionality you're intending to provide, and the way you're intending to provide it! This information will be gathered through user testing, so let's review several types of test that you could carry out:

Usability testing (or *user testing*) is used to confirm that your product is suited to your target market and that it is easy to use and understand.

There can also be an aesthetic element to user testing – does the design of your product appeal to people? Do people like the way it's presented? Is it pleasant to use?

Usability testing should be repeated as new functionality is built into your product, so you can continue to make important adjustments.

User acceptance testing (UAT), confirms that a product is "acceptable" to the group who are going to be using it. It is often used as a final check to confirm that a product meets the needs of the users and does not contain any outstanding bugs or issues. UAT should not result in any nasty surprises if you have user tested your product regularly.

A/B testing (or split testing) is a method for comparing two different designs to see which one is the most popular, or effective; version A, or version B? Examples of A/B tests include testing two versions of a home, or landing page design for your web or mobile app, or different versions of the same user journey.

How to run a user testing session and record your findings

We discussed ways to find participants for your user tests back in chapter 3, so let's continue, assuming that you've found several people willing to be involved in user testing your prototype.

Firstly, what exactly do you need to know?

The tests, or exercises you ask participants to perform during the session should cover all the major parts of the prototype. It will be important to do this before you pay to have any functionality built, so you can avoid investing your money in the wrong functionality. Try your best to get answers to fundamental questions, such as:

"Do people *understand* the way this [insert functionality] works?"

"Do people *like* the way [insert functionality] works?"

"Are people able to complete this user journey quickly?"

"Does this functionality truly make life easier or better for my target market?"

"Does the product solve their major problem(s)?"

Follow these tips to help you manage user tests that involve more *interactive elements*:

Prepare your questions and exercises (these are tests, but to avoid making people feel nervous about being "tested", you can refer to them as tasks, scenarios or exercises) and run through them until they're arranged in the order that makes most sense to you and has a logical flow from simple activities to more complex ones. The **Top 10 do's and don'ts** for running customer interviews and user tests and the **Plus, Minus, Interesting (PMI) log** for recording feedback (from chapter 3) will come in useful again here. You can download the PMI log here:

http://www.mylanderpages.com/donthireasoftwaredeveloperuntilyoureadthisbook/Free-resource-3-pmi-log

Provide clear instructions. Explain that you'd like people to complete several exercises and introduce each one with a set of clear verbal or written instructions. Encourage people to voice suggestions or ideas about how *they* would do things, or about what *they* would prefer.

Make a point of emphasising when each exercise starts and ends - it's easy to forget to explain things because they are so obvious to you. The user has never seen the prototype before, so explain everything fully and ask if there are any questions before you allow each test to start.

Once the session begins:
- **Listen carefully to the responses given** and watch how the user interacts with the prototype.
- **Watch for non-verbal communication.** Observe the user's facial expressions and body language, as well as what they say in order to get the full picture of what they are thinking *and* feeling and what pleases or frustrates them. Actively encourage people to say what they are thinking as they work through an exercise. This is fascinating, as people often say things like "Oh! What happened there?" or "Why can't I....?" Follow up, and ask what people were expecting - would they have preferred the app to do the thing(s) they have in mind, or what you offered them instead? Be sure to find out why!
- **Note how easy it was for the users to perform each task.** Did they experience any issues along the way? Watch for any journeys that do not seem very smooth or appear to be inefficient. You may have missed them before, but when you watch someone interacting with the prototype, they will become evident! It could be that there are too many clicks or taps involved in performing the activity and the journey could be tightened up. Alternatively, the order of the steps in the journey may need rearranging.
- **Identify other problem areas.** If you have to intervene to help a user or show them what to do, this is a sign that there is an issue. If your product is easy to use, your help should not be needed. Review why

this happened and think about different ways that you could resolve the issue. If the users *can* complete your user journeys without assistance from you (and without hesitation), this is a positive sign. Whenever people slow down, or waver during user testing, you can ask them questions like: "It seemed as though you hesitated then. Can you tell me what you were thinking?" or "You seemed to pause for a few moments back there. Can you talk me through what happened?"

- **Watch out for "polite" silences as you speak.** Does this mean the person you are speaking to dislikes, or disagrees with your proposal? Or, are they just confused? Pause frequently after discussing functionality to ask: "What do you think?" or "Would that work?"
- **Consider the aesthetics and the "look and feel" of the app.** Aim to find out whether they liked the look of the prototype and how it was presented. Did the colours and layout appeal to them? Why? Why not? *(It's best not to begin this type of testing until you have held other sessions to test your app's functionality and user journeys as the priority.)*

Towards the end of the session:
- **Give the user some free time.** I like to give users a few minutes at the end of a session to "click around" an app, ask any questions and explore it on their own terms, without any directions. Which parts of the app do they return to? A-ha! There are insights to be had there. Just watch what they do and make mental notes. When they have finished browsing around, ask them what they were looking for (or at) and why.
- **Thank the user and discuss next steps.** At the end of the session, ask users if you can stay in touch by phone, email, social media etc. to show them how the product is progressing. Ideally, you need a pool of people from whom you can get feedback, ideally quite quickly. If your developer has questions and you're not sure what the correct answer is, you may find it helpful to speak with individuals from your target market to get answers. Consider setting up a Facebook group as a way to obtain feedback and to remain in contact with people.
- **Hold a debrief and end the session.** You can acquire very useful information by holding a post-test debrief with users to discuss their thoughts and feelings about the session. If you'd like to give this a try, allow 5-10 minutes for this at the end of the testing session. Hand over a short questionnaire, which includes questions such as:

CHAPTER 13
How to test your prototype

i) The best and worst things about the app. (Which functionality should you put to one side and not pursue? Which should you focus your energies on? Remember Pareto's 20%!)

ii) Things which they expected to be able to do, but couldn't. (This will help you to identify gaps in your product, where useful or important functionality is missing.)

iii) Parts of the app that were confusing. (This will help you to improve your user interface and user journeys.)

iv) Any apps they know of that do something similar. (This will bring you extra market research data.)

v) Their recommendation for the number one thing that you could do to make your product idea better.

vi) It is also *very* interesting to ask the question "Which people would this app be most useful for?" Assess how closely your product fits your target group from *their perspective*. Do they think the product is ideal for them, or do they think it would be better for some other group? Is it time to review your avatars and customer profiles, or have you found the right *product – market fit*?

You could also write a set of statements for people to comment on and use happy / unhappy face ratings, or ratings from 1-5 or 1-10 to represent very happy / very unhappy or strongly agree / strongly disagree as other ways to gather feedback.

If you like this approach, try making statements like "I enjoyed using this product," "This product is useful," "I found this product easy to use," "I would not use this product." and "I would not buy this product" and asking people to assign a number to each statement to show how strongly they agree or disagree with it.

Mixing positive and negative statements is a tool used by researchers to make sure that people are not answering questions on "auto-pilot" and are taking the time to consider each question. Decide whether you want people to fill out a questionnaire on paper, or online.

If you make the feedback anonymous, you are more likely to get honest responses – remember that most people will not want to give you negative feedback, but you need it to improve your product!

There are links to survey and questionnaire tools you can use to collect feedback in chapter 24.

CHAPTER 13
How to test your prototype

If one or two people have an issue with something, you should test with a few more to get more conclusive results. If three, four or five out of five all agree on the same things, then that is a strong indication that you need to pay attention to that feedback.

If the same comments keep coming back, (whether good or bad) then you will need to think about what this is telling you.

What action(s) will you take to build upon your product's strengths and minimise its weaknesses?

An example of an interactive user testing session

Here's an example of a user testing session to review specific aspects of a *social media* app. You might ask the people testing it to perform the following tasks:
1. Sign in to your app and create a profile.
2. Upload a profile photo.
3. Post one comment from their profile.
4. Post one video from their profile, along with a comment.
5. Post one image from their profile, along with a comment.
6. Post one link from their profile, along with a comment.
7. Search for an imaginary friend (set this up in the app in advance) and ask them to "like" their friend's post (prepare the friend's post in advance.)

The structure will be almost the same for any testing session:
- Prepare the tasks or scenarios for the user, covering all the user journeys and functionality that you want to test.
- Prepare the app for user testing. Set up any information or data in the app that your users will need to complete their exercises.
- Know your do's and don'ts for running a session from chapter 3, and review the steps from the section above.
- Have your recording tools available, whether these are digital or an old-fashioned pen and paper.
- Have some online or paper-based questionnaires prepared in advance, if you've decided to do a post-test debrief.
- Set out the instructions for the session.
- Run through the tasks (from 1-7 in this case), introducing each one and giving the user the time they need to work through them.

- Give the user a few minutes "free time", ask them if you can follow up with them in future and debrief them using your questionnaire.
- Do your post session analysis and complete your PMI log, if you would like to use it to help you examine what you've learned.
- Create an action plan based on the verbal *and* non-verbal feedback you received and any other items of learning that you got from the session.
- When you have more functionality to test, arrange further user testing sessions and prepare new exercises.

Please note that many of the questions in this section are relevant whether you are testing physical software, or a paper prototype.

Project pitfall!

Don't focus on only one type of device.
Don't assume if your product works well on one type of device, it will work well on others.
Native mobile apps need to be tested on smartphones and tablets.
Web apps need to be tested on a laptops or PCs, smartphones and tablets via a web browser.
Ask users which devices they have access to and request that they use a specific device when they test. If you will be in the room for the sessions, bring different devices with you for testing and alternate between using a laptop, a smartphone and a tablet when running user tests with different users. See chapter 23 for more information about testing your product.

Testing with a paper prototype

If you're testing with a paper prototype, you will first need to prepare your screens and tidy them up if necessary. Arrange the sheets of paper in order, starting with the simplest journey first. Run through all the screens (or pages) for that journey, from start to end and then do the same for the next journey and so on.

Talk through each screen, or sheet of paper and the functionality on it and discuss all your annotations, explaining what each icon is for and what happens when the icons or elements on the page are interacted with.

CHAPTER 13
How to test your prototype

There are always items of functionality that the owner of the app (or the technical team) think are brilliant. When you user test *your* brilliant items, watch carefully. Is the user as excited as you, or do they get excited over different functionality?

Carefully explore feedback that is at odds with your current beliefs and assumptions about your product. This will help you get aligned to what customers really value, so you can continue to tailor your app to suit them.

How many people should I approach?

Try for a minimum of 5 user tests per avatar to be sure you've understood the needs of each target group. In other words, if you have 2 avatars, like Robert and Sam from chapter 10, then you would want to speak to 5 people like Sam who are administrators or office juniors and 5 people like Robert who are HR Managers.

To get 5 people to say yes to you, you may need to ask up to 25 people, but this depends on how persuasive you are!

If you're interested in the theory behind this, back in 2000, The Nielsen Norman Group published an article confirming that 85% of usability issues are found with 5 users.

You can see from the *diminishing returns curve* in the table to follow that if you test with 15 users, you will identify 100% of your usability problems. However, the increase in issues found is only marginal with between 6 and 15 users

Fig 69. "Why You Only Need to Test with 5 Users" by Jakob Nielsen (March 19, 2000). Article: https://www.nngroup.com/articles/why-you-only-need-to-test-with-5-users.

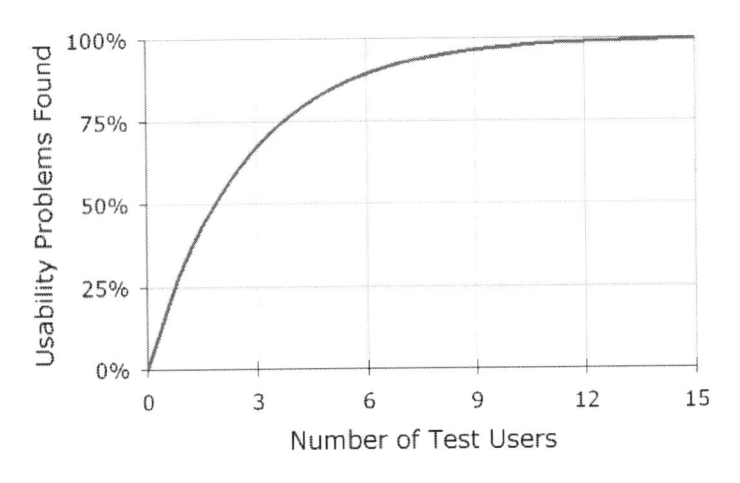

Screen recorder software

When running a user test, there will be quite a lot you'll need to pay attention to. You'll be asking questions, watching users' facial expressions and body language, observing what happens on the keyboard and / or screen and where the user is typing, tapping, swiping or clicking and possibly making notes too!

Use technology to make your life easier and to make sure you don't miss any important data.

Screen recorder software can be used during user testing. This may record users' faces and their mouse or cursor activity. Make a note of all the issues you spot during each session and study the video footage later. It's always an eye-opener to watch playback of users performing activities, you can see them thinking, frowning or looking relaxed, depending on how complex they find your tasks to be!

I'm reluctant to include links to free screen recorder software, because of the possible security risk, (most require you to download software), so here are two well-known names:

- Adobe Captivate. www.adobe.com/Captivate
- Camtasia. https://www.techsmith.com/camtasia.html

You could also use a mobile phone on a tripod, or video camera to record the screen of the device that you're testing on, or do a voice-only recording.

In some countries, it is illegal to make recordings without permission, so make sure your user testers agree to this before you go ahead.

Instagram case study: A product pivot that paid off

You may well need to pivot based on the user feedback that you receive.

The verb "to pivot" became widely used in the startup world in 2011, following the launch of the book "The Lean Start-up." Pivoting describes a change of business strategy based on new information coming to light. Instagram's rise to fame involves a major pivot:

CHAPTER 13
How to test your prototype

From **burbn** to (Instagram logo)

Even from the start, Instagram was huge. A week after launch they had 100,000 users, at two weeks 200,000 users and just three weeks in, the figure stood at 300,000.

Instagram's co-founders, Kevin Systrom and Mike Krieger spent about a year building a mobile app for the App Store called Burbn, offering "a new way to communicate in the real world", but weren't happy with the app, believing that it was too "cluttered, and overrun with features." Taking a huge gamble after a year of hard work, they slashed away all the functionality in the app - except for the photo uploading, commenting and "like" functionality and *that* was how Instagram came into being. Instagram was bought by Facebook for $1 billion US dollars back in 2012 and as of April 2016, Instagram had over 400 million active users.

Congratulations!

- You've done some excellent work covering user journeys, user experience and gathering feedback using prototypes, to highlight issues and opportunities.
- Repeat the prototype and test process several times over, if you can, updating the prototype each time based on your findings, ideally until no further significant issues are reported and all major problems are resolved.
- With a clear idea of the functionality you need, how the product will work, how the customer will use and interact with it and their likes and dislikes, you should be able to provide a clear list of requirements to a developer that are detailed enough for them to begin working on.
- Next, let's start pulling together and prioritising all the elements needed for the launch of your app - and then we'll talk about hiring your developer. We are cooking with gas!

CHAPTER 14
How to select and prioritise your MVP

"Things which matter most must never be at the mercy of things which matter least."
— Johann Wolfgang von Goethe

In this chapter:
- The power of having an MVP
- The MoSCoW prioritisation process
- Getting what you want from the development process
- Free resources
- Project pitfalls and pro tips
- Chapter challenges

What is an MVP?

MVP stands for *Minimum Viable Product*. Creating one (and sticking to it!) will keep you focused on the essentials required for the initial launch of your software. MVP describes a basic, "no-frills" core product, and the philosophy behind it is to get the first version of your app built as quickly (and economically) as possible, so you can start generating revenue!

The Minimum Lovable Product (MLP), concept has appeared more recently and those who support it say that the first release of a product should delight and excite customers rather than being basic and "just good enough." Getting the right balance is important and this can be tricky even for product management professionals, but there is still a lot to be said for clearing the hurdle of getting your product built and launched quickly.

To increase the chance of your app being well-received when it goes live, focus on the critical things that your product needs to do, based on *facts* and *data*.

Refer back to the market research, customer interviews and user tests that you have already done, then continue to consult with your target market throughout the build process to make sure that your product remains useful, usable and valuable to them.

MVP is all about making tough decisions
Every item of functionality that you decide to build should:

CHAPTER 14
How to select and prioritise your MVP

- **Be prioritised.** You will need to understand why different items are important relative to each other in order to make the right judgement calls on what you should do first, next - or never!
- **Have a clear purpose** and value for your customers.

Put everything else to one side and come back to it later, if you must!

It's o.k. if your MVP has a few niggles and annoyances initially, however, it should *be free of any serious bugs when you present it to customers.* I would define niggles as functionality or user journeys that "do the job", but could be improved, or the absence of useful, but non-critical functionality which has been deferred beyond your initial launch. Bugs and managing product quality, are topics discussed towards the end of the book, between chapters 19 and 23.

Project pitfall!
Don't bite off more than you can chew...

There's a common misconception that it's a good thing to build a product containing every type of functionality you can think of. It seems like a logical way of avoiding mistakes and keeping your options open. If you build a product with a huge range of functionality, surely you'll have a better chance of succeeding? *Everyone* will love it!

Unfortunately, this is not true!

This is a rookie mistake and a good way to create a lot of problems for yourself.

The risks involved in attempting to do too much include:
- *Overcomplicating* the product and making it more complex to build.
- *Overspending* on development work, due to an increased volume of work.
- *Overwhelming* yourself (and probably your developer) in the process, with so much to build, test and "get right."
- Delays to your launch. You will be slower in bringing your product to market if you have more work to do.

More is not always better, and building excessive functionality can waste time and money.

You also risk reducing the value of your product if the best parts of it become diluted by all the non-essentials.

CHAPTER 14
How to select and prioritise your MVP

> As you saw in Chapter 13, Instagram became successful after they decided to *remove* functionality and focused on doing a few things very well.
>
> Often, trying to build a lot of functionality seems like a good idea because not enough is known about customers wants and needs. Make sure you know what the "deal breakers" are - those items that your customers will not or could not use the product without.
>
> If you have worked through the earlier chapters in this book and followed the exercises, you should have a good idea of what is and isn't core functionality.

Methods for storing and prioritising your requirements

Now we've talked about the issues that come with trying to build too much functionality before you launch, I'm sure you're keen to avoid this! Your MVP should have a *scope* and the scope defines the work that you are going to do. This will include all your technical tasks, functional requirements and non-functional requirements. Let's run through a few techniques to help you manage your scope and define what your MVP is going to be.

Firstly, your MVP needs a home.

The most low-tech option for storing all the items on your MVP, and the details of the work that you want a developer to do for you, is probably an Excel spreadsheet. Alternatively, *Mingle*,

https://www.thoughtworks.com/mingle/

And *JIRA* https://jira.atlassian.com/secure/Dashboard.jspa are specialist task management and tracking systems used to store project requirements. They also allow work to be assigned to team members and can be used as issue tracking tools, so that *bugs* and other product faults can be either assigned to, or "claimed" by members of the team for fixing. Another tool you might consider is *Trello* https://trello.com/.

Trello and Mingle are both *freemium* products (you'll know about this from chapter 8) - both have a free basic version. The basic version of JIRA costs $10 USD per month.

CHAPTER 14
How to select and prioritise your MVP

I need to make a very quick announcement here.

Trello is versatile and great for managing projects, so I'm going to use it for *all* the task management examples in this book from this point onwards. I have no connection with Trello, but it's simple to use, there's a free version, it's a pleasure to use on the mobile web, it has a useful Google Chrome extension and is also available in the Google Play store and the App Store:

https://trello.com/platforms.

I have provided other alternatives that you can use, but for consistency, and the reasons given, I'll be demonstrating with Trello. Right, let's continue!

The Trello interface

Trello has a simple *drag and drop* interface and you can get set up in minutes. Trello has the concept of *boards* and *cards* and I've created a sample board for building a mobile app called *My App*. You can make boards private or share them, and there is a feature which allows you to send information to an email address linked with your boards. Once it is received, Trello will automatically-create a card for you. You can find out how to do that here;

http://help.trello.com/article/809-creating-cards-by-email

Now is a good time to gather the information you have about how the app should work and store it in one place for easy access. Attachments can be added to cards, so your wireframes, notes, process flows and other documents can be uploaded to them. Simply click on a card to add text or documents to it. Documents can be uploaded to Trello from your computer, *DropBox, Google Drive, OneDrive* or *Box*. Trello also has the concept of *Power-ups*, which offer useful extras that you can bolt-on to your Trello experience. The Business Class power-ups come with the paid version of Trello, but there are several free power-ups available with the free version, including the calendar power-up for setting reminders, which I'll demonstrate in chapter 22. You can find a list of power-ups here, https://trello.com/power-ups

Next let's look at two concepts together, the *storage* of your requirements and the *prioritisation* of them.

MoSCoW is a prioritisation method. It is used widely in Agile software development to help both the clients requesting software and the teams delivering it to stay focused and to manage scope.

CHAPTER 14
How to select and prioritise your MVP

MoSCoW consists of four priority categories; Must, Should, Could and Won't. Put every task you can think of that needs to be worked on by a developer into one of these 4 categories:

Must. This category is for core work that *"must"* be done. This list should include:

- Your essential functional requirements. All the essential functionality your customers require. These are core, integral pieces of functionality that the product would be useless or have limited value without. Your "musts" should always be high-value, high-benefit items.
- Your essential non-functional requirements - including those related to security, performance, availability and compliance. See chapter 6 for a refresher on non-functional requirements and to download your NFR checklist.
- Any technical items required to set-up the project, (including any tools a developer needs to install or activate in order to do their job; such as automated test tools or a source code repository system, we'll pick this topic up in the next chapter) and to maintain or support the product from a hardware or software perspective.

Should. It will feel a bit uncomfortable not to do these things. These are your important, but non-essential requirements. Your product will work without these items, possibly using *workarounds*; alternatives or methods for dealing with product gaps or limitations.

Any workarounds will need to remain in place until the "should's" can be built and made available to your customers.

Could. You *could* do these things. Some of them will be "nice to haves" or just ideas that you've come up with that may, or may not be of value to your customers.

Won't. These items *won't* be done. They can still be logged and kept for reference in case you want to remind yourself of the ideas you have already considered and dismissed and the reason(s) why.

Now we've covered MoSCoW prioritisation, let's come back to Trello to see how you can make MoSCoW work for you on a practical level.

CHAPTER 14
How to select and prioritise your MVP

Fig 70. The "My App" product backlog, prioritised using MoSCoW.

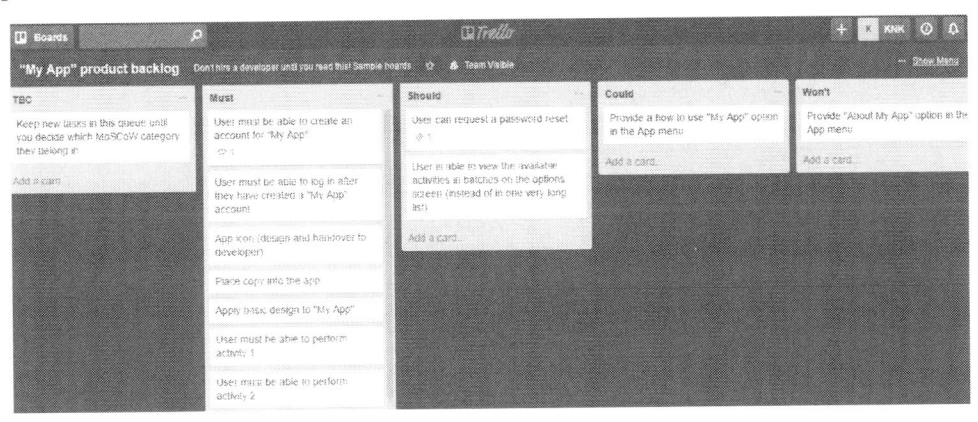

You can copy this board, and get access to the other 9 Trello boards featured in this book here:

http://www.mylanderpages.com/donthireasoftwaredeveloperuntilyoureadthisbook/free-resource-2-trello-boards

The *cards* are the small white entries on the board, and the *columns* (or *queues)* are the four vertical lists you can see on the board (five in total, if you count the *Won't* queue, which is off to the right and not shown here.) *Cards* will be used to represent simplified Agile user stories within this book.

This is the "at a glance" view of all the functionality that I *might* build and the Must list represents what I *will* build. To keep the process simple, you could use this as your *product backlog* (your product to-do list), so that all your tasks are kept here. (See Chapter 5 to recap on Agile projects and terminology.)

You will no doubt have more entries than this, but to keep the Must list as short as possible, keep all your thoughts and ideas about what you might wish to build, and any non-essential tech-tasks that your developer tells you about and assign them to the correct queue - either Should, Could or Won't. If they're *essential,* put them in your "Must" queue.

I've also created a "to be confirmed," TBC queue. You can place cards in this queue if you're not yet ready (or able) to decide which MoSCoW queue they should be assigned to. When you're ready, you can put them in their "proper" place!

> **Project pitfall!**
> **Watch out for the insidious scope creep.**
>
> *Scope creep* is dangerous, so beware! It occurs when the scope that was agreed upon gradually starts expanding to include more and more items. This process starts innocently, but always causes problems if it goes on unchecked.
>
> *Sticking to your MVP can hurt.* You'll face constant temptation to be *"just adding this"* and *"just adding that,"* to your Must list, but the end result is extra work, time and cost added to your project. It is far too easy to burn resources this way - when you're paying staff to work for you, time really is money, so this approach is issued with a financial health warning!
>
> Remember that you are making tough decisions in order to keep a tight rein on the project and your expenses.
>
> *The things that you can't do right now aren't necessarily "no's" forever - they are just "no's" right now.*
>
> If keeping your "must" list small is a challenge, try and imagine the worst that could happen if you DON'T get certain functionality built. You'll need to decide if the outcomes you imagine are risks you're prepared to take (Should, Could or Won't) or whether the potentially "bad" outcomes are too serious to take chances with (Must).

Adding acceptance criteria to your requirements

The next stage of the process is to take each card on your "Must" list and break it down into more detailed requirements. (Details can be added to each card by clicking on it.)

The more vague or high-level your requirements are, the more likely you are to get poor quality work back from a developer. The requirements written on the cards need to contain enough information and a sufficient level of detail for a developer to be able to sit down and start work.

Please heed this advice - it will save you a lot of time, money and hassle!

Let's run through a few examples:

Imagine instructing a builder to build a house for you (the app), with three bedrooms, a kitchen, two bathrooms and a living room (the *requirements*). Would that be enough detail for you to end up with your dream home? Hmmm, not really. You'd get a house, but goodness knows what the interior would be

CHAPTER 14
How to select and prioritise your MVP

like! To have each room designed and built the way you wanted it, you'd need to provide a lot more information.

Here's another example.

Do you remember the red cars that we spoke about in Chapter 10? The imaginary one which was your vision and the one with all the parts? If you wanted to buy a car, you might first think about the age, make, model, colour and its features. However, the engineers that build the cars spend their time thinking about nuts and bolts, engines, hydraulics, the laws of physics, gears, brakes, suspension and the relationships between all the components!

The same gap will exist between you and a developer.

The way you think about the project and the way they view it will be totally different. Thinking about the app is one thing, but building it from nothing requires a different perspective!

This is why it's so important to dig beneath the surface and really think about what it is you need your developer to build for you and how your app needs to behave.

Here's one more example, describing something we have all done at some time in our lives - visit a supermarket!

Imagine sending someone you know shopping for food and asking them to bring back cheese, milk, bread and tea. They arrive with the items you asked for, but you're disappointed. Why?

Well, you had a craving for mozzarella, to make a home-made pizza and you got Edam cheese instead.

You got a carton of cow's milk, but you're allergic to it and usually buy almond or soy milk.

You got a white uncut loaf and you usually buy brown bread which is sliced.

You wanted to wash it all down with some Earl Grey tea and you got a box of peppermint tea bags instead.

In this example, we didn't even get into brand preferences, pack sizes, how many packs or units of each you wanted and whether the items should be organic or non-genetically modified!

The devil, as they say, is in the detail.

CHAPTER 14
How to select and prioritise your MVP

The basic requests for "bread, milk, tea and cheese" are like looking at the tip of an iceberg.

When considering all the things that you need your app to be able to do, look beyond the more obvious and straightforward requirements to those that exist at a deeper level.

Fig 71. The assumed vs. real level of detail required to build an app.
https://commons.wikimedia.org/wiki/File:Iceberg.jpg By Uwe Kils.

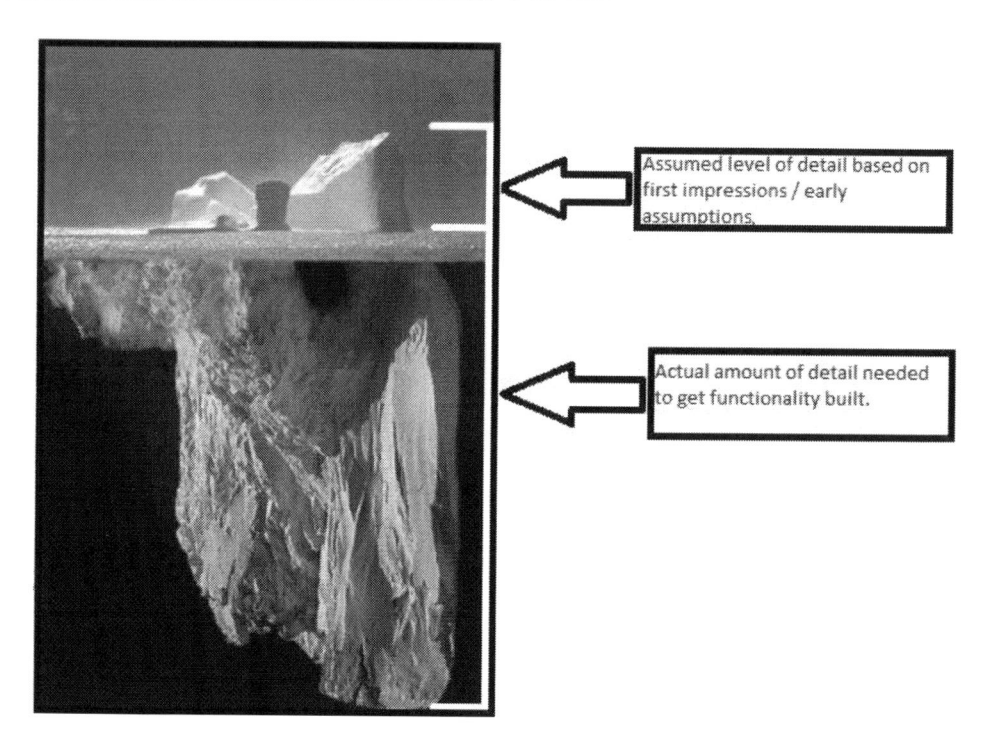

[Iceberg image with annotations:
- Assumed level of detail based on first impressions / early assumptions.
- Actual amount of detail needed to get functionality built.]

> **Pro tip!**
> **Use detailed acceptance criteria to get what you want from the development process.**
>
> Agile teams reduce the risk of confusion and set out their expectations for the work to be delivered using *acceptance criteria*. These are a set of conditions associated with a card or a task and the development team must fulfil these criteria in order for you to "accept" the work. The card contains written evidence of the work that was agreed and everyone knows where they stand, with no "mind-reading" involved:

CHAPTER 14
How to select and prioritise your MVP

> *If you didn't ask for it, you won't get it and if it was asked for, it must be delivered!*
>
> On delivery of the work, a tester will check that the developer did not miss any of the criteria and check for bugs and issues with the work. If anything is missing, it's easy to identify what this is and to send it back "into development" to be finished.

Covering both positive and negative scenarios

Unhappy path scenarios, are ones where things don't go according to plan when an app is being used. People naturally consider the *happy path,* which is what happens when actions or processes are completed without any issues arising, but as we know, in the real world things can go wrong and unexpected or undesirable events happen. Therefore, software teams also think about all the things a user might do on the *unhappy path,* so developers can make sure the app knows how to handle such events.

Each field in an app where a person can type or paste in some information should be set up with some *rules,* or in-app *logic* which tells the field what kind of information it can and cannot accept and the team thinks about how to *warn users* and *help users* should these events occur. They will also think about how to help the user avoid such issues completely.

Think of your app as being powerful, but also quite stupid!

All it does is follow the instructions you give it, via your developer. If you don't give it instructions for all the important scenarios it might face, it will get stuck whenever there's a gap in those instructions - it won't know what to do and may crash, or behave strangely as a result.

Let's look at a few common scenarios. How should your app respond if:

- A customer fails to enter information into your app that absolutely *must* be provided? (This is usually called *mandatory information* and fields that hold mandatory information are called *mandatory fields.*)
- A customer enters the wrong data in the wrong place (or the right data in the wrong place)?
- A customer tries to make the app perform an activity for them without performing other essential steps first?

CHAPTER 14
How to select and prioritise your MVP

You can have text in your app which is visible in the app all the time, called *inline text,* to advise users (a pro-active measure), or *contextual help*, which appears to help users at the relevant point in a process (also pro-active), or you can display an error message *after* something goes wrong (a reactive measure.)

Thinking these things through will improve the usability of your app, and the experience customers have when they interact with it.

You've now completed section 4! Next, we'll be spending several chapters reviewing the technical skills needed to build apps, discussing where to find professionals with suitable experience and I'll be showing you how to manage the interview process and hire yourself a developer!

Get them done and check them off! Chapter 14 challenges:

- ☐ Gather together and review all your data - market and competitor research, customer interviews, user testing feedback, prototypes, your avatar(s) / customer profiles (updated to include all that you have learned so far) - what do you need to build and what might be able to wait?
- ☐ Why not get yourself set up on Trello? Create a board with your TBC, Must, Should Could and Won't columns, or copy mine by making a copy of the board via this link.

    http://www.mylanderpages.com/donthireasoftwaredeveloperuntilyoureadthisbook/free-resource-2-trello-boards

    Create Trello cards for everything you can think of that you might need, assign them to the right queues based on your current understanding of where they belong, and add, or attach any important information to each card.

    If you don't feel ready to try MoSCoW for your cards yet, try using MoSCoW on anything from the items on your shopping list to your work tasks. Ask yourself whether each task is a deal-breaker and must be completed, or if some tasks can be downgraded in priority, or removed completely. Once you've practiced, complete the 2 action points above.

    Download the chapter challenges workbook and activity log, so you can keep track of important tasks:

    http://www.mylanderpages.com/donthireasoftwaredeveloperuntilyoureadthisbook/Free-resource-1

SECTION 5
FINDING A DEVELOPER

CHAPTER 15
Finding developers with the right skills

In this chapter:
- Common programming languages
- Identifying the skills required to create web and mobile apps
- Operating systems
- Front-end, back-end and full-stack developers
- Development frameworks
- Saving time and money through 3rd party tools and software
- Other useful skills for development

In order to hire a developer with the right expertise, it will be important to know more about the programming languages, technical skills and development tools available, and which ones might be suitable for building your app.

You'll also need this information when you start writing job adverts and reviewing developers' CVs and profiles. We're going to get a little more "techie" in this chapter, but stick with me and we'll keep things as straightforward as possible!

Which are the "best" programming languages?
Unfortunately, there is no straightforward answer to that question!
In defining "best", we would need to ask: *"Best for what?"* What I *can* tell you is that it will be beneficial if the skills of the person you hire naturally fit with the type of app you are trying to build. There is nothing worse than trying to fit a "square peg into a round hole" and *forcing* a programming language to do what is needed - you'll need the right tools for the job.

Some languages are more appropriate for certain tasks, or types of project than others - gaming, website building, number crunching, or in the scientific world, for example. Picking the wrong programming language *could* set the scene for future problems, such as an increase in the cost of building (and maintaining) your product, because of the limitations of the language selected.

CHAPTER 15
Finding developers with the right skills

There is no such thing as a single, definitive "top 10" or "top 20" list of programming and scripting languages. Rankings are determined by factors such as popularity; statistics from employment websites, the estimated number of professionals using the language and the number of searches carried out in relation to that language. Taking data from a range of sources into account, including the *Tiobe Index,* (Tiobe operate in the software quality arena), a list of the most popular ones from a choice of hundreds of languages, looks something like this:

- PHP (Hypertext Preprocessor)
- Java
- CSS (Cascading Style Sheets)
- Python
- Ruby
- C++
- C#
- JavaScript
- iOS
- Swift
- Perl
- Microsoft.net

Project pitfall!

Beware of technologies which are not (yet) very popular, or just emerging.

Don't overcomplicate your project by deviating from tried, tested and well-established programming languages! Leading or cutting edge technologies are sometimes nicknamed "bleeding edge" because their reliability has not yet been fully proven.

Technical projects are challenging enough – avoid adding more "unknowns" into the mix!

Here are 5 very good reasons to leave new technologies alone:

1. It will be easier to find new staff if you are using mainstream tools and technologies.

2. The pool of available talent will be larger (and therefore, less costly.)

3. Developers often rely on their particular development community for information and support. The newer, (or less popular) a language is, the more limited the support, documentation and other resources available will be. If your developer gets stuck, it will be harder for them to get help which could cause delays, or mean that the quality of your app could suffer.

4. Developers are generally intellectually curious people who enjoy experimenting with new technologies and gaining new skills. They may be more than happy to try new tech - just bear in mind that *you* will be the one funding the experiment!

Is this a good commercial decision? Do some *due diligence* research to see if this "investment" is really worth your time and money. Huge, (and wealthy) companies like Google fund experimental project teams, but they are prepared to write off the cost if things don't work out. If you're on a budget it is best to avoid this approach!

5. If things don't work out with the experiment and you need to change the programming language your product is written in, be aware that it will probably have to be re-built from scratch, possibly by a different developer. Ouch. This will be a drain on your time, and a real budget-killer.

Programming languages for building web apps

You may be interested to know that the *YouTube, Dropbox* and *Google* web apps were written in Python, *Shopify, Kickstarter* and *Airbnb* in Ruby, and *Facebook, Wikipedia* and *Yahoo!* in PHP.

These languages are suited to the web; (in fact, PHP was created *specifically* for it), have decent sized developer communities, (meaning that your developer has somewhere to turn if they need to discuss a problem) and they are not obscure - there are large numbers of developers using them. PHP boasts the largest community of the three by some margin.

Each language has its own strengths and weaknesses.

Ruby is recognised as having a large selection of re-usable widgets (pre-written code is convenient for developers, and for you!), but may not be as fast as other languages.

Python is considered to be a flexible and easy to learn language, but is regarded as being a slower language to code in, (in terms of productivity and how fast code can be produced). The Namcook Study, 2013 reviewed a number of programming languages and their relative productivity.

PHP is known as a language which is flexible and easy to pick up, but apps written in PHP have been identified as having security vulnerabilities. Security risks can occur due to a lack of programmer experience or awareness. One consequence of PHP being easy to learn is the large number of semi-professional PHP developers that exist, who arguably may have picked up uncorrected bad habits through self-tuition without mentorship or training.

Operating systems

Before we go any further, we should spend a brief time talking about *operating systems*.

An *operating system*, (or *OS*) forms part of the system software in devices such as computers, smartphones and tablets. OS software manages basic functions such as memory and task management. Software applications and programs usually require an OS to be installed and running on a device in order for them to work. Examples of operating systems include *UNIX, Windows, Mac OS, Linux, Android* and *iOS*.

Users interact with an app, or application, the application requires an operating system in order to run, and the operating system is installed on the hardware device.

CHAPTER 15
Finding developers with the right skills

Fig 72. A diagram showing the relationship between hardware, operating systems and applications. https://commons.wikimedia.org/wiki/File:Operating_system_placement.svg, Golftheman, derivative work: Pluke

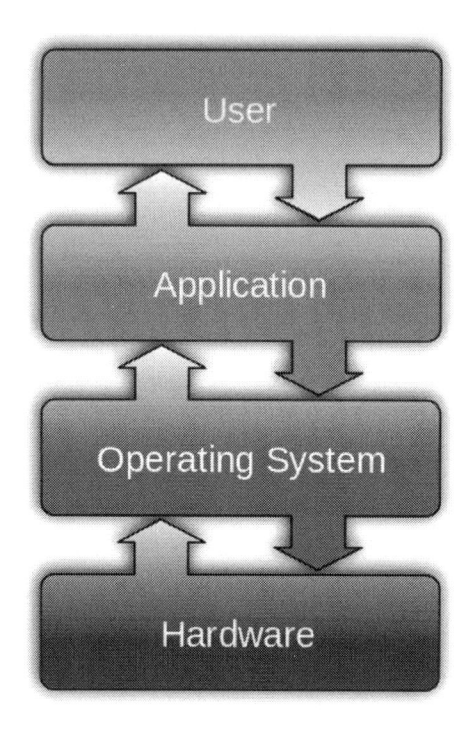

Programming languages for building mobile apps

Android is the operating system created by Google. Apps created to run on the Android OS are sold in the Google Play store. The Android OS is itself *written* in Java and if you want to create a mobile app suitable for Android mobile smartphone and tablet devices, then you will need a *Java developer.* (Note that C and C++ can also be used to build Android apps, but this is not promoted by Google - Java is the recommended language.)

iOS is Apple's operating system for the iPhone, iPad and iPod touch. (The operating system for the Mac is called OS X.) Apps compatible with the iOS operating system are sold in Apple's App Store. If you wish to create a mobile app for Apple mobile devices (and Macs and wearable devices too), then you will need a *C, C++, Swift* or *Objective-C developer.* C and C++ are Microsoft products, whilst Swift and Objective-C are owned and licensed by Apple. If you hire a developer with C or C++ skills, be aware that you'll be "mixing and matching" to some extent in using tools created by Microsoft to build a product for Apple, instead of using tools designed *by* Apple *for* Apple. However, there are no laws against this and C or C++ developers with a good track record in building iOS apps could be considered.

Development aides

How are you doing so far with the terminology? Stay with me - if you're going to be hiring a developer, there are some useful free resources towards the end of the chapter and there are still some important things that I need to tell you!

In this section, we'll discuss a few other key terms, *SDKs* and *IDEs*.

Tools exist which allow developers to create applications for different purposes. These are called SDKs (Software Development Kits.) There are many types of SDK, including ones for Facebook and Spotify, as well as those for specific programming languages.

The iOS SDK was created by Apple to build apps specifically for Apple mobile devices. The "kit" comes with a set of tools for developers to use, including an *iPhone Simulator,* which mimics the look and feel of the iPhone on a laptop or PC. There's a visual example of this in Chapter 23. The *Android SDK* contains tools used to develop applications for Android platform.

SDK's *may* include an *IDE (Integrated Development Environment),* additional software which provides extra tools and a more visual environment for a developer to work in. *IDE's* help developers create and test software in convenient, fast and efficient coding environments. The iOS IDE is called Xcode. It contains a suite of tools developed by Apple:
https://developer.apple.com/xcode/

Android's IDE is called *Android Studio*. This is the "official" IDE for Android and it supports the build of apps for all Android devices:
https://developer.android.com/studio/index.html.
Eclipse is an IDE used for Java development; Eclipse and Java can also be used together to create Android apps.

Other IDEs include Xamarin Studio, which can be used to create both Android and iOS apps, however just as you might think twice about using languages other than Java to build Android apps or using non-Apple languages to create apps for

Apple, using IDEs that were not built specifically for either Android or iOS may be something to think about, although Xamarin is certainly flexible!

Fig 73. Programming languages, SDKs and IDEs compatible with Android and iOS app development

Company	Operating System (OS)	Languages	SDKs	IDEs
Apple	iOS	Swift, Objective-C, C++	iOS SDK, Xamarin Studio	Xcode
Google	Android	Java, C, C++	Android SDK	Android Studio, Eclipse

Development options can be complex, but this is normal!
We've spoken before about straightforward answers being difficult to find sometimes in the software development world. This is head-busting stuff and even developers can get confused! To make good decisions technical folk will do a *lot* of research to deepen their understanding of the topic, look at the pros and cons of various options, consult their communities and seek advice and then come to a decision. Online developer communities and sites like *Quora;* https://www.quora.com/ are great for posting questions and evaluating options. I will give you the details for some popular developer communities in the next chapter.

Areas of expertise - "front-end", "back-end", "full-stack" and development frameworks

In many cases developers will have a specialism, focusing more on "front" or "back-end" development skills.

Front-end (or *client-side*) skills are used to create the parts of apps that the user is able to see and interact with. Front end expertise might include controlling the layout, fonts, colours, *call to action* (*CTA*) buttons, such as "back", "next" and "Go" and styling.

The positioning and integration of copy, images, video and logos are also "front-end" tasks, as are boxes that "pop-up" on mobile screens and web pages. Interactive elements like social media icons that connect the user to Facebook or Twitter or show the number of people who have 'liked' or 'tweeted' a post are also the domain of front end developers.

Common examples of front-end skills include: *CSS, CSS3 (the most recent version of CSS), JavaScript, jQuery, HTML, (Hyper Text Markup Language) and HTML 5 (the most recent version of HTML).*

Back-end (or *server-side*) skills are used to perform actions which take place at the back-end, (also known as the server.) A back-end developer's work might include capturing the information entered into an app by a user and storing it in a database and the retrieval of that data when a customer requests it via the app. Their skills ensure that the database and the app's *front-end* can communicate with each other. Back-end developers generally handle *configuration* tasks and the *logic* or *business rules* coded into the app, which tells the app what it needs to do and what limits or rules apply when it comes across particular scenarios. Do you recall the configuration example I provided back in Chapter 8?

A back-end developer will be skilled in a programming language; PHP, Python, Ruby or Java for example, *and* have experience with databases (nicknamed *DBs*). *Oracle, Microsoft SQL Server* (usually referred to as SQL Server), *MySQL, MongoDB* and *Postgres* (also known as PostgreSQL) are some of the most common databases that developers may have on their CVs.

Full-stack developers are multi-skilled developers, experienced and competent in both front and back-end technologies. However, it is challenging to maintain such a broad-skillset, especially as technology moves at such a fast pace. Consider the pros and cons of breadth of experience vs. depth of experience. You can certainly advertise for a full-stack developer and if you interview any, try to understand where their strengths (and interests) really lie.

Development frameworks

Developers may have knowledge of both programming languages and different *frameworks* for those languages.

Experience of using frameworks is a positive thing - they have common pre-packaged elements that can make development quicker and more straightforward.

Frameworks also introduce and maintain consistency and continuity, both in the way that your developer works, but also *between* developers - you could decide

CHAPTER 15
Finding developers with the right skills

that each developer you hire must have experience of the same framework(s) as their predecessor.

Frameworks exist for both front end and back end programming languages.

GitHub, one of the largest developer networks on the web, name frameworks such as *Bootstrap, Foundation* and *Semantic UI* as some of the most popular front-end frameworks. When considering back-end frameworks - *Laravel, Cake, Symfony* and *Zend* for PHP, *Django, Pyramid* and *Flask* for Python and *Sinatra* and *Rails* for Ruby are all well-known. Many frameworks may exist for each programming language, these are some of the most common ones.

Other important skills and tools

Revision control and continuous integration

The *source code* for your app needs to "live" somewhere and that place is called a *source code repository* or a *Revision Control System*. Often described in the development community as a *repo,* this holds all the files that your app needs in order to run and may be used for *version control* too, which involves storing, retrieving and merging changes to code. Popular repos include *GitHub* and *BitBucket* (owned by the company that created JIRA).

Revision control also makes it easier for multiple developers to work on your product at the same time and to add or *check-in* their code without affecting the work of other developers on the team. Repos *may* also help to get you and your developer out of crisis situations, by helping them "undo" mistakes (by *rolling back* to a previous version of your product) or possibly to recover deleted files.

If you have multiple developers, then *Continuous Integration,* (CI) experience may be useful too. Popular CI tools include *Travis* https://travis-ci.org/, *Jenkins* https://jenkins.io/ and *Codeship,* https://codeship.com/. CI is the practice of *integrating* and merging code from different developers into a shared repository (such as Git or Bitbucket). Automated testing is done before the code is merged, to confirm that the code to be added to the shared repository has not broken any functionality or caused any issues.

Full project life cycle experience

It will be advantageous if you can find developers who have experience of working on projects from beginning to end. This is called *full project life cycle experience*. Many developers will have this experience, but it is not a given.

You'll need someone who knows how to set up a development project from scratch, build the app and release it into the public domain successfully, so look for evidence of this.

3rd party tools and resources

You may not have to build all the functionality you need from scratch.
If they have the know-how, developers can make use of 3rd party tools including *APIs, code libraries* and *open source software* and adapt or integrate with them for your benefit. These 3rd party tools can be used to enhance your product, or to speed up delivery of your project. Be sure to investigate any costs attached to using these tools before going ahead. However, if they are reliable, then using them may well be cheaper than paying your developer to create the same functionality from scratch. See Chapter 19 for tips on reviewing and managing 3rd party tools and providers.

APIs. An *API* (Application Programming Interface; pronounced ay-P-eye) is a set of programming instructions and standards for accessing web or mobile based software applications. As an example, Google Maps, Facebook and Twitter all have their own APIs, which allow other companies to use elements of these apps alongside their own functionality.

Code libraries. Experience with *code libraries* may also be useful. These are collections of code available as resources that can be used to develop software. Familiarity with code libraries can save developers time and make the development process more efficient.

Open source software. Lastly, proven experience working with *Open source software* could be very beneficial. This type of software is created by a 3rd party, but the source code is made available publicly via a license.

Those holding a license usually have the right to *use, change, and distribute the software for commercial or private purposes free of charge*. There are many licenses associated with open source software such as the MIT License and GNU license. If you wish to use or modify open source software, make sure that you apply for the relevant license and understand the terms of use. The terms and license details are usually available from the website the source code is downloaded from.

Standards and protocols

Focus on the skills you need the most as the priority, however, it *may* be useful if your developer has experience with the following:

XML (Extensible Markup Language), pronounced ex-m-el, is a simple way of storing or transferring data between systems.

JSON (JavaScript Object Notation), pronounced jay-sun, is a format for sending or receiving data that can be read and understood by humans or machines.

RESTful Services *(Representational State Transfer), or SOAP (Simple Object Access Protocol.)* REST is not a tool, or software, but an approach used to help computers to communicate with each other. Some APIs are RESTful *because* they conform to REST standards. An alternative to REST is SOAP, which has a different set of communication standards.

You can certainly look out for these on profiles and CVs. They suggest, (but do not guarantee) that the developer has a good range of experience and is probably not a junior.

Join me in the next chapter, where we'll discuss where to find a developer and how to prepare for the interview process.

CHAPTER 16
How to hire a developer

In this chapter:
- Quiz: Are you ready to hire a programmer?
- Hiring Q & A
- Using freelancer hiring sites
- Free resource
- Writing and posting your job description
- Tips and Project Pitfalls

If you're feeling a bit nervous about hiring someone, that's understandable - this is a critical part of the process! When hiring for any position, there is an element of risk involved. I've interviewed staff to join software teams, reviewed thousands of developer's CVs as an IT recruiter, and attended many meetings where developers have discussed how they will handle the hire of a new colleague. Even developers hiring developers do not always get this right! This book was not intended to sell a dream of "magically" hiring the perfect developer, however, it *is* possible to increase your chances of finding a good developer, and this is what we will focus on.

Over the next two chapters we'll review some processes that you can follow and some important points to be aware of to help you make sound hiring decisions.

Hiring Q & A

Do you remember when I told you about the clients who had effectively left the meter on their "development taxi" running because there wasn't enough information to start the build process yet?

If you start the development phase of your project with too many unanswered questions, be aware that you will be working out the answers on your own dime.

CHAPTER 16
How to hire a developer

Is now the right time to hire?

The right time to start the hiring process is when you have clarity on what you want to build and have at least some detailed requirements. This will help you stop your project costs from escalating.

How about a **quiz** to see how prepared you are?

- ☐ If you've fine-tuned your idea, done market research, know who your competitors are and understand the wider context of the market, sector or industry you want to operate in, tick the box. (Chapter 2.)
- ☐ If you know who your target market is and have confirmed that there is interest in your product idea, tick the box. (Chapter 3.)
- ☐ Give yourself another tick if you've user tested your wireframes, prototypes and user journeys and have reached out to people to "sanity check" your idea. (Chapter 13.)
- ☐ If you have a Trello board (or other repository) set up to hold your requirements, process flows, user journeys and wireframes and you have cards with written requirements added to them, tick the box. (Chapter 14.)
- ☐ If you've prioritised your requirements using MoSCoW and have a good idea of what your MVP is, tick the box. (Chapter 14.)

If you have 3 ticks or less, you've made a good start, keep going!

If you have 4, you've worked hard to minimise a lot of project and business risks! Great job!

Got 5 ticks? You're a well-organised superstar. You deserve a huge well done - you'll reap the benefits of all your great prep-work. Excellent effort!

Now you'll be less likely to start build work only to find there are gaps in your user journeys and processes, or that the ideas you have do not work in practice.

I'm not saying that things must be perfect; the start of a project is when you will know the least. You will still discover more about your requirements *and* your customers as you go along, but at least you'll have the foundations in place. It is those situations where there are *too many late discoveries of essential information* that result in difficulties in making progress.

If you haven't yet done the exercises in Chapters 2, 3, and 10 -14, please complete them as soon as you can.

Who should I hire?

Here's a summary of the technical skills discussed in Chapter 15:

- For Apple / iOS mobile app development, hire C, C++ or Objective C and / or Swift skills. Look out for use of the iOS SDK, Xamarin studio or other SDKs.
- For the Google Play store / Android, hire Java developers, (possibly with additional C++ and XML skills). Look out for Android SDK, Android Studio or Eclipse IDE experience.
- For back-end development, consider Ruby, PHP or Python developers with knowledge of frameworks (e.g. *Laravel, Cake, Symfony* and *Zend* for PHP, *Django, Pyramid* and *Flask* for Python and *Sinatra* and *Rails* for Ruby) and solid database experience with DBs such as Oracle, SQL Server, MySQL, MongoDB and Postgres.
- For front-end developers, core skills will be *CSS / CSS3, JavaScript, jQuery, HTML / HTML 5* and knowledge of front end frameworks such as *Bootstrap, Foundation* and *Semantic UI*.
- "Full-stack" developers should have a mix of both front and back-end skills. Look out for REST or RESTful services (or SOAP), APIs, JSON and / or XML, open source development and use of code libraries.
- If you are developing other types of software app, you may need to do some research to find out which programming language(s) will meet your needs. Start by trying to find out the languages your competitors' products are written in, paying special attention to those known to have decent or highly rated software. You can also run Google searches or visit the developer communities listed below using keywords like: "best programming languages for + [insert type of product, industry sector or task]" or "top programming languages for + [insert type of product, industry sector or task]."

Leadership experience has its benefits. It can be a good idea to look for developers with experience of leadership in their previous roles. This should be hands-on management, rather than pure man management, however, the skills gained from running a team can be very useful – communication skills, a responsible nature, the ability to explain complex concepts to other people, patience and maturity, in addition to their technical skills and expertise. Experience of this type suggests (but does not necessarily guarantee) competence.

How many developers do I need?

It may be best to start with one hire first, even if you think you have a large amount of work to do. This will give you a chance to:

- **Get used to the hiring process,** and make adjustments if you need to.
- **Observe the pace of progress** with your first developer to get a better sense of whether you need extra assistance, or not.
- **Think about how you might divide up the development work.** You'll see from the pro tip to follow that some planning needs to be done when there are several developers on a team.

If you wish to hire additional developers, ask those you have already to help you with the onboarding process by explaining the technical environment and processes to them. Decide who should give the new joiner the relevant passwords and tools that they will need access to.

Pro Tip!

2x developers does not mean 2x the output.

It's a common misconception that doubling the number of developers will double the amount of code that can be produced. This is not always the case, because some work can only be done *in sequence.*

Where a relationship exists between tasks, and one must be completed before another can begin, this is called a *dependency.* At certain points in the project, tasks which have dependencies will result in one (or many) developers needing to wait for that task to be completed before they can begin a new one. In other words, this work must be done *in sequence.*

Tasks that can be done *in parallel* are more flexible.

Let's look at some examples of dependencies, sequential and parallel tasks. We'll use a house renovation as an example.

A workman due to fit new bathroom flooring cannot start work until another contractor first rips out and replaces the shower and toilet in that bathroom. This is a sequential task.

An example of a parallel task might be engaging a builder to fit a new kitchen for you, whilst another paints a bedroom. In this case both tradesmen can work independently and at the same time.

Teams usually look at the work to be done and agree a plan to minimise delays and maximise output as far as possible.

Three tasks run in *parallel*. Tasks 1, 2 and 3 can all be coded at the same time.

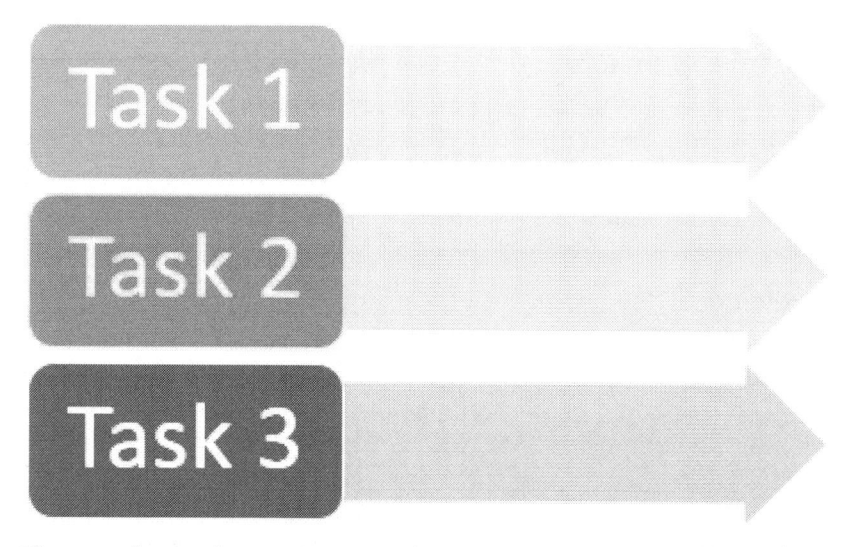

Task 1

Task 2

Task 3

Three tasks run in *sequence*. Task 1 must be completed before task 2 can start and tasks 1 & 2 must be completed before task 3 can start.

Task 1   Task 2   Task 3

How do I find a developer?

There are several ways to achieve this:

Recruitment agencies. You could consider hiring a developer (or testers, UX consultants or designers) through a recruitment agency, however, this method isn't cheap. Recruitment agencies generally post adverts to help them fill their client's vacanc*es and this is done via online job boards including Indeed.com, Indeed.co.uk, Monster.com, Jobserve.com or Totaljobs.co.uk.* Websites like these have millions of job hunters visiting their sites every month, so you're likely to get a good supply of CVs to consider. On the downside, the average daily rate for a commercial back-end PHP or Ruby developer in the UK hired via this method could range from around £250-£550 per day, excluding agency fees.

Permanent salaries for developers range from around £35,000-75,000+ dependent on skills, experience and location (and as much at $60-$80,000+ in the Silicon Valley region of the US.)

If you hire through an agency you will be charged a finder's fee – usually this is a percentage of your new hire's annual salary.

Some agencies will meet prospective hires before they recommend them to you for an interview. This may screen people out based on their communication and interpersonal skills and suitability for the role, however, the majority will expect you to have your own technical testing processes in place, although they may administer written tests for you.

Free / low-cost job sites such as Workinstartups.com, will allow you to post ads for full and part-time workers, freelancers, interns or co-founders: http://workinstartups.com/

Co-founder websites and meetup groups. Finding a co-founder and offering them a share in your business rather than paying directly for work to be done is another option. If you go down this route, agree early on which roles you and your co-founder will play in the business, and who will get what in terms of equity as well as what will happen if you decide to part ways. Here are a few global groups where you can network:
- **Meetup.com** can connect you with local groups. Try searching on the keywords "developers and entrepreneurs", "co-founders", "entrepreneurs" or "startups," http://www.meetup.com
- **Founders nation,** http://www.founders-nation.com,
- **Founder2be,** https://www.founder2be.com/index.php/ideas
- **CoFoundersLab,** https://www.cofounderslab.com/

Developer communities. Developer networks and online communities are both a lifeline and an excellent resource for developers. They can also be used as a way of hiring developers. On many of these websites, developers get points or gain status or kudos within the community by answering questions and supporting other members. If you create an account on these sites you may be able to reach out to potential hires and post questions in the forums. Popular communities for developers include:

- GitHub: https://github.com
- Stack Overflow: http://stackoverflow.com/
- Google+ communities: https://plus.google.com/ (then search for the individual community by name e.g. Android, PHP, Python etc.)
- DZone: https://dzone.com/
- CodeProject: http://www.codeproject.com/
- Codingforums.com: http://www.codingforums.com/
- Programmer's stack exchange: http://programmers.stackexchange.com/
- There are also lots of Facebook groups for developers, usually set up according to the name of the development language and sometimes also by location e.g. The PHP developer's zone or PHP developers in the Philippines.

Here is a guide which explains how to locate talented developers using GitHub: http://www.socialtalent.co/blog/how-to-use-github-to-find-super-talented-developers

Word of mouth. You may find good freelancers that are working for themselves through word of mouth, so let your personal network know that you're looking to hire.

Freelancer / outsourcing websites. Large and small businesses worldwide are now using freelancer websites to find staff. There are a variety of well-established sites based in the US, Australia and the UK that will allow you to hire talent located anywhere in the world. Most are set up so you can explore freelancers' profiles and previous reviews. In addition to finding front-end, back-end or full-stack developers, you should also be able to find designers, software testers, content writers and other roles covered in Chapter 5 using these sites:

Upwork. Upwork was formed from the merge of Elance and Odesk. Up until recently, clients weren't charged a fee for hiring using the site, but fees were introduced as either a one-off payment or as a monthly transaction in 2016. https://www.upwork.com

Freelancer.com (formerly Rentacoder.com). Freelancer.com describe themselves as the world's largest outsourcing marketplace, you can hire programmers, web developers, designers and admin staff via the site on a freelance basis. https://www.freelancer.com

CHAPTER 16
How to hire a developer

Guru.com. Guru report having a global network of over 1.5 million freelancers able to work on technical, creative or business projects. http://www.guru.com/

Toptal.com. Toptal has come onto the scene more recently and have positioned themselves as a high-end supplier, providing freelance staff to a lot of big-name and international companies. They will carry out interviews and technical tests for you and pledge that their developers are in the top 3% globally in terms of their technical abilities. https://www.toptal.com

Peopleperhour.com. This is another community of freelancers / remote workers. Web and mobile designers appear on the site in high numbers. These designers generally focus on the "look and feel" of the app and not the actual building of the app itself, so clarify in detail what will actually be delivered to you. https://www.peopleperhour.com/

99designs.com / 99designs.co.uk. This company can find you a designer to create a logo, design your website (or web app), mobile app, business card, Facebook page and more. Their revenue generation model is unusual – you submit your request and designers from around the world will compete to provide you with the best design. You pick your favourite, and if you don't like any of the designs, then there is nothing to pay. https://99designs.co.uk/, https://99designs.com

Fiverr provides a huge range of services, whether it's a Virtual Assistant (VA) to handle your Social Media, marketing or admin, a designer to create your logo, a mobile app developer, or someone to do work on an existing website...or build it from scratch! Most jobs (known as "gigs") start from $5. https://www.fiverr.com/

Payment methods

Hourly fees for developers hired via these sites can range from about $18-$100 USD+ per hour, excluding any amounts due to the freelancer websites in commission, introduction or transaction fees. There is often an option to pay a fixed project price or to pay an hourly rate. Most of these companies have built-in ways to make payments to freelancers via their websites and discourage or forbid "employers" from making direct payments.

Time tracking tools

Upwork.com has a built-in time tracker, but if you use a freelancer site that doesn't have one, then here are a few alternatives. Both of these tools have nice start / stop timers, making it simple to track the time spent on tasks.

https://myhours.com free, or $2-$3 USD per user, per month

https://toggl.com/ $10 USD, per user per month.

> **Tip!**
>
> **Don't make large financial commitments too soon.**
>
> Initially, you could pay your developer in instalments, based on their delivery of an agreed set of tasks at various stages of the project based on agreed milestones, or else hourly whilst you monitor how the arrangement is progressing. Don't agree to pay large amounts upfront - at least until you've had time to properly assess your working relationship and the quality of the work that you're receiving. To avoid misunderstandings with milestone-based payments, remember to be clear about what should be delivered at each stage.
>
> It is true that a flat fee may help you budget more easily, although getting a flat fee deal will be no good if the work, or worker is unsatisfactory. Consider offering work on an initial probation period and offering a fixed fee after the trial period ends, if you've had a positive experience.

A brief word about exploitation

The availability of sites like those we have discussed mean that smart, capable people from all over the world are now able to serve a global market. They can choose which sites they offer their services through and to set their own rates. You will need to decide whether these options are right for you, however, if freelancers can freely decide who they work for, when they work and how much they will charge, then the power is in their hands, which can only be a positive thing.

CHAPTER 16
How to hire a developer

Should you hire an agency or an individual?

Some of the hiring sites have both individuals and "agencies" looking for work. These agencies are usually either "real" companies or freelancer collectives of individuals with a range of skills who have banded together to deliver varied services to customers. A full-service agency may take your requirements and build and test your software for you.

Let's consider both sides of the argument.

The advantages of using an agency:
- Your developer may have more time to focus on programming tasks than if the two of you were working alone together. This is because a project manager or team leader is likely to be assigned to assist you with admin and queries, without involving them.
- If your developer is hired directly, then they will have to be an excellent problem solver. They'll need to rely on their own knowledge of online resources and contacts within their community to get help if they are stuck. At an agency, your developer may have other people to consult and brainstorm ideas with.
- If you need to hire other IT professionals and your agency has them, this could be convenient, so long as you are happy with the standard of work provided. Arrange for a trial period to be put in place, possibly with a rebate or form of compensation if you're not happy with the work that has been done.
- Build work will come to an abrupt stop if your directly hired developer is unwell, disappears without warning or suddenly decides to move on. An agency may be able to supply a replacement if this happens.
- Working with an agency will give you additional escalation points if any issues arise that you cannot resolve directly with your developer.
- If you hire a lone developer, there won't be anyone else to check the quality of the code they produce, for example via a *code review*. This is not guaranteed at an agency, but you could try asking for it.

The disadvantages of using an agency:
- Your developer *could* be replaced by someone else without your knowledge or approval. Manage this risk by insisting that you keep the same developer throughout the project (unless you specifically want to change.)

- The portfolio of work shown to you by an agency before you engage them might *not* be the work of the person assigned to work with you. This should not be the case with an individual, if they are genuine.
- Ask for direct contact with your developer, otherwise, you may be assigned a go-between. This is fine for admin or general queries, but not so good for discussing requirements or giving feedback. Information passing via a 3rd party could become distorted or diluted by the time you or your developer receive it.
- You may be less able to build a close relationship with your developer via an agency.
- You may pay more via an agency, although from what I have seen, agencies aren't always more expensive.

Tip!

Always have a plan B.

Contingency planning, project management techniques and running a team are things we'll talk more about in chapters 18 and 19, but whether you hire an individual or an agency, your backup plans for finding a replacement developer, or dealing with issues might include:

* A few promising developers or agencies on a reserve list. Many of the freelancer sites have ways to "favourite" freelancer or agency profiles that you like the look of.
* A clear idea of how long you will wait before you call an end to a working relationship that is not working out. See chapter 18 for more information on this topic.
* An emergency cash buffer and "padding" around any deadlines that you might have.

Writing and posting a job description

Here's a sample job description in blue text, with annotations and tips in italics.

Experienced PHP or Ruby developer required to build a photo sharing web app.

[Write a title for your job description. List the main skills you require and describe the project in a few words.]

CHAPTER 16
How to hire a developer

Hi,

I'm looking for a reliable [PHP]/[Ruby]/[Python] / [Java] / [Swift]/[Objective-C] *delete as appropriate* developer with 3 - 5 years' full project lifecycle experience to build a [insert type of app] from scratch.

[Elaborate on the essential skills you require and the number of years of experience you want. Note that Swift has only been available since the Summer of 2014, so it won't be possible to get 3+ years' experience with that, but you could ask for 3 years with a combination of Swift and Objective C or 12 - 18 months' Swift experience. Briefly discuss the project and the type of app you want built.]

Ideally, you should be able to start work within the next [4] weeks.
[State how soon you need someone to start.]

You will have used frameworks such as [Laravel, Cake, Symfony or Zend for PHP], [Django, Pyramid or Flask for Python], [Sinatra or Rails for Ruby.]
[Leave in the frameworks related to the correct programming language and delete the rest.]

You should have a minimum of 2 years' experience using any of the following databases: MySQL, MongoDB, Postgres, Microsoft SQL Server or Oracle.

You should have solid experience of CSS (including CSS3), HTML (HTML 5), JavaScript (jQuery or Backbone.js), ideally used with a front-end framework such as Bootstrap, Foundation or Semantic UI.

[Add these front-end skills if you're looking for a front-end developer or a full-stack developer.]

Experience of leading a small team would be useful, but not essential. [Earlier in the chapter, I explained why this skill may be useful. Leave this line in, or remove it as you see fit.]

You should be experienced with Agile ways of working and test driven development (TDD) / automated testing. You will also have experience of version control / revision control systems such as Git, Bitbucket, Travis or Jenkins. *[Add any other requirements here. List any desirable skills and any non-technical skills that are also important.]*

You should also have experience of developing responsive web apps.

[Leave this line in if you want to build a web app, because your app must work on smaller devices like smartphones and tablets, but it is not relevant if you're building a desktop app or a native mobile app.]

Please include any available links to your portfolio.

Many thanks,

[Your name]

Important: Please quote reference *XYZ*.

[Create a reference here. This is a small test to see if a developer has taken the time to read your entire advert and if they are thorough and pay attention to detail.]

You can use this ad to hire a back-end or full-stack developer as it asks for front and back-end experience.

If you want to advertise for a front-end developer, then put the focus on the front-end skills and frameworks and request 3 - 5 years' experience with those and remove the database skills. If you have multiple developers or believe you are going to need to hire more in future, then Continuous Integration, CI experience will be useful, so ask for that too.

Click the download button below to get a version of this job description in Word that you can edit and use.

http://www.mylanderpages.com/donthireasoftwaredeveloperuntilyoureadthisbook/resource-6-sample-job-advert

Should you post your ad, or invite developers to apply?
Choose the sites you wish to advertise on, then:
- Write your ad (or copy and paste my version) and post it to the freelancer website(s) of your choice so that interested parties can apply, or
- Post the ad, but to send it to specific developers that appear relevant and *invite* them to apply.

My opinion is that the invite-only route will allow you manage the process more easily.

CHAPTER 16
How to hire a developer

If the ad is open to all, you could have lots of people applying that are not relevant, but you will have to review all their profiles and messages! They will also be chasing you to follow up on their applications.

Guru, Freelancer.com and Upwork allow you to "hide" your advert so that only those you invite can see your advert and contact you. The downside to the invite-only approach is having to run keyword searches to find developers with the right skills that you can invite. Once you find some, check their profiles and decide whether they are a i) "yes", ii) "maybe," or iii) "no" by:

i) Sending them a message and a copy of your job advert,

ii) Marking them as a favourite, or

iii) Moving on to the next one.

Reviewing profiles and applicant responses

When reviewing profiles, consider:

- **Feedback ratings.** Consider the number, and quality of ratings.
- **How recently the ratings were given.** Prioritise those in the last three months vs. older ones.
- **The type of work that has been done for previous clients.** How complex does the work appear? Was it a very large project or did the job just involve writing a small amount of code? Do they look like they have solid and relevant experience in the areas *you* require?
- **Written communication skills.** Would you be happy to read emails or other messages from this person on a regular basis?
- **The evidence of the skills you require.** Look for the skills that have been mentioned in the last two chapters and look across the projects the developer has listed on their profile. When and how were the technologies used? How often have they used the skills you are looking for over the last few projects? Which versions of the technologies have they used? Please refer to the project pitfall example below. If you choose to interview the person, be sure to get the answers to these questions.

> **Tip!**
> **Relevant experience can make a big difference.**
> If you can find a developer with a history of working on similar projects, who has already faced the sort of challenges that are going to arise when creating an app of your type, this could be a huge benefit.
> If you can't find anyone who has built a similar product, the best you can do is make sure you hire an experienced developer so they can draw on that experience when issues arise.
> Try and look for developers that have used the key skill(s) you require on long-term, as well as short-term projects, where they may only have used the skill(s) occasionally or only dabbled with them more lightly over a period of years.

> **Project Pitfall**
> **Watch out for dated skill-sets, or infrequent use of key technologies.**
> Pay attention to the version(s) of a programming language that a developer has used. Googling *"latest version of [insert programming language of interest]"* will give you the answers you need.
> The "current" versions of some of the languages we've discussed are: HTML5, CSS3, PHP 5.6, Ruby 2.3.1 and Python 3.5.2.
> Professional developers will try to use the latest version of a programming language, or the version that came immediately before it, otherwise their skills will become out of date. If your developer hasn't kept up, they may have trouble finding assistance within their community if they need it. It will also mean that your product has been built in an "old" version of the language, which is already outdated. Over time this will happen anyway, but try not to begin your project in this way.

When you get responses back from your posted ad or personal invite, note how well they communicate, how quickly they respond and how relevant their reply is to your ad. Developers may reply with details of their portfolio, which you can review and ask questions about.

Compare each developers' relevance based on their skills "on paper," previous projects and your initial impression. Shortlist at least 5 for interview, although I would shortlist more if you can because:

- Some may look good in theory, but may not come across well during their interview.

- Not everyone you invite to interview may accept. It's common to have people "drop out" of interview processes for various reasons, including taking other positions, or other changes in circumstances.
- You are trying to find the best developer you can afford!

Now you have 5+ developers on your shortlist, it's time to invite them to interview with you.

In the next chapter, we'll cover the interview and selection of a developer to build your app!

CHAPTER 17
The interview process

In this chapter:
- Preparation, and interview questions
- Technical testing
- Running a work trial
- Qualities to look out for
- Chapter challenges

Are you ready to hire a developer?
We're going to start off with some planning and preparation pointers, then move on to holding interviews and selecting a successful candidate!

Preparing for the interview

Will you be holding interviews online, or in person? If you are planning to interview remotely. *Skype* and *Google Hangouts* are quick and easy ways to hold voice only or voice and video calls for free, whilst *GoToMeeting*; www.gotomeeting.com and *Cisco WebEx*; www.webex.co.uk, both allow one-to-one (and three-way) video conferences on their free plans.

If your interview candidates are based abroad, discuss time zone differences with them as early as possible. This will be the first test of how easy it is to contact each other and how a business relationship might work in practice. Real-time meetings with freelancers in the Philippines and China might be tougher than India, for instance, depending on where you are in the world.

Have a notebook, spreadsheet or similar that you can use to store notes about each interviewee, including:

- Written and verbal communication skills.
- Their responses to your questions and how satisfied you were with what you heard.
- Your thoughts about the quality of working relationship you think you could have with them.

CHAPTER 17
The interview process

A quick reminder...
If you want to go into detail about your project during an interview, or share user journeys, process flows and other information, then it may be best to get an NDA signed *before* **the interview takes place.**

The interview questions

Here are a large set of questions you can use, divided into 3 parts. You can ask any combination of these, or cover them all for an in-depth overview of each candidate. Allow at least an hour for the interview.

Introduction

- **Provide relevant information about yourself and explain the format of the interview**, for example, a basic question and answer format with some scenario based questioning.
- **Explain what the project is,** what stage you are at and the information you have gathered so far. This could include prototypes, process flows or requirements. Remember that the developer has to choose you too, so demonstrate that you are organised and collaborative!
- **If you have any important deadlines to meet, say so up-front.** You'll want to confirm whether any dates or timescales you have in mind are realistic.
- **Request a summary** of all the information you have just given them. *This is a test*. You can say something like, "I'd like to confirm that you got all that, and everything was clear. Could you please summarise my requirements?" Note how they handle this. If you get the right information back, or if they got most of it, but ask you to clarify a few points, this is all positive. You've got someone who pays attention, listens well and knows when to ask for clarification. If they start to "play back" your information to you before you even ask, that's great, they're pro-active too!

Middle

- **What challenges do you foresee on a project like this?** This is a great question to see what kind of insights and knowledge the developer has and whether they have the right personality, experience and skills to be able to help and advise you, or if they will just follow your instructions and write code. These are two *very* different types of developer and the former will be great for your project: they are confident, will share their knowledge and are not shy about speaking up and giving their opinion.

- **Do you have any experience working with apps (or on projects) of a similar type to this one?** If so, ask them to tell you as much about the project and products as possible. The project's duration, team size, their role and the part they played in the project and the key skills they used. This will give you a sense of whether the part they played was major or minor. Ask for website addresses or the names of any mobile app(s) they have worked on. Next, select some other projects from their profile or CV and ask them to talk you through them using the same questions (the project, the product, its duration, their role and the skills used, etc.). If they *don't* have experience of working on a similar app, ask them to run through at least 3 projects they have worked on. Ask the same questions about each one. As they run through them, listen for evidence that they played a significant part in each project and note the key skills involved in each project. Do they match the skills you requested in your job description? Does their use of the skills you need seem comprehensive, or light?
- **I'd like to ask you a few more questions about your technical skills...** Ask your questions in priority order, starting with the most important skills in the job description you posted, and ask how long they have been using each one. Next, ask them to name their top 3 strongest technical skills, along with a rating out of ten for each. (Scoring is subjective, but it is a good indicator of the developer's confidence and where they feel their strengths lie. If the top 3 skills mentioned were not skills that are essential for the role, this should be a red flag that the developer may not be a good match.) Ask about any other skill that you think may be relevant to the job, from Chapter 15 or elsewhere and seek examples of when these skills were used, how they were used and how long for.
- **I'm very keen on having monitoring and analytics in place for my app...** (See the NFRs in Chapter 6.) Are there any products you can recommend? What types of monitoring do you think are most important, and why?
- **I want to make sure that my app performs quickly when people are using it, and that it will cope if many customers are using it at the**

CHAPTER 17
The interview process

same time... How would you help me achieve this? What types of performance testing have you done in the past?

If you can't find developers with strong performance testing skills, you may need to hire a tester with specialist experience in this area. (See Chapter 6, and review Chapter 23 before you do your interviews, so you're aware of some of the terminology that you might hear about.)

- **Maintaining a secure app is important, can you tell me which sort of hacks my app may be most vulnerable to?** How would they prevent, or minimise the risk of these hacks occurring? Ask about their experience with creating secure apps and what role they specifically played in any security work. Find out what security measures they recommend when building apps like yours. (If needed, refer to Chapter 6 for a recap.)
- **Please provide some examples of challenges you have faced whilst building apps. How did you deal with them?** In asking this question, you are trying to get a feel for whether you think the developer is proactive or not. Did they solve the problems they mention, was it a team effort, or did someone else in the team resolve the issues? Listen for any other indications they give about what kind of worker they are.
- **Do you have any automated testing experience?** If you would like to have automated testing in place on your project, ask which tools they have used, how long for and how they used them. Who set up the tools? Was it them, or someone else? Ask their opinion about automated testing and its pros and cons. Can they provide a detailed explanation?
- **What do you do when you encounter a challenging technical problem?** How would the developer try to solve it? Here you are looking for evidence of any networks, forums or communities that the developer uses to solve issues quickly and accurately, and how proactive they might be in seeking the right answers. This is very important as technical issues can become roadblocks that burn time and money: development work may slow or even stop completely if a problem is large or serious, and a problem which is not solved in the most effective way may reoccur.
- **Have you ever worked on an Agile project?** (See Chapter 4 to recap.) If they say yes, ask which framework(s) they have experience with.

Ask how long they have been following Agile development principles, whether they like them and any advantages and disadvantages of following Agile practices. Try asking for examples of how tasks were managed on Agile projects that they have worked on previously. You know some of the basic principles now, do they mention these? Did they seem confident and knowledgeable when discussing Agile, or vague and uncertain? You'll be given a framework you can follow to manage your project using Agile philosophies in Chapter 22.

- **What is your current employment situation?** Why are they leaving their current project? How many projects are they working on at the moment, and when will they be available to start yours? Find out how many hours per day and days per week they can dedicate to your project. You may want a developer full-time and exclusively, or just part time, so decide whether their answer is positive or not based on what you need. If a developer is running between two or more clients, bear in mind that it might be difficult for them to focus! What if both clients need the developer urgently at the same time?

- **What tools will you need in order to start building the app?** Ask why each item is needed and note these down any product names, so you can research these later. Before the project starts, you may need to sign up, or pay for tools and services that will support your project. These are potential sources of expenditure, so keep track of them in your finance app (Chapter 1) or expense log, noting how much they cost and whether the expenses are one-offs, or will recur monthly or annually. We'll talk about preparing a "technical shopping list" and taking stock of all the purchases you need to make in Chapter 21.

- **If you were to get the job, what are the first tasks you would want to do?** This question is to help you get a feel for how organised the developer is. Do they have a process in mind for how to start the project? Do they name a standard sequence of tasks? More than anything, the range of answers you get to this question should tell you a lot about each developer's thought processes. I'll explain how you can proactively kick-off your project in Chapters 21 and 22.

End

- **Do you have any questions for me?** Are you asked intelligent, insightful questions about the project? Note down all the questions raised. They *may* give you an insight into points you hadn't yet considered, or where you need to do more research or to gather more data before development work can start.

- **If you got the job, how would you prefer to communicate with me?** Find out which tools they like to use for communication and note these down. Are you happy with these? Tell them you would like a daily update (see Chapter 22) which will cover what they did "yesterday", what they will do "today" and any issues they are facing that are "blocking" progress. Check that the developer is happy to do this. Mention that you would like to use Trello (or whatever task management tool you've chosen) to store the project requirements and ask if they have any concerns or questions about that. (I'll show you how to use Trello to manage day-to-day activities in Chapter 22.)
- **Just to confirm, your rate is $, isn't it?** Sometimes this can change, so check just to be sure! Ask how they normally track the hours they work on a project and any software they recommend. Some of the freelancer sites have tracking built into them and the details for a few time tracking tools were provided in Chapter 16. Either way, you may wish to keep an eye on the hours you are being billed for.

Take as many notes as you can, and don't be afraid to ask the developer to repeat the names of any tools or technologies they mention. You won't be able to research them later if you don't catch all the details. Click the download button to get a copy of an interview log that you can use to store your notes.

http://www.mylanderpages.com/donthireasoftwaredeveloperuntilyoureadthisbook/resource-7-interview-log

---

Tip!

Keep the interview process tight.

Bear in mind that interview candidates may have several options to consider. Other startups and businesses are looking for developers too and a good one can be snapped up in a matter of days, or less.

If you want to carry out multiple interviews with the same developer, get them done within two or three days to make sure you don't waste time interviewing people who have already found other jobs by the time you get around to speaking to them again.

Technical tests

Technical tests may comprise of:

- **A programming aptitude test.** These can be used for developers of any level of seniority. They assess logical reasoning skills and the ability solve numerical problems.
- **Written technical tests**, which assess the developer's grasp of the fundamentals of programming and their understanding of good coding or database practices, or tests with questions about specific programming languages or databases.
- **A practical tes**t which involves writing code to solve a specific problem assigned by the interviewer.
- **A verbal technical interview,** used to assess understanding of specific topics in the form of a "technical chat."

If you know anyone with the same skills as the developers that you are interviewing, ask if they could do a technical interview on your behalf.

There are technical tests available online for most languages. Technical tests can be obtained via

https://tests4geeks.com, https://www.interviewmocha.com/pre-employment-testing/software-development, and

http://www.w3schools.com/php/php_quiz.asp. Bear in mind, however, that the answers to most technical tests can also be found online! If you'd like to ask developers to sit a test, you could try sending them a link to the specific test you want them to take and ask them to send back a screenshot of the test results within a time limit - so for instance, if the test is supposed to take 45 minutes, you could ask them to send you a screenshot of their results within 45 minutes. To solve this problem, *Mettl* will email test results directly to you when a test has been taken: https://mettl.com/pre-built-tests/Test, Types/TechnicalTests

Now you will be able to make a decision based on a review of your interview notes, your opinion about who you'll work best with and any technical test(s) that were taken.

Running a work trial

One approach which is not particularly cheap, (but with the potential to save you money and hassle in the long-term), is to *select several developers who passed your general interview and invite them to work for you for a trial period.*

The proof of the pudding is in the eating as the saying goes, and this is one of the best ways to assess a developer's work. If you know anyone who can look at the quality of each developer's code, even better as this will identify any bad habits and show whether a logical approach was taken in terms of the way the code was written.

Discuss some simple tasks that the developers could do from the MVP "Must" list that you created in Trello in Chapter 14, that could be prototyped quickly. Agree on *exactly* what you are expecting to see. Give all the developers in the work trial the *same* piece of work to do so you can compare one result directly with the other.

To manage your costs during the trial, agree on a strict time-limit with your developer - anything from a few days up to a week, and agree on a fixed price, since this is a short-term agreement. Confirm that you'll provide feedback within a few days of the end of the trial period and ask them to check in with you during the work trial to update you on their progress.

Check if there is anything else the developers need from you before the work trials can start. You will also need a way to test the work done during the trial, so ask each developer how they intend to give you access to it.

Assessing the outcome of the trial

Once the trial period comes to an end, test the work you've been given, asking the following questions:

- Have the task(s) been completed correctly? Does the work done match what you both agreed would be done? How were your requirements interpreted (or misinterpreted)?
- Was the work done within the agreed time-frame?
- Did each developer check-in with you during the trial period as you requested? Were you happy with the way they communicated?

- Did they ask any questions to check they were following the instructions you provided correctly? Did they contact you to seek confirmation if in doubt? A good sign. Or, did they just go ahead and guess what was needed without checking in with you? A bad sign!
- What were your impressions? What was it like working with each of the developers? Were they resourceful, with a can-do attitude, or difficult to communicate with? Did they seem professional and organised? Did they seem to know what they were doing?

There may be a gap between what you asked for and *what you should have asked for*.

Are there some lessons you can take away and reflect on for when the project begins? The level of communication needed to get software built is far more detailed than most people are used to. You could view this as a dry run to get used to how much information you need to provide in order to get the right results.

Hire the developer that impressed you the most, or if you weren't happy with any of the developers, keep interviewing, or refer to your shortlist of "maybes." This will be disappointing, but it would be a costly mistake to hire a developer whose work is of a poor standard. You *may* have to consider hiring developers who are a bit more expensive to find the quality you're looking for.

Qualities to look out for

If you find a developer with these qualities, keep hold of them!

- **Knowledgeable / skilled.** The developer is aware of a range of technologies and tools relevant to your project and your requirements. They can explain the advantages and disadvantages of them in the context of *your* project. Their past projects are relevant to the type of app you wish to build, and the developer appears to have played a significant role in these projects.
- **Consultative and communicative.** Communicating with the developer is easy. They listen carefully and address your concerns, and can explain concepts to you in layman's terms.
- **Friendly.** You feel at ease with them. Working together is a positive experience.

- **Flexible, and a good problem solver.** They make suggestions which are helpful or relevant.
- **Direct.** Getting a "yes" to every question isn't always a good sign. Software development isn't simple, so if someone says yes to every question without providing much information I would be a little concerned! If you are hiring people from a different part of the world, be aware that in some cultures it is rude or frowned upon to say "no" and this can cause people to skirt around an important issue or to avoid answering a question directly. Look for developers from any culture who *won't* skirt around problems and are comfortable telling you the truth, warts and all, whilst giving you decent explanations! Your developer should be able to tell you if more information is needed from you in order for them to do their job and you should also ask this question regularly to check that your developer is in the best position to do a good job for you.
- **Reliable and competent.** Does what they say they will do, acts on your requests, and puts in the agreed hours. Provides regular progress reports and delivers quality work.

Get them done and check them off! Chapter 17 challenges:

☐ Get any employment and NDA contracts signed by the developer you've chosen. Make sure you've acted upon any relevant legal or intellectual property related advice you need to follow. Review Chapter 1 for a recap.

☐ Use the time before your developer starts work with you to really get on top of things. Focus on resolving issues with your processes and user journeys, and getting more clarity about what the product needs to do. Gather together answers to all the queries the developers raised during the interview process, and address any issues or observations that came out of the work trial(s) that you did. Look out for any remaining "leaps of logic" or missing or incomplete steps and user journeys that don't flow well.

Remember, this is your last chance to do a review before your thinking time will be on a paid meter and you will have someone waiting for you to supply them with a steady stream of work and to answer their questions!

Download the entire set of chapter challenges as a workbook with an activity logs to help you keep track of important tasks:
http://www.mylanderpages.com/donthireasoftwaredeveloperuntilyoureadthisbook/Free-resource-1

SECTION 6

PEOPLE, PITFALLS AND PROJECT LIFE-SAVERS

CHAPTER 18
People management, and productive working relationships

"Coming together is a beginning. Keeping together is progress. Working together is success."
- Henry Ford

In this chapter:
- Communication on projects
- The benefits of being a "good" client
- Pro tips
- How to "help *them*, to help *you*": comments from freelance developers
- Deal breakers: parting ways with your developer
- Technical documentation

In this chapter, we'll be looking at the human side of software delivery. There are practical steps you can take to make sure that your working relationship with your developer is productive and harmonious, and we'll cover them here. Whether you have a tiny team or a large one, you can benefit from fostering a positive and cooperative team spirit. We'll also look at what you should expect from your developers and what they should expect from you. Fair is fair, after all!

Communication on projects

Follow these pointers to avoid some common causes of conflict and confusion, and to create an environment where information is pro-actively shared within the team.

Ask questions… and make your expectations clear.
"No? What do you mean, 'No'?!"
Friction can arise where there are difficulties in providing the desired solution.

CHAPTER 18
People management, and productive working relationships

If your developer comes to you and says something you've asked for "can't be done", what they probably mean is that given the project's budget, timescales or other restrictions such as the technologies being used or even the boundaries of their own knowledge, the work cannot be done.

It may also mean that they do not support or recommend the course of action, but it is unlikely that it is completely "impossible" to perform the task. Try to get to the heart of the problem. Ask them to explain why there is a problem and to tell you what the key issues are.

Quality information is essential. You'll need it to make good decisions for your product and your business.

Even if you cannot progress with a particular course of action, this decision should remain in your hands and not be made for you. Explain that you'd like to know *why* it's not possible to complete the task that you have requested.

Consultative developers will come to you with this information without you having to ask, but if the information isn't offered, here's an example of a decent, professional explanation:

*"Unfortunately, there is a problem delivering item **A** for reasons ------------- and -------------.*
*We could do item **A** if we had ------- and ------ but you need to be aware of possible issues such as -------------if we go ahead.*
*What we could do is try alternative **B**, or alternative **C**.*
*The pros, cons and costs of doing **B**, are -------------.*
*The pros, cons and costs of doing **C**, are ------------- and in order to do **B** or **C** we will need -------."*

This is a logical and thorough way to present a problem and set of solutions and it gives you the chance to fully explore your options.

Always ask for several alternatives if there is a problem with delivering what you have asked for.
When you have all the facts, you can discuss the possibilities and make an informed decision.

Make this your standard approach, and the people who work for you will come to understand that you expect detailed explanations.

CHAPTER 18
People management, and productive working relationships

You can also use this process to investigate project delays: *"We have a delay for reasons --- and ----, if we tried ---- and ----- we might be able to speed things up... The pros, cons and costs of doing----- are ------, and -----."* In fact, it's a good way to break down any business problem.

We'll talk about techniques for managing your project in Chapter 19, and how to estimate the building blocks of your product in Chapter 20.

Welcome all information, both good and bad. No news is not always good news on a project! It's important that your developer feels that they can point out any errors or leaps of logic you have made. They should also be able to come to you with bad news about the project. No-one likes to hear bad news, but rather than being kept in the dark and having to deal with a problem which has grown bigger or more complex because it has been left to fester, take the approach that whatever is wrong you want to know about it a.s.a.p.

Make it clear that you will be more annoyed if people DON'T speak up. Anything else is totally self-defeating.

If a problem is reported to you, stay calm, thank your developer for their honesty and move on to discussing how to resolve the issue. This sends out the message that being honest with you will not lead to the end of the world(!) and they will be encouraged to repeat this behaviour in future.

If you have hired a sensible, knowledgeable professional, you do not want them to keep quiet, you want them to speak up, and add value to your venture!

Minimise confusion... and clarify what you want, and what you mean.
People talk cross-purposes. They also mishear, or misread instructions.
These misunderstandings can be costly in a project environment.
You are more likely to experience these issues if you send instructions in emails, verbally and via Twitter, Skype and so on - this is a recipe for chaos!
A good way to handle this is to freely discuss topics via whatever modes you like, but to ensure that the *final outcome or agreement is always logged in your task management tool, along with all the relevant information and details needed by your developer.*
Agile teams use the phrase "card, conversation, confirmation," which means that before new tasks are started by a developer, they should be briefly discussed and the requirements confirmed. This is a simple, but effective quality management technique, which can save hours or days of unpicking mistakes.

CHAPTER 18
People management, and productive working relationships

Create a safeguard against forgetting important items. When talking with your developer about tasks or functionality, try to make it a habit to check what may have been forgotten and what else might be important or relevant before you end the conversation.

There are so many reasons why people don't express everything on their minds - nervousness or fear that their comments won't be welcomed, not wishing to appear too pushy, uncertainty about whether to highlight potential problems... To get all this extra information out into the open I have some questions that I like to ask developers and other team members when running a project. My *safeguard questions* are:

- *Do you have any questions or concerns?*
- *Is there anything missing?*
- *What issues do you foresee?*
- *Is there anything else I/we need to know, or consider?*

Strangely, asking these questions often results in important points suddenly coming to light. It's surprising what people will start to tell you!

Pro Tip

Spend quality time with your developer.
You already know that if developers don't understand what they need to do, or if they make unqualified assumptions, this will have a negative effect on your product.
Professional software delivery teams spend a lot of time reviewing requirements and asking questions of each other and of their client until they fully understand the work to be done. Even with limited resources, the principle behind the time investment is the same: *If you're paying someone to work for you, it makes sense to do what you can to help them succeed.*
Get regular feedback from your developer's perspective via daily micro-meetings (see Chapter 22) and weekly catch-ups. Ask them how they feel things are going and regularly ask them if they have everything that they need from you to do their job and take action where needed. Put some time in your diary on a weekly basis to answer questions and discuss the upcoming work to be done. The act of reviewing and discussing tasks together *will* lead to a better product.

The benefits of being a "good" client

After your MVP is built, you may want to extend your developer's contract, or you may need their help again for maintenance or emergencies. Maintaining your end of the bargain in the following ways will keep your developers motivated and contribute to a positive relationship:

Respond promptly. Answer questions as quickly as possible when your developer asks. This will help maintain their momentum, prevent them from context switching (see *avoid task overload* below) and keep the development of your MVP progressing.

Pay promptly. Don't expect staff to be o.k. with late payments. Everyone has bills to pay and disputes can be ugly and time-consuming.

Be clear and consistent in your communication. Provide clear, detailed requirements.

If you are regularly changing your mind about very fundamental elements of the product, you may have hired a developer too soon.

Excessive to-ing and fro-ing on a project can be de-motivating for a team. Have you ever had a boss who changed their mind frequently? How did you feel about it? No-one likes being given tasks which are vague, or where priorities change from day to day without good reason.

Avoid task overload and creating an environment where your team exists in "emergency mode". Constantly providing developers with lots of tasks that need to be done "right now!" can lead to frustration and burnout. Development work requires deep concentration as there is a huge problem-solving element to it. There is scientific research on the inefficiency of context switching and multitasking: when performing a task, every time you are disturbed (or disturb yourself!), it will take time to gather your thoughts and gain momentum before you can get back to where you were before the interruption.

This problem can be solved by *prioritising tasks* before assigning them to your developer. Each task should be "slotted" into your developer's work queue according to its importance and the level of urgency it carries. Refer to Chapter 22 for information on task prioritisation and scheduling.

CHAPTER 18
People management, and productive working relationships

Feedback from developers

I'd like to share some feedback from developers based in countries from Eastern Europe to the Indian subcontinent that were asked about the types of issues they experience when hired to work on development projects, and what clients could do to make the build process more efficient and effective.

These are the challenges that they raised:

"The biggest issue is a lack of communication / lack of project clarity, which results in incomplete or poor understanding of requirements. To make exactly what you need, we need to clearly understand what you want. Describe the whole picture so that the developer can imagine what has to be at the end."

"The most challenging thing is…proper requirements. Flow [workflow] should be clear on both sides and we must be on the same page."

"[Provide] clear guidelines about the functionalities of the website or app, how should it work, what it should do."

"Proper task management - tasks should not be given via email…or via chat."

"[Clients should be] answering questions as well as asking questions."

"There should be daily or weekly communication to check progress and to clear issues."

"I think using task or project management tools and messaging apps is a good idea."

"The UAT [User Acceptance Testing] phase [should] be given more importance by the customer."

"Use several channels for communication (email, Skype, Redmine, Trello etc.)"

CHAPTER 18
People management, and productive working relationships

Did you notice any common themes?

Thankfully, these are less likely to be issues on your project because you know how to help your developer to help you! We'll be talking about ways to manage team communication and how to manage the build of your product in Chapter 22.

Deal breakers

We'll close this chapter by talking about freelance agreement deal breakers. The following issues should signal the end of your working relationship if they continue to happen, and you have not been able to resolve them through discussion:

Consistent slow progress / lack of progress. You can't get a clear reason why you aren't seeing progress, or the reasons given are not acceptable to you.

Incompetent behaviour. Your developer seems unwilling or unable to follow written or verbal instructions. They do not build functionality or perform tasks according to the written requirements provided to them.

Unreliable behaviour. Your developer "disappears" and you are unable to contact them during agreed working hours. He / she does not do what they say they will do and does not check in with you at the agreed time(s).

There's a personality mismatch. They are inflexible and difficult to work with, or you find it hard to get on the same page about tasks. If you have more than one developer and you notice that one is causing disruption, investigate and get to the bottom of the issue as soon as you can. Weigh up the situation and if the balance is more towards pain than gain, then take action.

"Executive decision making" by your developer. They may be trying to help, (and if you're busy this might seem useful at first), but unless you've found a mind-reader who can anticipate your every need, then this is not positive. Do not delegate decision-making. Questions arise frequently during the development process; expect to be consulted – you can seek your developer's opinion, but it's *you* who gets to make the final call. There is also an issue if someone you hire fails to listen to, or respect your requests and wishes.

CHAPTER 18
People management, and productive working relationships

Slow communication. You find it hard to get responses or updates in a timely fashion.

Poor communication. You have a hard time understanding the options available to you and your developer cannot communicate in terms you can understand, either in writing or verbally.

Lack of interest. Your developer does not seem interested or enthusiastic about the project. Unfortunately, you won't get the best from someone who is disengaged.

Software quality issues. There always seem to be a lot of issues with the software being developed - it is either not doing what it should, is buggy, or displays other unexpected or undesirable behaviours. Even when you send the issues back to be fixed, there are *still* multiple problems.

There are issues with time sheets or claims for payment. If you regularly have to dispute the number of hours being claimed, then trust (or lack of it) is going to become a problem.

If you've raised your concerns and have not seen any improvements, then it might be best to start interviewing again. Be wary of doing this immediately before or after launching your product, unless there is a serious problem with your developer's competence or conduct. At this time, you'll need someone who understands your app to help you if any bugs or issues arise.

Before they leave you may want your developer to finish particular tasks, do a "show and tell" and technical handover for their replacement, and provide technical documentation about the project. Make sure your *new* developer signs any relevant NDA and employment contracts before they start work.

If it really is hopeless, you probably won't want to spend any more of your budget on development until you hire someone new. Request access to your source code and files if you don't already have this, and change any passwords.

If you wish to terminate the employment agreement immediately, check that this will not breach the terms of your contract.
Alternatively, serve notice to confirm that you wish to end the agreement.
If your developer is a permanent employee, then other rules may also apply. If in doubt, please seek legal advice.

Technical documentation

Whilst *technical documentation* can be extremely useful (especially during handovers), producing it can be expensive. Time spent preparing documentation must be paid for and is time taken away from building your software. Documentation can also become outdated as your app is built, which means an ongoing commitment to keeping it up-to-date, or taking some time *after* your MVP is built to do a full write-up. If you would like documentation to be provided, create a card for it in your task management system, (because it's still a piece of work that you'd like your developer to do). Here are some fundamentals you might ask to have delivered to you in a document:

1. The architecture of the system and its components including databases, servers, hardware and any other critical parts. If possible request diagrams as well as a written description.
2. Any APIs, plug-ins or other 3rd party tools and services your app relies on (monitoring tools, performance management tools, web hosting services, analytics tools etc.) Your developer should explain what each service does, and how it is being used in the context of your app.
3. Any important technical information and any configuration settings (system settings) that have been put in place and what they are for.
4. All account information, logins and passwords related to your product. (You may wish to use password manager software to keep your passwords safe: http://www.techradar.com/news/software/applications/the-best-password-manager-1325845.)
5. Any important, or useful links and reference information and access to all *release notes*. (Release notes are discussed in Chapter 22.)

In the next chapter, we'll talk about the role of project manager and we'll cover a number of ways that you can steer your project *away* from issues.

CHAPTER 19
Project management, pitfalls and perils

"A little risk management saves a lot of fan-cleaning."
- Anonymous

In this chapter:

- Project management: mindset and fundamentals
- Project plans
- Project management tools and tips
- Risk assessment exercise
- Risk mitigation case study
- Common pitfalls: Death by 1000 cuts and Suicide missions!
- Managing 3rd party relationships

In this part of the book, we'll look at some project planning, monitoring, prevention and risk management strategies that you can use if you don't have a project manager to assist you. We'll also review some major project pitfalls to look out for.

Project Management: mindset and fundamentals

Project planning

Having an outline plan of where you're going and the steps you need to take to get there can help you stay focused. This can be a rough outline to start with and can be filled in as you learn more. High level plans for a project or product are also called *roadmaps*, because of the sense of direction they provide.

Your plan doesn't have to be overly complex, especially with a small team. An example plan might include key events in the project, starting from your initial idea through to the post-launch phase of your app (after it has gone live.) The list might look something like this:

CHAPTER 19
Project management, pitfalls and perils

- Develop your product idea, carry out customer interviews and do competitor research
- Create prototypes, prepare user journeys, run user testing sessions
- Decide on a visual design
- Gather and prioritise requirements for MVP
- Hire your developer
- Estimate MVP
- Build and test MVP
- User test MVP
- Launch MVP and run beta test
- Reflect, review and decide on next steps
- Post-launch bug fixes and adjustments (usually done between 1-4 weeks after launch, depending on feedback and the severity of any issues found)

Bitrix24, https://www.bitrix24.com, Trello https://www.trello.com or Excel could be used to store your project plans, however, there are a wide range of free and low-cost project management tools available.

Here's an example using Trello. This is one wide board, split across two images (figs 74 and 75.)

You can add any number of high-level activities and extra weeks to the plan (see the W/c, or week commencing markers at the top of each queue), or represent the roadmap in months rather than weeks - it all depends how detailed you want your plan to be.

In this example, I've colour-coded the tasks to make it easy to identify them.

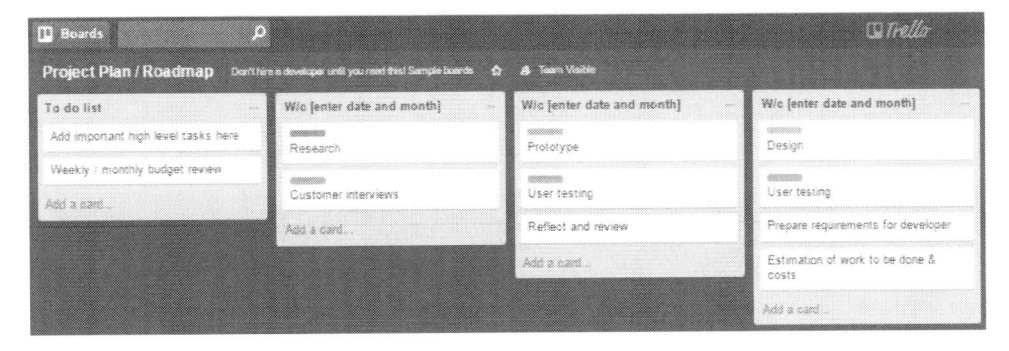

Fig 74. Trello project plan / roadmap example, part 1.

CHAPTER 19
Project management, pitfalls and perils

Fig 75. Trello project plan / roadmap example, part 2.

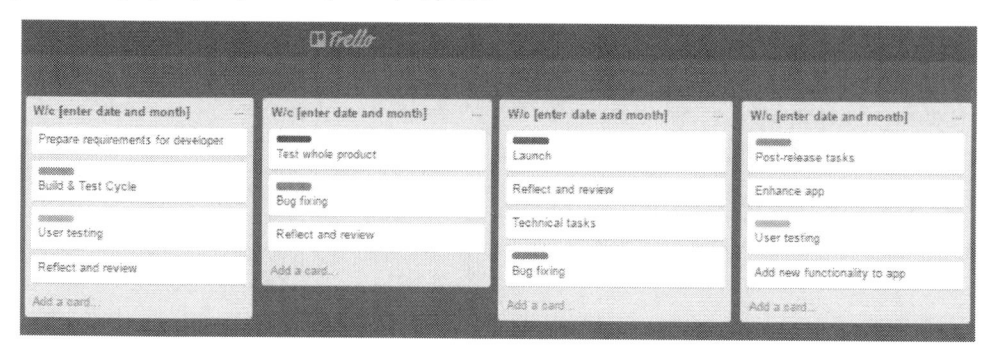

You can get access to all the Trello boards shown in this book, via the download link below:

http://www.mylanderpages.com/donthireasoftwaredeveloperuntilyoureadthisbook/free-resource-2-trello-boards

If you prefer to use Excel, a standard project plan layout is to:

1. List the tasks in the first column
2. List the people who need to action the tasks in the second column
3. Put the status of each task in the 3rd column (pending, in progress, done / complete, overdue, etc.)
4. Map the task's duration over the correct number of days, weeks or months, by highlighting the relevant fields in Excel.

Fig 76. Work plan template, http://www.tools4dev.org/resources/work-plan-template/

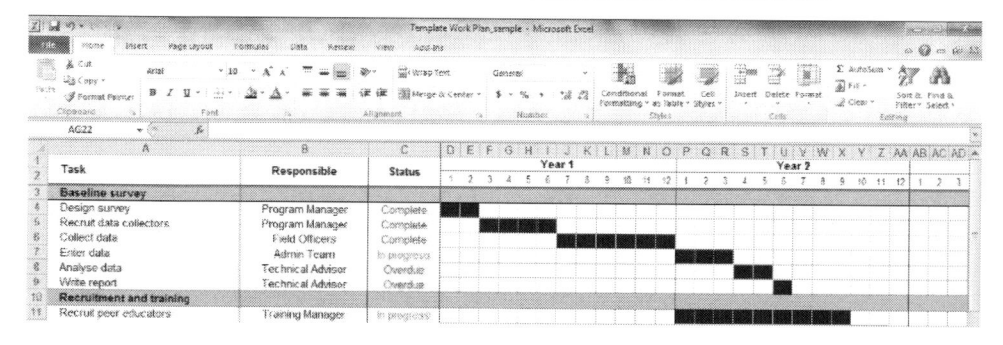

CHAPTER 19
Project management, pitfalls and perils

Project management tools and tips

There are some important points to bear in mind when wearing the project managers "hat":

Deal with the tough tasks first

It may seem logical to do all the easy technical tasks within the project first, but this is counterproductive. Dealing with the challenging elements of a project is part of *risk management;* the action of identifying risks and then acting to minimise their impact. As far as technical risk goes, if we pick all the simplest cards first (wherever possible), then all the more challenging tasks would still remain and the project would become *more unpredictable* and face *more risk* as it progresses. This is a PM's worst nightmare! Even if it is slow going at the start, if we do as many difficult tasks as we can as early as possible, then the project becomes *less risky* and *more predictable* as we progress.

This means that the worst is now theoretically behind us, and not in front of us. That's a better position to be in, isn't it?

Later in this chapter we'll review risk management in more detail, and I'll provide an exercise that you can use when managing your project.

Factor buffers into your plans

You can also protect your project against shocks by building in *buffers* (extra padding added to an estimate) within your plans. There are very good reasons for having *buffers* in place:

- **Development work is notoriously difficult to estimate accurately**, so whilst the estimation of the work involved in delivering your MVP is worthwhile, you should add a margin for delays and unexpected events to whatever estimate you and your developer arrive at (More on this in the next chapter.)
- **Project managers may also add contingency to the expected cost or time to complete a project**. Adding a 10-15% margin is fairly standard, but if you're new to this AND are forming a relationship with a new developer, you should leave a BIG margin. I would recommend at least 35%. There are always challenges on software projects, so factor this in!

CHAPTER 19
Project management, pitfalls and perils

Shield your project from risks

Have back-up plans in place, to keep your project afloat.

A PM spends time thinking about what might go wrong so they can prepare for negative events, or prevent them from happening. It's a role where you need to scan the way ahead for issues.

When operating in PM mode, you'll regularly need to consider worst-case scenarios. Don't feel like you're being overly negative or cautious - when you're in PM mode, this is how you are *meant* to think, and this means being prepared for delays, unforeseen costs, and problems:

What if the project over-runs?

What if your developer leaves (or you have to fire them)?

What if you need to spend more money than you intended?

If you're worried about any aspects of your project, this is a sign that you need to do some *risk management planning* (also known as *risk mitigation,* or *mitigation of risk)* in that area.

Risks have the potential to turn into issues that can harm your project, so give them the attention they deserve for long enough to work out how to deal with them and to prevent them from happening, or escalating. To avoid becoming overwhelmed by a potentially large number of project risks, PMs will usually categorise risks and deal with them according to priority. Let's run through how to do this.

How do you assess risk?

To assess project risks, you'll need to consider the following:

1. What might go wrong? List all the issues you can think of.
2. What is the *probability* or *likelihood* that each item on your list might happen? Low, medium or high? Put a likelihood rating against each risk.
3. How badly might your project be affected if the worst were to happen? Would the *impact* on your project be low, medium or high? Put an impact rating against each risk.

Review your list and prioritise the risks based on likelihood and impact, assigning them to one of the 4 quadrants shown in the diagram in fig 77.

CHAPTER 19
Project management, pitfalls and perils

Next, do a quick brainstorming exercise and note down some solutions or alternative courses of action to help you deal with the risks. Start with the ones that are the most likely to occur, with the highest impact - the orange quadrant, then move on to the blue and then the green quadrants.

Fig 77. Risk assessment quadrant. Risk and Impact.

https://opentextbc.ca/projectmanagement/wp-content/uploads/sites/3/2014/06/risk-and-impact.jpg

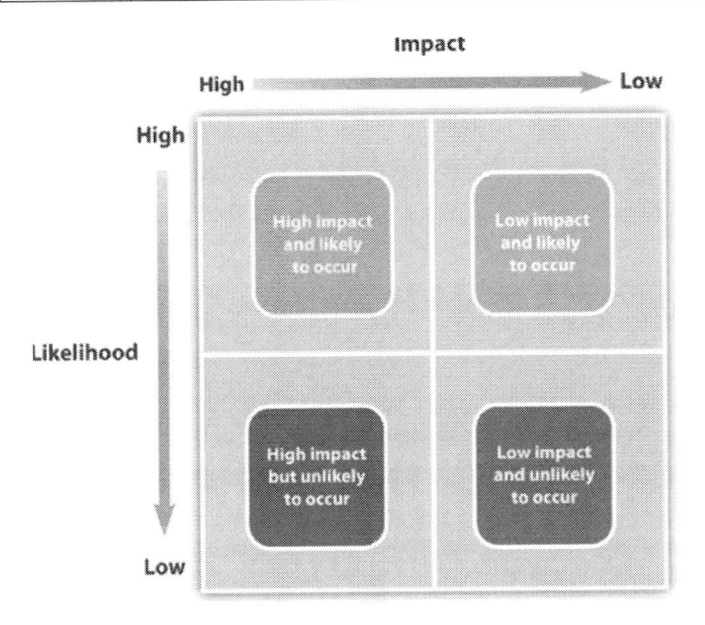

If the *impact* is high *and* the *likelihood* is high for any of your risks, then you will need to proceed *very* carefully as your project faces a *high degree of risk*.

These type of risks should be big red flags.

How should you handle project risks?

- **Do a quick brainstorming exercise** and write out all the solutions or alternative courses of action to help you deal with each concern.
- **Select the one(s) that you will act on**, and keep the others as a back-up plan that you can refer to, if needed.
- **Ask your developer for their input too.** Call a meeting and assign dedicated time to the problem if you need to. Thinking time can be very important on tech projects, so take time to think about your options if you need to.

CHAPTER 19
Project management, pitfalls and perils

Generally, the management of risks can be put into one of 4 categories and you can choose to *avoid, mitigate, transfer* or *accept* risks:

Fig 78. Risk management options. By Barron & Barron Project Management for Scientists and Engineers, http://cnx.org/content/col11120/1.4/

Avoid. Risks can be avoided completely, or by choosing to pursue safer alternatives. For example, abandoning all attempts to build a particular item of functionality because you know it is going to be very time-consuming or expensive to build, or choosing to take a totally different approach instead. Another example of risk avoidance would be to rule out working with a 3rd party that you know has a bad reputation or slow response times.

Mitigate (*lessen* the impact) of a risk, by taking action. Taking out business insurance is a form of risk mitigation as is *user testing* and collecting feedback about the functionality you intend to build before you spend money on building it.

Transfer. You might choose to transfer risk by outsourcing it. For example, rather than trying to manage and hold people's credit card details and making sure you have fulfilled all the regulations for holding payment cards, you may decide to sign up with a payment processing service such as *Stripe* https://stripe.com/, to handle this element of your business for you. As I mentioned earlier, you'll still need to be confident that the 3rd party that you're transferring the risk to can do a respectable job on your behalf, if not, then choosing to work with them has just added *another* risk to your list! Humph.

Accept. You may choose to proceed knowing that certain risks exist that you cannot avoid, mitigate or transfer. Despite this you can still make sure you fully understand the possible negative outcomes associated with the risk. Monitor the risk and take any actions that might neutralise it if the opportunity arises.

Because situations and circumstances change during projects, it's worth repeating the *risk assessment process* at least every few weeks. The more rapidly things are changing, the more frequently you should review your risks.

Case study - A successful risk mitigation plan

Risk mitigation planning really does work! I'd like to share a personal example with you, if that's o.k.

It comes from a software project I was asked to run, that had failed at least twice before under different project managers. A new team was formed, but the stakes were high; the budget was tight and the team was under a lot of pressure and could not afford to make any mistakes.

The project was complex and I had recurring worries about things going wrong, so I decided to call a team risk management meeting. I shared my fears and encouraged the team to share theirs. We wrote out a long list of horror scenarios, prioritised the ones that might have the biggest negative impact and were most likely to happen and brainstormed the simplest ways to mitigate each of them. Two issues arose after the software was released, but we were saved by the defensive planning we had done, the board members of the company were happy and the team won an award. (Oh, and my head remained attached to my neck, which was very nice too!)

Managing budgets

PMs also need to keep a close watch on project expenditure. Let's pause here and examine the 35% contingency margin mentioned in the previous section.

If you needed to add 35% to your current project budget, could you do it?

Your budget will not just be spent on paying developers to build your product - you may also need to pay for a range of tools and products, including: hosting, monitoring, analytics tools, hardware, data storage and more. See Chapter 21 for more about these costs. Throughout this book, I have included details of free or freemium software you can use, but you will still have some monthly or annual business costs to consider.

CHAPTER 19
Project management, pitfalls and perils

If you don't have the scope to add an extra 35% as a buffer, this means that there isn't much tolerance within your project for things which might go wrong. As a result, it will be even more important to cut your MVP down to the absolute bare minimum and to minimise project risks and delays.

Here are some tips for managing your finances:

Keep a close eye on your expenditure. In Chapter 1 we discussed using spreadsheets, mobile or web apps to plan expenditure and track what you've spent.

Know your monthly *burn rate* – how much money will it take to run your business each month? If you are tracking all your costs, you will be able to work this out.

Monitor progress and take action if necessary. A key element of project management is monitoring whether things are going according to plan, and *swiftly* taking the right action if they're not. Several things to watch out for include:

- Tasks or cards (in other words, your requirements) constantly taking longer to build than expected **and running** beyond their due date. The cumulative effect will be a longer time to complete your MVP and additional expense if you are paying your developer by the hour. (We'll talk about how to track and manage development progress in Chapter 22.)
- A build-up of untested tasks / cards. Cards are not really completed until they have been tested and signed-off as being acceptable by you, or by a manual tester. When cards come to you for testing, always check them as soon as possible so any bugs you find can be fixed, freeing your developer to start work on new cards.

Plan for future expenditure. If you'd like to enhance your product further in the months after your launch, then you'll need a budget for that too. As a minimum, be prepared to have some development budget available to fix emergency bugs post-launch, just in case.

CHAPTER 19
Project management, pitfalls and perils

Testing cards completed by your developer

Your approach to testing your app can have an impact on your budget and increase the level of risk in your project.

Can I give you an example? (If you are unsure about the concepts of cards and tasks, please review Chapter 14.)

*Let's imagine you score 1 point for every card from your MVP "must" list, which is **completed**.* There is no other way to score points - cards must be completed first.

Next, we need to define what completed, or done actually means. In this example, a card is only completed, or done when:

- Your developer has performed all the technical tasks and built all the required functionality connected with the card *to your specifications*, has checked it over and sent it to whoever is taking on the QA or tester role), to be manually checked AND
- The QA / tester has checked *all* the requirements relating to the card and confirmed that they are all present and working correctly, and that there are no bugs or issues that need fixing and agrees to sign-off the work.

If you have 20 cards waiting to be manually tested, and none have been completed, that's 20 cards' worth of uncertainty and 0 points. There could be bugs, issues, errors, unfinished work and all manner of problems lurking within those 20 cards.

Even though your developer has built the functionality, that's not enough to score a point because we don't yet know if what has been built is acceptable.

Now imagine your QA has tested 10 of the cards and confirms that they can be accepted. You now have 10 points and 10 cards' worth of uncertainty.

When you finally have 20 cards accepted, you have scored 20 points. There is no lingering uncertainty from any outstanding cards.

The main point here is that even if you have 100 cards that have been worked on by your developer, if they are not completed, you are not in a good position.

Keep this in mind and convert your cards from sources of uncertainty to point-scoring positives every few days if possible. (Definitely on a weekly basis as a worst-case scenario.)

Common project pitfalls

The pitfalls in this section have scary names because they *are* scary. It's frightening just how much time and money they will eat up and how they can send a project off track.

Unfortunately, at times you *will* be tempted to do these things, but they are the project equivalent of going down into the basement alone in a horror movie! When you're lured towards these activities, try to imagine hearing me calling out to you: "Noooo, don't do it!!!"

I hope that image will not only make you smile, but it will act as a reminder of the dangers involved. You could also put a reminder in a prominent place, or if you have a co-founder, agree to warn each other if you start getting sucked into these patterns of behaviour.

Death by 1000 cuts

The impact of these won't be felt initially, but over time they can be fatal to a project.

Burning your cash reserves trying to perfect parts of your product. *Spending too much time building functionality for one part of your product can cause you to run out of money, or to overspend… and other parts of your app will suffer as a result.*

Once you have estimates, *don't spend more than the allocated time on each card* and avoid going on the equivalent of a "spending spree" trying to perfect parts of the product *until* all the "musts" from your MVP have been completed. Once you have achieved that, if time and money permit, then return to areas of the app that you think need more attention. We'll talk about estimating the "cost" of cards in the next chapter.

Allowing your scope to "creep" and expanding your MVP. You will run out of time, money or both before you can build all the functionality you can think of, so practicality is essential to preserve your resources. Here are some tips for controlling scope creep:

1) Clear away unnecessary distractions. Only add essential tasks to your "must" list and don't spend time getting estimates for cards which are not "musts." All other tasks should go into your TBC or "should", "could" or "won't" queues.

2) Manage change by having a "1 in, 1 out" rule. This is standard Agile practice, but let's have fun with these analogies! You were the protagonist in a horror movie earlier, and now let's imagine that you're a discerning bouncer outside a nightclub! Only the most valuable functionality makes it in, and once you're at "capacity", for something else to be added, other functionality will have to move off your "must list" to make way for it.

If your "Must" queue starts to grow significantly and you're worried you may not have the budget to do all the work, before adding anything new to the queue, look for cards of an equivalent size and decide whether any of these are *less* important than the new card you want to bring in. If so, then add the new card to the "must" list and slot it in the right place according to its priority and remove the less important card and add it to a different queue. Ideally, the card you bring into the "must" queue should not cost more to build than the card you removed, otherwise the net effect is an *increase* in the work to be done.

3) Do the *"What's the worst that could happen?"* test on new cards. See Chapter 14 for a reminder.

Underestimating the work involved in making "small changes." Over time, underestimating the work involved in making changes and amendments can be harmful to your project. Changes may appear insignificant or small, but this is often a misconception. The functionality you wish to change may be tied to a number of other elements behind the scenes, which will then also need to be changed. All changes have a cost associated with them, and the impact of lots of small changes adds up over time, with the end result that your budget may not stretch as far as you'd planned.

Make sure that the changes and adjustments you ask your developer to make are really needed.

Cutting corners on requirements, communication or testing. Not investing time in putting together good quality requirements for your developer(s), not communicating often enough or clearly enough and not testing regularly or thoroughly, will all result in a slow (or fast!) decline in product quality. Set aside time each week to check the requirements on your cards to make sure they are clear, check that the work to be done is understood and stay on top of testing your product.

Over-optimism. "It'll work itself out" is not a strategy! Try to squash problems when they arise rather than waiting, hoping or procrastinating before you deal with them. There's no point in monitoring or tracking progress unless you act when you discover things that aren't right. Regular catch ups with your developer will give you a chance to ask questions and give feedback where necessary and for them to raise issues or concerns with you.

Suicide missions

Don't attempt these before you're due to go live with your product! They'll greatly increase the chance that you will be delayed, or lead to other business problems.

Suddenly squeezing in more functionality or changes shortly before going live. This is when mistakes often happen because "last minute" tasks are performed at the worst time - when people are already busy or under pressure. Before a deadline you should be focusing on testing and ensuring that what you want to release works well.

It is not the time to try and add in more work!

Don't be afraid of adding more tasks to your backlog, it's specifically adding them to your "must" list that is risky.

When changes are made to code, there's a chance that the changes can "break" something else in the app. This can start a vicious cycle where fixes can introduce additional bugs, which require fixing, then *those* changes can break something else and so on. If this happens, your app will be far too unstable to for it to go live.

Ideally, you should stop adding new functionality to the version of the product you intend to release 3 to 5 days in advance so you have adequate time to test it, assuming that you have kept up with testing. Allow much more time if not, because you are more likely to discover multiple issues.

Going ahead with a release even if there are outstanding issues.

If you do find multiple issues or serious ones that greatly reduce the quality of your product in its current state, then you should postpone your release. (Issues like these are sometimes known as *show stoppers.*)

Releasing a product with issues really is suicidal from a business perspective - the issues are likely to place strain on your resources - unhappy customers will contact you to report the problems that they are experiencing, may complain to you, or about you, and understandably, they will want you to fix the issues fast. This will only put you under unnecessary pressure. Instead of releasing the product, review what you need to do to increase product quality and to deal with all the most important issues.

Get the outstanding issues fixed, and *then* prepare to release the product.

Hiring additional developers close to a launch or release date to "speed things up"

It's a common misconception that you can accelerate progress by adding more developers into the mix in an emergency. Be aware that you will see progress slow down *before* you see any productivity gains, because the newcomer will need time to settle in, so this is not a quick fix strategy. If you think you may need extra help, start hiring well before the matter becomes urgent.

Managing 3rd party supplier relationships

In Chapter 15 we talked about speeding up the time needed to bring a product to market. This can be achieved using software, services and products created by 3rd parties.

Whilst external software and services can bring lots of benefits and opportunities, they are also a project risk. In addition to assessing how well a product meets your needs, shop around and compare suppliers to make sure you get the best deal in terms of reliability, price and service. Even if a product or service is free, if you're relying on it to deliver at least some of your services or features, then it must be reliable too. If your supplier lets you down, this could affect your product and cost you in terms of reputation, lost customers and wasted money and time invested in trying to integrate their product with yours.

Be prepared to walk away if necessary to avoid getting stuck in a bad (3rd party) relationship where you are dependent on an inflexible or unreliable partnership and carry out *due diligence checks*; to research potential partners:

- **Know who you're dealing with.** Do some research on the supplier. How well established is the service you intend to use?

CHAPTER 19
Project management, pitfalls and perils

- **How easy will it be to work with the 3rd party product?** Unfortunately, different tools and products may not just "slot together" seamlessly. Be aware that you may have to do a least a little (and maybe even a lot) of fine-tuning before things settle down and behave as you'd like them to. How much work might be involved in integrating, (fitting together) your software functionality with theirs? How flexible is their product?
- **How easy will it be to work with the company?** Get an idea of how responsive and helpful they are *before* you commit to using their services. Try making contact by phone and/or email to see how quickly they get back to you and check online to see what experiences others have had. If their customer service is slow even at the point of *gaining* new business, that's a bad sign.
- **Think about security.** Could your 3rd party relationship result in any of your customer data being exposed to the 3rd party? If so, what does this mean from a legal standpoint when *you* are responsible for how you protect and store your customers' data?
- **Timescales.** When you consider your project timescales, factor in time for 3rd parties to complete any integration tasks from their end. Bear in mind that you may not be their priority. If you need assistance, ask them for a timescale for them to play their part, and once you receive it, add anything from a few extra days to a week as a buffer!
- **Terms and conditions and legal agreements.** Do you need to sign any legal agreements or be granted a license to use the service? Ask to see a copy of the *SLA (Service Level Agreement)* and Terms of Business covering the service that you are going to be using and read ALL the small print! This should outline what the service covers, the expected reliability of the service and when and how the service is offered. It should also include response times in the event of an issue (think hours, not days) and any penalties or reparations if issues arise, or the 3rd party does not perform to the level of service expected under the terms of the agreement. If you're paying for the service, then don't be shy about asking for the agreement to be modified if you don't like what you see. If the supplier refuses, you will have to decide how comfortable you feel about having a business relationship with them. Try shopping around to see if better terms are available elsewhere.
- **Price.** Is the cost reasonable? Check how prices escalate as you use or consume more of the product or service. If the jump between one price bracket and the next is very large, will you be able to afford to stay with them at the higher price and how long do you think it will take you to

CHAPTER 19
Project management, pitfalls and perils

graduate to the more expensive plan? Do your sums before making a commitment.

This marks the end of section 6.

In the chapters to come, you'll learn how to calculate how long it will take to build your app, discover what sorts of things might appear on your "technical shopping list", and I'll show you how to run a development project, step-by-step.

SECTION 7

BUILD AND TEST IT

CHAPTER 20
How to estimate the cost of your MVP

In this chapter:

- What is estimation and why is it important?
- Preparing for an estimation meeting
- Estimation exercise: How to review your MVP with your developer and get time estimates
- Troubleshooting Q&A
- Assigning a duration and a $ amount to your development work

Once you have a developer on board, you'll understandably want to start working on building your MVP as quickly as possible, but before the build work starts, wouldn't you like to know more about how much it will cost to get your development work done... and how soon your product will be ready?

We've talked about the pros and cons of fixed price payments, paying by the hour and making milestone based payments. *If you are considering the latter two options, then you will want to know that your funds will last long enough to get your MVP built and delivered to you in a bug-free state.*

In this chapter, I will walk you through how to run an estimation meeting with your developer. This chapter will focus on your first estimation meeting, but you will be able to use the same steps for future meetings.

The benefits of estimation

Now, I will state honestly here that estimating the time it will take to complete development work is hard for developers to get right. Trying to predict what will happen during the course of a project is not easy, but for the following reasons it is still a worthwhile exercise:

Estimation creates accountability in several ways. Firstly, estimates provide another way of timeboxing work. When a developer estimates a task, they become accountable to deliver it by the due date. Secondly, consider the impact of *Parkinson's Law*. This law states that: "Work expands to fill the time available

CHAPTER 20
How to estimate the cost of your MVP

for its completion." *If there are no time limits or deadlines assigned to tasks, then there will be less urgency to complete them.*

The process of estimation aids understanding. Because the estimation process requires you and your developer to review and discuss the work to be done, your developer will naturally start to get a better sense of what you are trying to achieve in terms of both the building blocks (the cards) and the big picture vision! Would you agree that this is better than having a developer who doesn't really "get" what they are doing?

You'll be able to make better business decisions. Cost estimates provide you with data. You can find out how much work is going to "cost" you before you decide to do it. This will help you to avoid starting tasks only to realise later, that they will cost more to build than you first thought. Knowing the relative cost of different tasks in advance gives you an opportunity to reassess their importance.

If card **A** is estimated to take 4 times longer to code than card **B**, do we still want to do it? Is it worth the cost if it will take *that* long to build? The answers to these questions may still be yes, but this is an important evaluation process. Without this data, you would have lost the opportunity to consider alternatives.

You'll have a baseline. Even though a project estimate may not be precise, it will provide a baseline for you to work from. You'll be able to create a (rough) budget and make (flexible) plans in terms of delivery dates and knowing when you may be able to launch your MVP.

Previous estimates won't be accurate. Even if your developer has given you an estimate of some sort previously, this will be inaccurate (unless you have recently given them detailed information about the whole of your MVP.)

Over time, individual estimates *should* improve, as developers become more familiar with a project - we just need to accept that they'll be less accurate at the start.

Pro Tip!

Use completed cards to accurately estimate new ones.

Once you have some cards that have been estimated *and* built, you will be able to see how long these cards took to build *in reality,* and how close this was to the original estimate. When new cards are being estimated, look to see which completed tasks are *most similar* in complexity to the new ones

> and encourage your developer to use this information to help them estimate more accurately.

A brief reminder: To estimate the work required to build your app, your developer will need detailed information. If you want them to sign an NDA and they haven't already done so, now is the time to get this done.

Before you begin estimating your MVP...

Make sure you have ALL the essential items in your "must" queue, including all your *functional requirements* (covering the activities your target customers will want and need to be able to perform), *non-functional requirements* (performance, security, database storage, monitoring, legal requirements etc.) and any *technical tasks* you know your developer will need to complete.

Accidents happen, and cards can end up in the wrong queues, so run through the items in the TBC "should", "could" and won't" columns and rescue any cards that are in the wrong place!

With your developer present, start the estimation session:
First, summarise your MVP. Explain that you're using MoSCoW prioritisation and you only want to build the items in the "must" queue for MVP. Show your developer any prototypes that you have and answer their queries.

Next, ask your developer to list out all the work they need to do from a technical perspective in order to build and launch your app. Ask them to explain the importance of each one and what they're needed for. Add all the tasks to the correct queue - "must", "should", "could" and won't" based on your developer's recommendations and the importance of each technical task.

Before making decisions (or if you can't decide on which queue a card should go in), ask:

"What if I do this work?" and

"What's the worst that could happen if I don't?" then allocate the card based on the advantages and disadvantages that come to the surface.

Then, discuss your non-functional requirements (NFRs) in detail.

- Review all your NFR cards one-by-one (see Chapter 6).
- Invite your developer to comment about the relative importance of your NFRs and if they think any important ones are missing. If so, create new cards for them.
- Assign all your NFRs to the most appropriate MoSCoW queue. If in any doubt about which queue cards belong in, ask the *"What if I do?"*, *"What if I don't?"* questions to help you decide.
- Ask the *safeguard questions* – *"Do you have any questions or concerns?"*, *"Is there anything missing?"*, *"What issues do you foresee?"* and *"Is there anything else I / we need to know, or consider?"* to get issues out in the open *before* you start estimating.

The estimation exercise

Here's a 3-step overview for getting a simple estimate for your MVP. Allow an initial 60+ minutes for the discussion and follow up as necessary:

1. **Review the cards on the "must" list in detail and add any important or missing information to each one.** Discuss each card, one by one and explain what functionality you require. Read through any notes and details you've written inside the card. A consultative developer will be able to explain where they think you need more information or detail in your cards. If they don't offer this information, then ask them to provide it so you can learn as you go along. Note any questions your developer has that you don't yet know the answer to, or that you need to clarify. Add any important points or missing requirements which come up as you read through each card. *Your developer is going to build your product according to these details, so add as much relevant information as you can.* Remove any non-essential cards from your "must" queue as you go along.
2. **Ask your developer to estimate each card in your "must" queue.** There are many ways to estimate tasks, but **a** quick way to do this is to use t-shirt sizing. This is a popular estimation technique used by Agile teams. Estimates come in sizes XS, S, M, L, XL and XXL representing the T-shirt sizes, extra small, small, medium, large, extra-large and extra extra-large. Hopefully, your developer is familiar with T-shirt sizing, if not you can explain that you'd like some high-level estimates for the time required to build your MVP based on the number of days or half days required to complete each card. Ask them to be realistic, and to err on the side of pessimism if in any doubt about the time it will take to complete each card. Have you come across

CHAPTER 20
How to estimate the cost of your MVP

Hofstadter's law? It states that things always take longer than you expect, even when you take into account Hofstadter's Law!

3. **Revisit the priority order of the Must column.** Change the priorities of cards or switch them between MoSCoW queues if you need to, based on the estimates you received in step 2. If the *cost* of a card is much bigger than the *benefits* it brings, then save yourself money and time and park it! Next, ask your developer whether the ordering of the items in your "Must" column is logical from a *technical perspective*. Drag and drop the items into an order that you're happy with.

The order should take into account:

Any technical tasks that need to be prioritised in order to start, or complete project work.

That challenging work should be done first. (Revisit chapter 19 for a refresher on the reasons behind this.)

Your own preferences and the functionality you would like to see built first.

Now let's focus on step 2 in more detail. Let your developer know that you expect each estimate to include:

1. Thinking and preparation time.
2. Writing any automated tests (if your developer is going to be doing this for you).
3. Writing the code needed to complete the card and all its requirements.
4. Testing the code / cards, (including running it through an automated test tool if you have one) and doing a basic sanity check before telling you the item is ready for you to look at.
5. Fixing and making right any bugs found in relation to the card.

> **Project pitfalls**
>
> **Include ALL activities in estimates and make sure ALL activities exist on a card**
>
> Your estimates will be inaccurate if parts of the work involved in delivering a card are forgotten or left out of estimates.

CHAPTER 20
How to estimate the cost of your MVP

> *You run the risk of your project becoming chaotic if you cannot account for all the work that needs to be done, or that has been done.*
>
> Create new cards for all the work to be completed, no matter how small. Otherwise, you will be left with tasks floating about which all have a time and cost associated with them, but do not exist in the task management system you are using.
>
> Just thirty minutes work a day done on tasks which are unaccounted for works out at over ten hours per month. To make this more manageable, really small tasks of a similar type can be bundled together and put into a single card.
>
> This isn't the only issue - if you want to build a decent product, any code that is added to your product must be tested for quality checked by you, or by a manual tester. If some parts of your product do not have cards associated with them, you will have no information about them - no requirements, no acceptance criteria, no point of reference, and no reliable way to confirm what was actually done. Don't allow stray and untested code to get into your product and cause problems!

Take the first card. Ask your developer whether it is a XS, S, M, L, XL, XXL*.

Don't debate about the first one too much. This is a relative scale, so the task will get easier as more cards are estimated. They just need to go with their gut as to its size.

Note the estimate given and move to the next card and the next until all the cards have been assigned to a T-shirt group.

Keep a note against each card of which T-shirt group they belong to.

Now ask your developer whether they want to make any changes and if they are sure each card is in the right T-shirt group. Give them a few minutes to think and review the cards and categories again. You can facilitate the process by asking questions such as: "Is this task definitely bigger than that one?", "Are you sure that all the cards in this group are of approximately the same size? Make any adjustments needed.

Next, we need to link the T-shirt sizes to time.

This could be time blocks such as 1/2 a day, 1 day, 2 days, 3 days, 4 days and 5 days.

CHAPTER 20
How to estimate the cost of your MVP

Let your developer decide the number of days that should be associated with each T-shirt size: XS, S, M, L, XL and XXL. (Estimating work is a subjective exercise and as they are doing the work, this is their own personal estimation scale.)

Now you can note down the T-shirt size on the front of each Trello card and calculate the number of days, weeks or months' worth of work ahead.

Fig 79. Trello board with t-shirt sizes assigned to cards. In this example, Small =2 days and Medium =4 days.

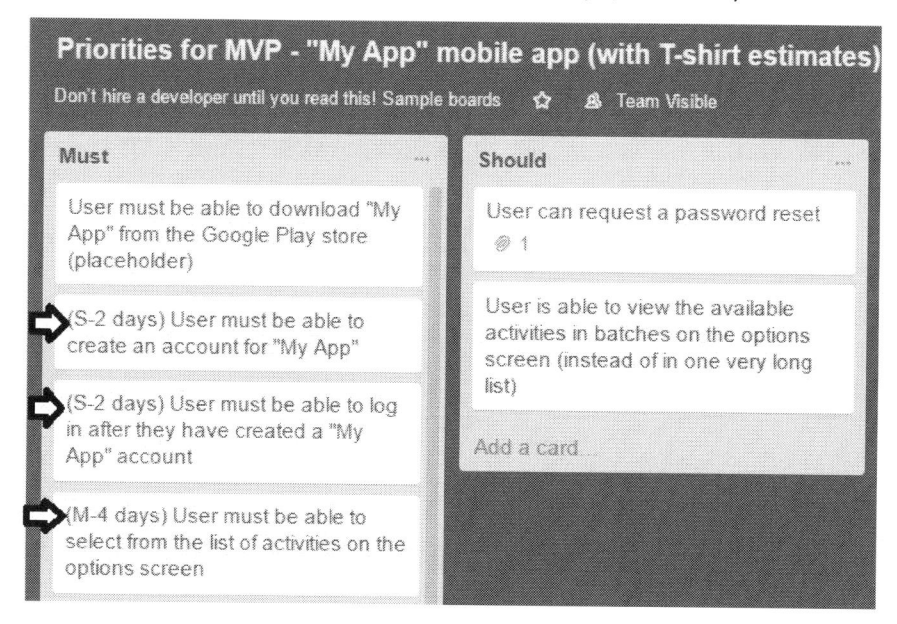

Troubleshooting Q&A

Any issues?

Yes! We got stuck on some of the cards, my developer says we need more information.

If your cards were still missing some detail when you dug into the detail, you might not have enough information available for your developer to estimate them. *If there are cards at the top of the queue without enough detail for the build work to start, then your project is going to face delays while you gather the information required,* so work on getting the details as soon as you can, starting with the cards at the top of your "must" queue. This is the position of your top priority cards. Focus on these first, so development work won't be held up.

300

Once this is done, your developer will be free to start work on the top cards in the queue, whilst you work on getting cards that are further down the queue ready. This is a cycle that you will repeat throughout the build process until there are no cards left in your "must" queue and your product is built! The key things are to keep the cycle going and to make sure that your developer is never waiting for you and you are quick in getting the information they need.

My developer says this card is XL, XXL or more!

*If any of the cards are bigger than XL, then the card is way too large and needs to be broken down into smaller more manageable pieces of work. Small, well-defined tasks are easier to define, estimate, build and test and there will be less chance of your developer getting stuck or lost whilst working on "smaller" cards.

Always break large cards which are complex and have a lot of functionality, down into their smallest *useful* components. The card has got to deliver some value to you, but should still be as small as possible.

Assigning a duration and $ amount to your development work

Once your MVP has been estimated, you can calculate (approximately) how long it will take to build it.

Note down the cost estimate for each "must" card, add them up and then add your project management contingency value of 35% (see chapter 19):

For example, if you have 7 cards each taking three days to build, that would be 21 days, plus 35% extra added as contingency, gives us a total of 29 days.
21 days x 35% = 7.35.
*21 days + 7.35 contingency days = 29 days, rounded up to the nearest whole number.
Given there are approximately 22 working days in a month, then the project will take just under 6 weeks to complete.*

Assuming you have one developer that costs $30 US dollars per hour:
If they work 7 hours per day, they would cost you $210 per day to employ.
7 hours x $30 per hour = $210 per day.

CHAPTER 20
How to estimate the cost of your MVP

Apply the worst-case time limit of 29 days.
A 29-day project x $210 per day = $6,090.

You could also use these figures to calculate that you will spend $4200 *every 4 weeks* (20 days x $210 = $4200), or approximately $4620 *every calendar month* (22 days x $210 = $4620).

Assumptions
These calculations are based on some working assumptions:
1. You only have one developer. You may want to hire additional developers or other technical staff, but note that if you have two developers, the cost will double if their hourly rate is the same, but the time estimate may not halve right down to 14.5 days. I explained why this is the case in chapter 16.
2. This is based on a *per hour* payment agreement, not a fixed, all-inclusive price, or milestone payments.
3. This calculation excludes any overtime that you might pay.
4. Other project running costs are excluded.
5. Your "must" queue will remain fixed and you won't add any more tasks to it, or will only switch cards with the same estimates in and out. If more cards are added, then the cost and length of the project will increase.
6. Cards on the "must" queue will not become any more complicated than they were when they were estimated. More complex requirements will increase the cost and duration of the project.
7. Your developer works 5 days per week.

To reduce the cost of your project:
- **Reduce the *number of cards* you have and**
- **Reduce the *complexity of the remaining cards***

Using placeholders to represent "unknowns"

If your budget can support them, there are a few other build costs you may wish to accommodate, such as changes based on feedback from user testing. If you receive feedback that will help you improve your product and you have no budget left to make adjustments, that would be disappointing! Create a few *placeholder* cards in your "must" or "should" queue(s) called "Changes based on user feedback" or something similar. We don't know what the cost of these placeholders will be just yet, because we don't know what the work will involve, but at least you have allocated time into your plan.

Rather than having cards with zero cost, you could assign a T-shirt size to each card as a temporary measure and have the cards estimated by your developer once you have all the details.

Work which arises following your product launch could become very important. There may be bugs to fix, improvements to make or urgent tasks to attend to. Therefore, it would be beneficial to allocate some of your budget to *post-launch tasks* too.

In the next chapter, we'll review some important project running costs, and the products and tools you'll need to invest in, to support your business.

CHAPTER 21
Preparing to build your product

In this chapter:
- The benefits of having a "Sprint 0"
- Confirming your list of "pre-build" set up tasks
- Setting up your communication channels
- Your "technical shopping list"
- Environments for building and testing your app
- Accepting customer payments
- Managing technical investigations
- App marketplace registration and fees

The immediate period before starting development work is often called *Sprint 0* (pronounced as sprint zero) in the Agile world. *Sprint 0* is actually a small, self-contained project in itself, which allows the team to lay its foundations ready for build work to start.

Why is a Sprint 0 necessary?

Developers will use a lot of tools and software in the process of building your product and there are hardware and networking considerations to be factored in too. As a result, there will be some essential tasks to complete before they begin writing code for you.

One of the biggest challenges of being new to software development is that you won't be aware of all the steps in the development process, or if anything important has been missed. You will be relying on guidance from your developer. We did our best to find a competent, proactive and communicative one in chapters 16 and 17, who will ideally be well-organised and great at explaining the "big picture" process to you and telling you what you need to do, when and what it will cost...

But if not, what happens then?

Well, they may need some prompting from you, so I am going to tell you what you need to know so you can do this.

Firstly, arrange a pre-build planning meeting. The objective will be to find out about anything and everything that needs to be set-up, ordered, paid for or arranged to support your project. The issue we are trying to avoid is having a developer start work and in 3 days' time, you are told that some software is needed, then in 1 weeks' time, you find out about an account that needs to be opened with a service provider, then in 2 weeks, there is something else that urgently needs to be set up. Stop, start. Stop, start. Deal with all that at the beginning, so once build work begins these distractions have all been dealt with. Now, there should be nothing to do, but focus on delivery.

That is the value of a sprint 0!

Setting up a task list for Sprint 0

Your pre-build planning meeting should give you an overview of the work to be done during Sprint 0, how long each piece of work might take and the costs of any tools or services needed for your project. If several are named as possibilities, talk through the options and do some research on the products and their costs before coming to a conclusion about which ones you will buy.

Whether you're using an app, spreadsheet or other method for tracking your project expenditure, you may find it helpful to start noting which products you will be using and any one-off or up-front costs, along with any monthly, quarterly, or annual fees you will have to pay.

At the meeting, ask your developer the following questions:

- "Before you can write and deploy any code, what software or tools need to be in place?" Find out about each task, the time required to get set up, and any associated costs.
- "Will you be running unit and automated tests? Which tools will you be using to do that?" Find out about the set-up details, the time needed to set up an *automated testing environment* and the cost of the product(s).
- "What other technical tasks need to be completed *before* development work can start?" Find out what needs to be done, the duration of the tasks and any associated costs.

- "Are there any tasks it would be better for us to deal with now, so that they don't disrupt the development process?" Again, get a sense of the costs involved, if any.
- Finally, wrap-up with the *safeguard questions* from chapter 18: *Is there anything missing? What issues do you foresee? Is there anything else I/we need to know, or consider?*

Next, organise all the tasks:

Create a new Trello board, then log and prioritise the work. Give the board a name, "Sprint 0" or whatever you prefer, and add all your information to it. You can use MoSCoW to prioritise the work that "must" be done, "should" be done or "could" be done before build work starts. Focus on the "musts" as the priority and put the most important and urgent work at the top of the must queue. (Ask your developer to identify any tasks that will need more than a day to complete. These should be started as soon as possible, so they don't cause delays.) Setting up developer accounts for the app marketplaces can take around 3 days, so if you want to build a mobile app, set up the account right at the start of Sprint 0 and then move on to other tasks whilst you wait for your confirmation to come through. There are some links provided later on in this chapter to help you with this.

Sprint 0 should be timeboxed to ensure that it runs on for no longer than necessary.
Agree what your timebox will be for completing the "musts". (Ideally, you will want this work to last for no more than a few days.)

Your technical shopping list

Are you curious about the sorts of things that might appear in your Sprint 0 "must" list? Depending on the type of product you're building, there are some items that you are very likely to need, so let's run through them. Some will require one-off or recurring payments to be made.

You'll need access to a source code repository / revision control system

Source code repositories, (or *repos*) can be used to "house" the code for your product. These repositories may offer additional services such as *version control management* (also called *revision control,* used to manage and merge changes to code), the tracking of changes made within the repo (history tracking) bug and issue tracking, and release management to assist your developer when they need to "release" code to the outside world, or to you for testing.

A number of these tools exist, including GitLab, SourceForge, Redmine, GitHub and BitBucket. GitHub and BitBucket are very user-friendly and reasonably priced. Git hub charges between $7 and $25 USD per month for private projects for teams of five or less and is free for public and open source projects. BitBucket has private repos and is free for up to 5 users.

https://bitbucket.org/

https://help.github.com/articles/signing-up-for-a-new-github-account/

Speak to your developer and decide which repo you will get an account for. You can sign up via the links above.

Repository tips and warnings

Whilst we're on the topic of repos, let's cover off a few very important points before we look at the next items that may end up on your shopping list. Please note the following points:

Be sure to retain access to your source code. Set up the account in your name and share the password with your developer. If new developers join, then they will need the repo password too. By setting things up this way, the code "lives" within your own repo account, which your developer(s) have access to. If a developer leaves, you should change any shared passwords.

Some repos have private and public / open source features. If your project is public, then others are free to view it, whilst open source projects have a special license which allows others to view, copy and download the source code and use and adapt it as they wish.

If you do not want your project to be visible to other repo users, then be sure to set up a private repo account.

Once you grant someone access to a repo, they will be able to clone the project to their computer. If you have access to the repo, you may revoke other users' access to it at any time. This will block access from that point, but will have no effect on any copies a person might have on their own computer, **so a degree of**

CHAPTER 21
Preparing to build your product

trust has to be involved in the process because developers must have access in order to do their work. Seek legal advice if you are concerned.

Let's get back to the shopping list.

You'll need developer account(s) for the app marketplaces if you're building a mobile app

You will need developer accounts for each marketplace you wish to submit your app to. These accounts need to be approved, this takes approximately 72 hours, so set them up as soon as possible. There are fees to pay:

- To submit an app to Apple's App Store, you need to join the Apple Developer Program, which costs $99 USD *per year*: https://developer.apple.com/programs/how-it-works/, https://developer.apple.com/support/compare-memberships/
- To submit Android apps on Google Play, you'll need to create a Google Play Developer account. There is a $25 USD *one-time fee*. https://play.google.com/apps/publish/signup/.

As these require payment, you may want to set up the accounts, pay for them and then share the login details with your developer, but discuss this with them before going ahead.

You'll need access to software and hardware services

"Renting" cloud-based services is cheaper and less complicated than buying and setting up your own hardware and infrastructure services.

Amazon Web Services (AWS) offers an impressive array of flexible, start-up friendly cloud-based services. You pay for what you use and benefit from working with a large organisation that gives your developer the freedom to scale the Amazon services you use up or down to meet increases or decreases in demand for services such as *bandwidth* and *memory (RAM)*. They offer networking, data storage, web hosting, analytics, security, database services and more. The types of services offered by AWS will be useful in helping your developer fulfil some of your non-functional requirements (see chapter 6 for a recap.) Let's look at a few of the AWS tools that may be of value to you:

CHAPTER 21
Preparing to build your product

Amazon Simple Storage Service (Amazon S3), allows you to store data / content, including videos, audio files, documents and images for your website, web app or mobile app, which can be retrieved by you or your customers as needed;

https://aws.amazon.com/s3/, http://docs.aws.amazon.com/mobile/sdkforios/developerguide/s3transfermanager.html

AWS Mobile Services offers a selection of tools that you can use if you wish to build a mobile app. The services offered for mobile app development, include analytics, Amazon SDKs for mobile app development (see chapter 15 for a refresher), app testing (find out how to use Amazon to test your app in chapter 23), sign-in services that let users sign into your app via Google+ or Facebook, storage of your users' data and management of *push notifications* that we discussed back in chapter 9: https://aws.amazon.com/mobile/?nc2=h_l3_ms

Amazon Elastic Compute Cloud (Amazon EC2) is a web service akin to a cloud-based supercomputer that will allow your developer to install and run software applications on it. https://aws.amazon.com/ec2/

Amazon Relational Database Service (Amazon RDS), offers what it describes as a "managed relational database in the cloud that you can launch in minutes https://aws.amazon.com/products/databases/?nc2=h_l3_db. Amazon RDS can be used to store, manage and retrieve your customer data. Confirm that there are no legal restrictions that would prevent you from keeping customer data stored on the servers of any cloud database that you plan to use. See chapter 6 for a recap about data protection laws.

AWS Elastic Beanstalk is a free service for web apps. It includes release management tools, statistics and alerting tools to help your developer monitor and manage various aspects of your product's "health."

If you are interested in building a *web app*, such as a *SaaS*, then a combination of EC2, S3 and RDS and other AWS products can be used together to cover the major services that may be needed to support your app. https://aws.amazon.com/application-hosting. *The AWS Free Tier Offers* access to EC2, S3 and RDS and several other products free of charge for 12 months within specified usage limits: https://aws.amazon.com/free/

You may also require tools that provide statistics about how your app is being used and early warning detection mechanisms if all is not well.

Please see chapters 6 and 25 for more information on monitoring and analytics tools.

Web hosting services

There are a huge number of web hosting companies that offer shared, partitioned and completely private cloud hosting services.

Virtual private servers and dedicated servers allow you to have your own partitioned space and resources, whereas shared services are well, completely shared! As you'd expect, prices increase the more exclusive the service becomes. Some of the well-known web hosting companies used by businesses include:

1&1, https://www.1and1.co.uk/

GoDaddy, https://www.godaddy.com

HostGator, httpww.hostgator.com/

DreamHost, https://www.dreamhost.com/

Technical environments for building and testing your app

Your developer will create some *technical environments* for your project. These environments will need to be hosted somewhere, so discuss this with them. Here are examples of the environments that your developer may set up for the project and what they may be used for. Find out how yours will be set up.

Development environment. This is the environment where developers write their code.

After your developer has tested their code in the development environment, they will make a "release," which can be any combination of functionality, additions or changes to code, non-functional or technical items or bug fixes. Releases may happen many times in a day and these releases *push* code into the QA environment.

QA environment (or test environment). QA exists so that further checks can be done on items released from the development environment. In this environment, you, (or a manual tester, if you have one) will be looking for bugs and issues with the released code, trying to "break" and strain the product to see if it can cope. You will also be checking against your Trello cards to see that the functionality released to the QA environment has been built according to your requirements and completed in full. *Ask your developer which environment you should do your testing in and make sure you have all the technical permissions you need to access it.*

See chapter 23 for more information about testing web and mobile apps.

Demo, demonstration or presentation environment. This environment may not be needed; however, it can be useful if you wish to allow customers to review and comment on new functionality that has been tested by a manual tester in "QA", but has not yet gone public.

Staging environment. If provided, this environment should be an exact copy of your "live" environment and is there to protect it. Before functionality is released to your live environment, it can first be released to staging and tested. If issues are spotted in the staging environment, then the planned release to the live environment is postponed until the issue is resolved. If staging did not exist, the issue would have passed undetected into your live environment and may have had a negative impact on your customers.

Live environment (also known as the production environment or "prod"). A live environment must be set up. If you are building a web app, or are setting up a website, you will need to buy a *domain name, e.g. http:// or https://* (if you want a secure site), *www. productname.com.* (Many native mobile apps have a website too.) You can refer to the hosting companies listed earlier in the chapter if you'd like to buy a domain name.

Payment services

If you're planning to accept *in-app* payments from your *mobile app*, or online payments via the web, there are a number of pre-packaged solutions that can be used, including:

Stripe, https://stripe.com/

PayPal, https://www.paypal.com/uk/webapps/mpp/home-merchant (UK), https://www.paypal.com/webapps/mpp/merchant (International)
Sage Pay, http://www.sagepay.com/online-payments
Worldpay, http://www.worldpay.com/, https://business.worldpay.com

Some charge a flat fee, plus a percentage of the purchase price of each item sold, however, pricing models vary.

Do your due diligence on the companies that you're considering, using the 3rd party tips in chapter 19, and consider the uptime (chapter 6) and reliability of each company. Shortlist 2 and ask your developer to assess them from a technical perspective to confirm that they can be integrated with your own and are easy to work with; sadly, it is possible to burn a *lot* of time and money trying to work with 3rd party tools that aren't very flexible. We'll talk more about technical assessments in the next section.

Technical investigations

Sometimes there are several approaches that could be taken in order to complete the requirements on a card, and it may not be obvious which option will yield the best results. In some cases, your developer may not even be sure how to approach building the item. Don't worry just yet if this is the case. This is where kudos should be given to developers. None of them can know how to build *every* type of app, with any functionality that can be imagined without doing at least some research or planning, but *if* they are experienced, competent and logical in their approach, in a short amount of time they will work out how to meet the challenge.

In these scenarios, rather than guessing the best course of action, Agile developers will undertake a technical investigation, (known as a *development spike* or *spike* for short), in order to delve more deeply into the issue. The investigation might involve Internet research, searching or consulting development forums, or speaking to the suppliers of 3rd party services to assess whether their tools could be used to bridge a gap. It could also include writing code to test out different technical approaches, creating a prototype, or trialling different 3rd party software that you'd like to integrate with your product.

Your developer may identify the need for a spike, but you can also suggest, or request that one is carried out if a clear way forward is not obvious, or to decide between several different options.

CHAPTER 21
Preparing to build your product

If a spike is going to be attempted, make sure that the time is used effectively:

- **Make sure the "terms" of the spike and its objectives are clear.** Agree on the objectives, or deliverables for the spike with your developer and confirm what the deliverables will be. Write any questions that need to be answered (in order for a decision to be made, or for the issue to be resolved) on a card. This is development work, so a card should be added to your board or task management system.
- **Set a timebox for the spike**. This could be anything from a few hours to a week or more for very complex investigations where code needs to be written, or where a prototype is built to "prove" what might be possible.
- **Follow through.** Based on the outcome of the spike, create card(s) for any new development work required, add the requirements and details to the card(s) and assign these to the correct MoSCoW queue based on their importance.

It's also worth noting that during Sprint 0, your developer may spend time considering architectural decisions which will set the direction for how your product is built. To get the foundations right, they may seek further information from you to help them make the right decisions.

Review your MVP again

At this stage, it's time to review and polish your requirements.

Aim to have all the known requirements for your MVP logged in Trello, or your task management tool of choice - JIRA, Mingle, Excel etc.

Write, or type descriptive titles on the front of your cards (so you don't waste time trying to recall what each one is about!) and detailed requirements and important attachments stored with each card.

Now you're all set up, it's time to get you app built! In the next chapter, we'll be talking about how to manage your project on a daily basis and how to track and maintain project momentum.

CHAPTER 22
How to manage your software project

"It is not enough to do your best; you must know what to do, and then do your best."
- Dr. W. Edwards Deming (management consultant, statistician and author)

In this chapter:

- Managing your software development project like a pro
- The build cycle - in practice!
- Quick and easy ways to monitor project progress
- Recurring check-points
- Project and task management tips
- Carrying out regular user testing

It's time to get your product built!

We're going to examine the practicalities of running your software project. A lot of important activities happen repeatedly in cycles on software development projects. If you have solid processes in place, you can make sure that you get the most from each cycle and make the next one even better, so there is continuous learning and improvement as the project progresses.

I'll also be bringing together information from the earlier chapters of this book, so you can see how to *practically* apply the knowledge you have gained to move your project along on a daily basis.

Let's start with the development cycle first.

Please note:
This chapter is a set of step-by-step instructions you can review on a regular basis to show you how to manage your project. There are many ways to "implement" Agile processes within a project. This is just one example.
The version shown below is probably closest to Scrumban, which favours "just in time planning," which I believe will be easy to follow for those new to the process, and for small teams.

The build cycle

Step 1

Refer to your product backlog and identify your "must" items.

- Your *"must"* queue should contain the essentials that you are going to build for your MVP; the first version of your product to be made available to customers.
- Make sure all your essential functional, non-functional and other technical tasks are in the *Must* queue, with the most important and urgent tasks at the top.
- The most difficult and complex items should be tackled as soon as possible to reduce project risk. (See Chapter 19.)

Step 2

Prepare the cards in your Must queue, so they are ready to be assigned to your developer.

To avoid misunderstandings and the likelihood of having to re-do work, the prioritised cards should be *prepared for build* before handing them over to your developer to work on.

You know that a lack of clarity about what is to be built causes issues for your developer, will slow down your project, could lead to an inferior product being built and may waste your money.

Let's revisit what being prepared really means. Your preparation should include pulling together all your *requirements,* in all their forms, to help your developer understand *exactly* what they need to build, including:

- **Non-functional requirement**s such as performance, accessibility, security, data storage, compliance etc. (Chapter 6.)
- **Functional requirements**. What the product needs to do and how it should behave in expected *and* unexpected scenarios. What you expect to happen and what should *not* happen, your unhappy path scenarios, and your most advanced process flows, mind maps, user journeys, diagrams, drawings and wireframes - whatever you have available! (See Chapters 10 -12 and 14.) Be sure to include other information relevant

to the build of your product, such as any important app gestures required. (Chapter 11.)
- **Any designs and styling** that you want your developer to apply to your app, including the relevant *hex numbers and colour scheme* and the way you expect any *widgets* in your app to look. (Chapter 11.)
- **Any *assets* that need to be part of your app, or its presentation**, including logos, company branding, mascots or icons you'll need for navigation inside your app, your app launcher icon (for mobile) and your favicon (for websites and web apps.) (See Chapters 9 and 11.)
- **The content for your app.** Don't forget the content for your web app, mobile app, website, or app marketplace sales page! This should be prepared and made ready for your developers to insert in the relevant places. (Chapter 11.) This includes text based content such as information, help text, warnings, anchor text https://moz.com/learn/seo/anchor-text, button text / calls to action and error messages. Remember to specify all your heading sizes (h1-h6), font styles and sizes, descriptions and alt tags for SEO purposes! (Chapter 9.) You'll also need to supply any videos, images or audio files, which should be available on your screens and pages. These count as "content" too.

Pro tip!

Set up a quick-access filing system.

Avoid wasting development time hunting for important documents. Keep all your assets, content, wireframes and designs organised in folders so that you (or your developer) can quickly and easily access them when needed. Consider attaching the relevant items directly to your Trello cards or include links to the right folders inside the cards to make the build process more efficient.

It is also very useful to have a *brand guidelines folder* which contains details of the font types and sizes you use for your app and website, any icons, logos and favicons you have, their dimensions and the hex numbers used for your app.

Unless you decide to change your branding, whoever updates your app, or makes changes to your site should always follow your guidelines.

CHAPTER 22
How to manage your software project

> This ensures that your app will always look and feel consistent.

> *Pro tip!*
>
> **Use your developer's time wisely and avoid duplicating effort.**
>
> To keep the process efficient, provide all *content* and *assets at the same time* that your developer is building the screen or web page where they will sit. If they have to come back to these again to add your content…and again to add your assets… and again to add other missing items…, this will add extra time and cost to the job.

Now make sure that all the information is transferred to the cards that your developer will be working on.

Attach all the relevant documents to each card.

To make the list of requirements in Trello easier to read, you can click on the "checklist" button to turn the requirements into a list that your developer can tick off as each sub-task is completed.

Fig 80. Inside a Trello card with the checklist option activated and 50% *of tasks completed*. Note that some tasks may take longer than others, so the card may be more, or less than 50% complete in terms of the *time remaining*.

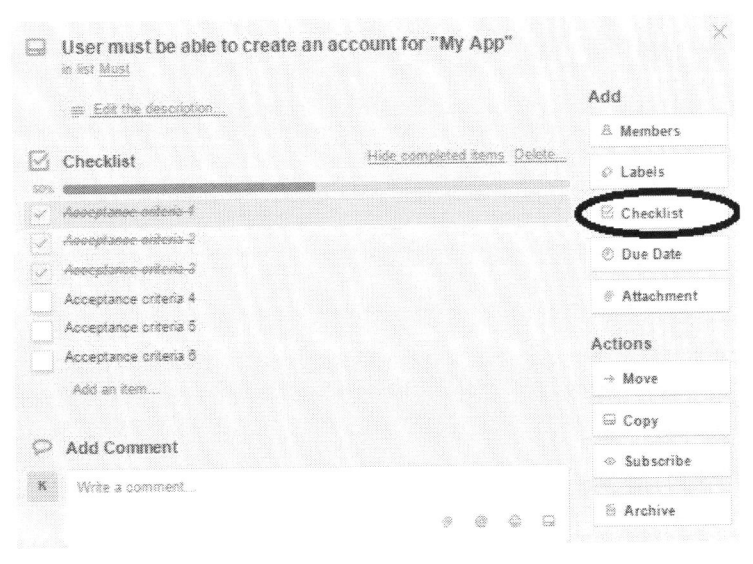

317

Step 3

Planning

Take the top 10 cards from your prioritised product backlog and discuss each one with your developer:

- Check to see whether they have any outstanding questions that need to be answered and that they understand what they need to do.
- Check the *time estimate* (see Chapter 20) on each card. Has it risen? If so, and your budget is very tight, discuss how the card might be simplified to reduce its complexity, and therefore its "cost."

Step 4

Assign tasks from your *product backlog board* to your *Development board*.

- Create a second Trello board to manage your development tasks. I've called my board the *Development board.*
- Move the *Must* cards from your backlog board to the *Ready for build* queue on the *Development board* and arrange them in priority order, with the most important, urgent and technically complex tasks at the top of the list. (Chapter 19.)
- Ask your developer to always work on the cards at the top of the list first.
- ***Monitor the queue and keep it filled with enough tasks to keep your developer busy without them having to wait for you to top up the queue again. To avoid project delays, ideally, you should have at least 5 cards in the queue at any time. When the cards in the Ready for build queue run low, repeat step 3 to top up the queue with new work that has been discussed and estimated.***
- Make sure that the work to be done for each card is clearly described and properly understood. Only cards with enough detail to be worked on by your developer should be put in the *Ready for build* queue. Have a quick conversation with your developer about the next couple of cards in the queue *before* they start working on them - this really does help to iron out the misunderstandings that can arise during the build process.

CHAPTER 22
How to manage your software project

Fig 81. The top priority card from the Must queue on the *product backlog* is moved to the *Development board*.

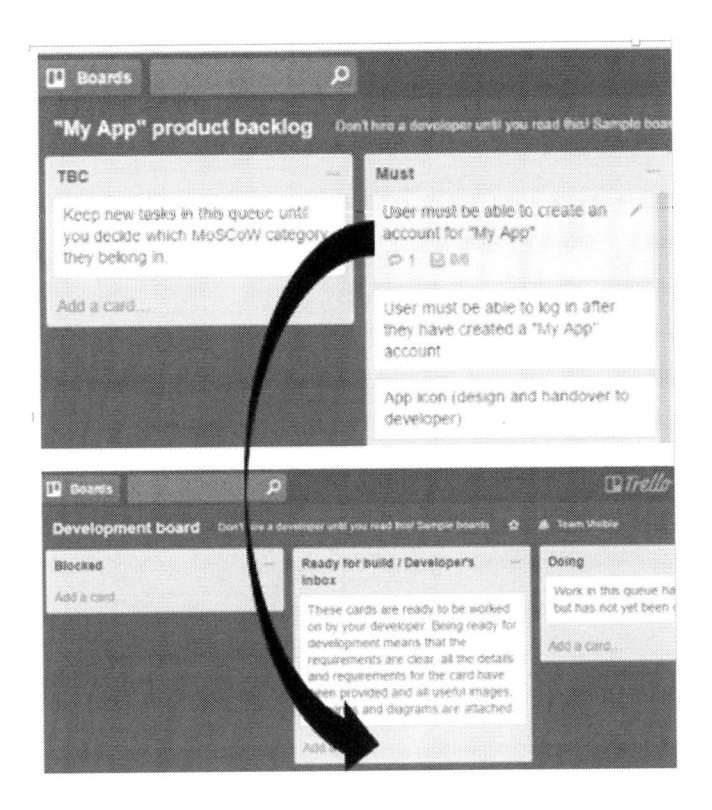

Fig 82. The card is transferred between boards using the **Move Card** functionality.

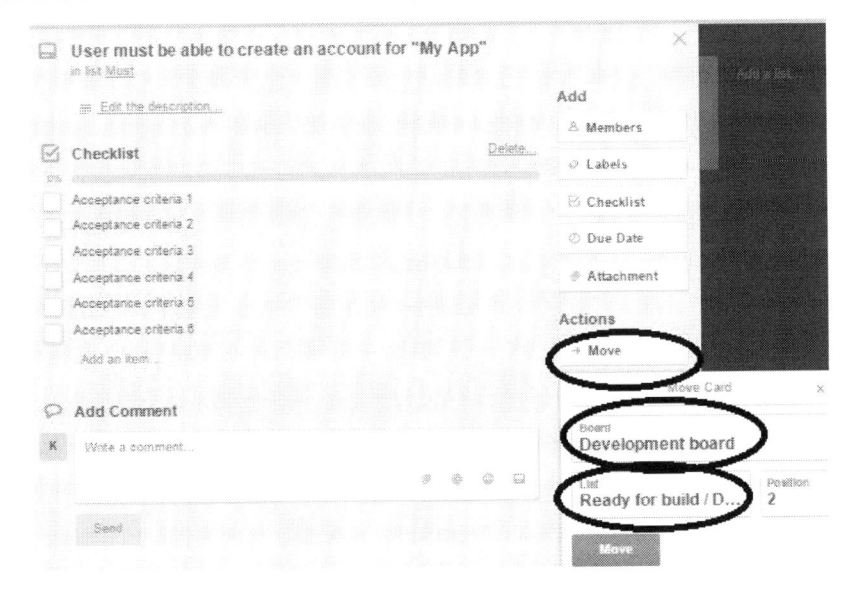

Step 5

Build

Your developer will work on the cards in their *Ready for build queue* working from top to bottom, and will build them according to the requirements and attachments provided with the card.

If your developer *cannot* work on a card assigned to their *Ready for build queue*, then they (or you) should move it to the *Blocked* queue.

This queue exists to highlight important items that require your attention.

Cards are usually *blocked* because there is insufficient information to start work, an issue has arisen which cannot be solved immediately, or because there is an outstanding decision is to be made. *These items will slow down development if they are not resolved swiftly - ideally, this queue should always be empty!*

Organise the blocked items in priority order and deal with the most urgent and obstructive ones first.

Whenever your developer begins work on a card from the *Ready for build* queue, they should move the card into the queue marked *Doing*. Once the work has been finished and all the requirements on a card have been checked off and translated into code, your developer will check their work (including testing the card using the automated unit or functional tests they have written, if you've agreed to that.) Once they are satisfied (and if the automated tools do not flag up any problems), they will then *release the code to the QA / test environment* prepared in chapter 21, so manual testing can be done. At this point, your developer should move the card to the queue named *Released for testing* and should prepare a simple set of *release notes*.

What are release notes?

Release notes are simple documents written by developers to accompany an internal or external (i.e. public) software release. They outline the contents of each release and are sometimes made available to customers via email or online, as a way of updating them about new functionality, changes, bug fixes and work done in response to customer feedback. Some of the *repos* discussed previously can be used to store your release notes. Make sure you know how to access them so you can refer to them at any time. In the future, they will provide a useful summary of all the work ever done on your app! Release notes may contain:

CHAPTER 22
How to manage your software project

The number (or version) of the software release. Software releases are given numbers so they can be easily identified. Version naming conventions differ, but whichever format your developer uses, they should be consistent. A common convention is *major, minor, patch* as shown in Fig 83, which covers; *major* changes to the software, *minor,* less significant changes or new functionality and *patches,* or small changes and bug fixes, respectively.

The date (and possibly the time) of the release. Multiple releases can be made in a day, so this additional detail can help to distinguish one release from another.

The name of the person who made the release, if you have more than one developer.

A list of the items released. There should be a couple of sentences describing each item and its purpose. For example, n*ew functionality, a change or update to existing functionality, a bug fix,* or *resolution of an issue*, or a *technical, housekeeping* or o*perations task.*

Release notes are a useful accompaniment when testing, as the notes should include all the work that was done in a release.

Here is a public-facing version of a company's release notes. These are from *Proto.io;* https://proto.io/en/changelog/.

Fig 83. Software versioning. An example of the *major, minor, patch* convention.

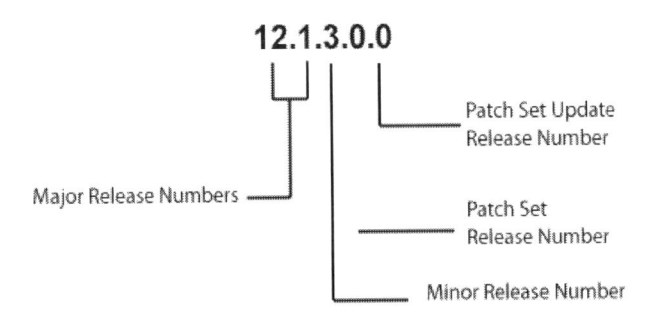

12.1.3.0.0

- Major Release Numbers
- Patch Set Update Release Number
- Patch Set Release Number
- Minor Release Number

321

Step 6

Test

Once the code has been released into the *QA / test environment,* it's time to start your manual tests to check if the work done matches the details on the card. The tester confirms whether the card is "Done" or not based on:

- Whether any issues are found, whether visual, functional, or of another type.
- Whether or not the requirements on the card were: i) missed completely or ii) are partially complete.

The tester then either approves the card, and moves it to the *Done* queue, or creates a bug card for each issue found, including a screenshot of the issue, (where this is useful), explaining the problem(s) found and what you expected to see instead, which of the cards the bug originated from, and how to *reproduce* the bug and make it happen again, (so your developer can observe the bug "in action" for themselves.) The bug card is put into the *Ready for build queue in order of importance.*

Once your developer has fixed the issues on the bug card and released the changes, the card should be moved back to the *Released for testing* queue to be tested again.

Now you can confirm that the problems that were identified have been completely resolved. If all is well, the bug card can be signed-off and moved to the Done queue. If there are still issues, it should go back to the *Ready for build queue in priority order,* with an explanation of what the issues are.

If a card has issues but they are only minor and you can live with them, then you can move it to the *Done queue.* Spending time fixing low-value issues can burn development time that might be better spent elsewhere, so you will need to be pragmatic, especially if time or money is tight. It's not the individual fix that is the problem, but the *cumulative effect* of doing this numerous times over the course of a project. See Chapter 23, *Keeping track of your bugs,* for information on how to create bug cards.

Do you remember the phrase from chapter 14?

If you didn't ask for it, you won't get it and if it was asked for, it must be delivered!

So, it's not a "bug" if you forgot to ask for what you wanted, or the request was unclear or incomplete.

If this happens, you have 2 options:

Plug the gap between the work you received and what you actually wanted. Create a new card, or cards covering the missing items and if they are essential, put them in your "Must" queue so they can be worked on by your developer.

Take any items like these as a lesson learned and make sure your cards very clearly state what is required in future, otherwise you'll be constantly creating extra cards to plug gaps in your requirements and you may run over budget!

Keep moving. If you have a very tight budget, then if you've forgotten some of your requirements, unless the app is useless or severely compromised without them, *don't* go back and add the missing items, just press on.

You can always create a card for the missing tasks and put them in one of the MoSCoW queues, and revisit them in future, time and money permitting.

Testing mobile apps

Testing on a physical mobile device is the most reliable way to test your mobile app. See chapter 24 for information about tools like *TestFlight* that will allow you to test your mobile app on smartphones and tablets. There are also tools that will help you test your app via a web browser. These are called *emulators,* or *simulators*. Software testing is a huge topic on its own, so Chapter 23 is dedicated to some of the ways that you may wish to test your app before it is launched to any customers.

Repeat

The cycle then begins again. Keep up the momentum by moving new cards from the "must" queue on your backlog to the *Development board* with detailed requirements on them. Repeat the cycle until all your "must" cards are built and marked as done, and any essential bugs and issues related to your cards are fixed.

As the number of cards remaining gets smaller, you'll be thinking about your readiness to launch your MVP, subject to some other pre-launch checks and a go / no-go review (see Chapter 24.) When all the functionality you require is built, this is called being *feature complete.*

Starting a new board to represent a new build cycle.

Each time a new build cycle starts, you may wish to create a new Development board.

This is useful if the number of tasks on your Development board gets too long and you'd like to start afresh, whilst maintaining the history of all the work done and bugs fixed previously. (These will remain on the "old" versions of the board.) Some development teams create a new board *at the start of each new development cycle* (also called *sprints,* or *iterations* by Agile teams) which will commonly last for 1 week, 2 weeks or 4 weeks. To do this either **copy** your Development board (and name it Development board 2, then 3, then 4, for instance) or create a new board from scratch and add the label for each queue to it, *Blocked, Ready for development, Doing, Released for testing,* etc. If you'd like to run sprints, choose a day of the week to consistently start them, for example starting on a Wednesday, would mean that your sprints will always finish on a Tuesday. Don't feel that sprints need to run from Monday to Friday. Agile teams sometimes *avoid* running sprints from Monday to Friday for productivity reasons. This is about maintaining a consistent level of effort throughout the sprint and avoiding a double psychological dip on Fridays because it is the end of the week *and* the end of the sprint on the same day!

Pro tip!

Give the functionality in your system a name.

Spending 5 minutes at the start of every conversation trying to understand whether you're talking about the same part of the app is an inefficient use of time. Confusion can be avoided when pages, functionality or parts of the app are described by the same names by all team members. Agree on common terminology for your app and stick to it. These names can also be useful when creating FAQs or product training materials for customers.

Try simple names like the "options page" or the "send email screen" - something easy to remember that describes the purpose of the functionality.

CHAPTER 22
How to manage your software project

Monitoring project progress

If you are using Trello, the movement of cards across the board from left to right will show you how quickly development work is progressing.

Please note that other task management tools may have different ways of checking progress.

Ask your developer to move cards to the correct queue(s); on the *Development board* as soon as they:

- Start work on a new card. (They should move the card to *Doing*.)
- Become aware that a card is *blocked*. (They should move the card to *Blocked*.)
- Finish development work on a card and it has been released for testing. (They should move the card to *Released for testing*.)

If they do this, you will have a 24/7 real-time view of your project! (Remember to add bug cards to the Development board and to move completed cards to *Done* when they have been tested and approved to ensure your real-time view is truly accurate.)

If you and your developer have worked together to estimate your cards, then you can also ask them to add a due date to each card on the day the card moves into the *Doing* queue, based on the *T-shirt estimate* they provided for that card. For example, if a card is started today and is estimated to require 3 days to build, then the due date should be set 3 days from now. In Trello, a *yellow badge* means that a task is within 24 hours of being due, *a red one* means it's due and a *pink one* means it is past due. Take note of how many cards are overdue in each development cycle and follow up with your developer if you have any concerns. See chapter 20 for more information about estimating the time it will take to complete development tasks.

If you and your developer have agreed to use the checklist functionality, you will also be able to see how many acceptance criteria have been checked off within each card.

Fig 84. Setting a due date in Trello.

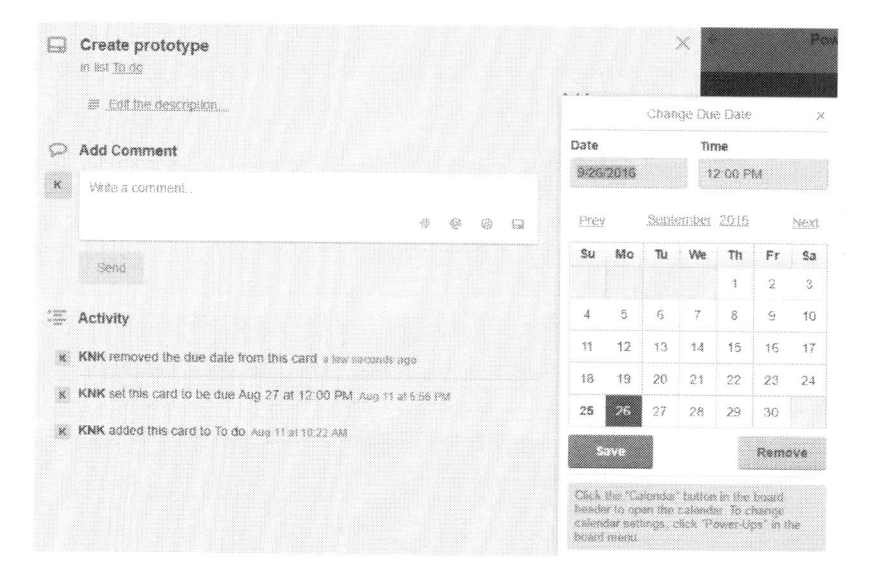

Fig 85. A yellow badge indicates that a task is due to be delivered within 24 hours

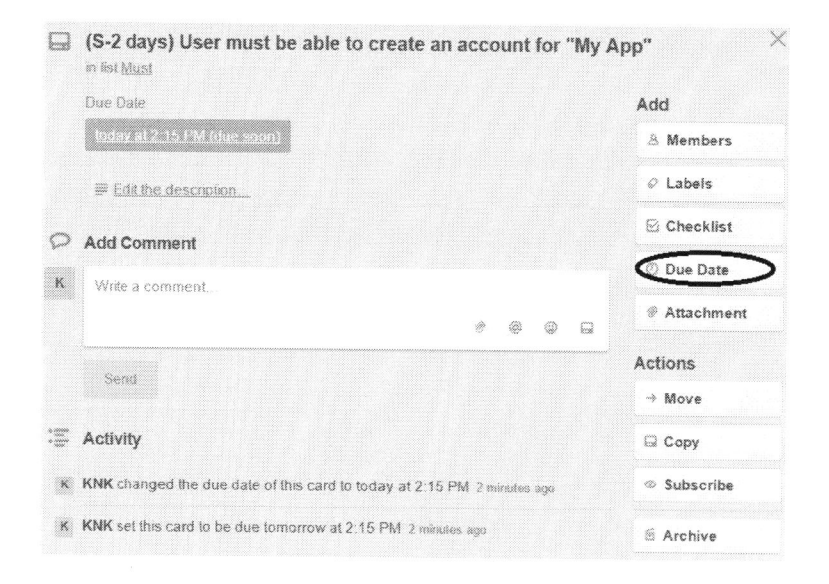

Recurring checkpoints and general communication

Consider requesting **daily progress updates** and holding a **weekly (or fortnightly) review** to discuss the tasks and functionality that your developer worked on during the previous week, and to resolve any project issues. Frequent meetings may seem like a hassle, but short feedback loops provide more opportunities for questions to be asked, and information and challenges to be shared.

These regular check-points will play a big role in keeping your project on track. If you don't have a Project Manager, then the role of Chief Troubleshooter belongs to you!

Daily progress updates

Make sure you're up-to-speed with any issues that could affect your project. If you don't know about problems, you can't begin resolving them and if you don't know about risks you won't be able to put contingency plans in place. The days of developers working in a "cave" with the customer not understanding what is happening, or knowing what progress has been made, are coming to an end. Don't allow your project to be managed in this way!

Agile teams usually have a short daily "stand-up" meeting every morning (a micro-meeting), which lasts for only a few minutes and focuses on 3 specific questions:

1. What happened yesterday?
2. What do you intend to do today?
3. Any issues which are "blocking" and impeding development progress. (This portion of the meeting should also be used to discuss any cards in your *blocked* queue)

Find out whether your developer needs your input and look out for tasks that seem to be taking much longer than anticipated. Be ready to ask questions and to help (where possible) with any issues that are affecting progress.

Remember: the quicker you developer gets what they need, the quicker your product gets built!

Ideally, this meeting should be done at a consistent time at the start of each working day, so it becomes a routine, although depending on where you and your developer are based, it may not be morning for both of you!
If the meeting can't be done by telephone or video conference, ask for an email summary instead. Make an email template which includes the 3 questions we've discussed, and ask for them to be filled out and sent to you each day.

CHAPTER 22
How to manage your software project

With a combination of estimated, or timeboxed work and daily check-ins, you will be much better able to manage your project, and prevent or minimise the impact of delays.

Let's look at 2 examples, the first with no timebox estimate agreed on the card and casual check-ins, and the second with daily check-ins, or stand up meetings and timeboxed work:

No timebox agreed...

- When will it be ready?
- Soon... A few days.
- When will it be ready?
- Soon... A few days.

- When will it be ready?
- Soon... A few days.
- O.k.
- "What?" Crying inside! "Oh, my budget!" Annoyance! Frustration!

Copyright K.N. Kukoyi
Don't hire a software developer until you read this book™, chapter 22

Timebox agreed, check-ins happen daily...

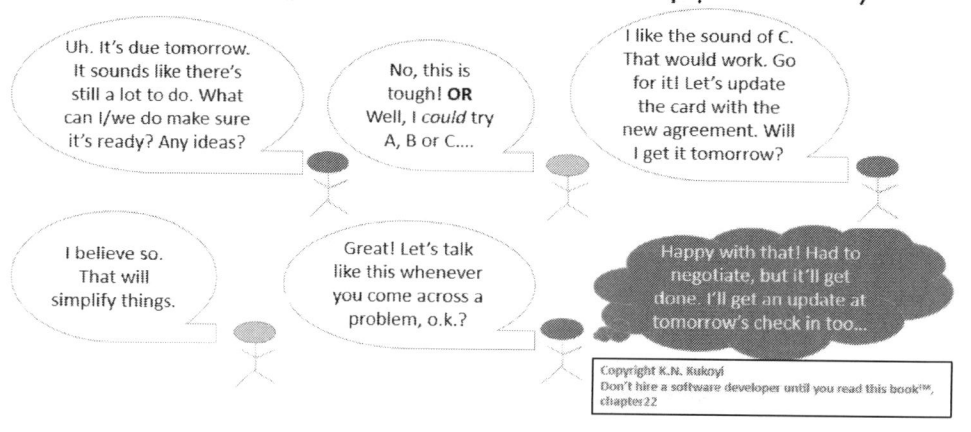

- Uh. It's due tomorrow. It sounds like there's still a lot to do. What can I/we do make sure it's ready? Any ideas?
- No, this is tough! **OR** Well, I *could* try A, B or C....
- I like the sound of C. That would work. Go for it! Let's update the card with the new agreement. Will I get it tomorrow?

- I believe so. That will simplify things.
- Great! Let's talk like this whenever you come across a problem, o.k.?
- Happy with that! Had to negotiate, but it'll get done. I'll get an update at tomorrow's check in too...

Copyright K.N. Kukoyi
Don't hire a software developer until you read this book™, chapter 22

Weekly (or fortnightly) reviews

The weekly review provides a forum where you can discuss and resolve issues on a regular basis. Agile teams often use exercises to help them reflect during these reviews or *retrospectives*, but for a small team, there are some simple questions you can use for this purpose:

- *"What has gone well this [week / fortnight]?"* Identify positive habits, activities and ways of working that should be continued.
- *"What hasn't gone well?" / "Where have we struggled this [week / fortnight]?"* This is your chance to get any issues that you've noticed out in the open and to discuss what isn't working and what needs to change. (But don't wait until a review to raise really important points.) Mention anything you're concerned about - delays, issues with communication, the quality of the product or any other issue(s) and try and get some resolution on these matters. Brainstorm some ways to solve the problems and decide on the solutions you like the best. Give them a try for a few weeks and see whether they're useful or not. If so, keep them, if not drop them and consider alternatives.
- Ask the *safeguard questions* at the relevant points in the conversation: *"Do you have any questions or concerns?"*, *"Is there anything missing?"*, *"What issues do you foresee?"* and *"Is there anything else I/we need to know, or consider?"*

Setting up your communication channels

Let's look at some popular communication tools used by technical project teams. There are a number that will allow you to perform activities including instant messaging, sending attachments, sharing links, searching and storing data, and making calls.

Google Hangouts, WhatsApp, and *Skype* can be used for video and voice messaging and sharing documents. Google Hangouts also has screen sharing functionality.

Slack has a free version which offers 5 GB of document storage and a 10k data allowance of searchable messages and call functionality for 2 people, https://slack.comhttps://slack.com

Bitrix24 includes a social network, video and chat, task and calendar management and a CRM (Customer Relationship Management system); useful if you are building a software app for businesses, https://www.bitrix24.com/.

> **Pro Tip!**
>
> **Have a communication agreement in place.**
>
> You will be a far more effective (and happy) team if you do this! I'm not suggesting anything too formal, just a 5-minute verbal discussion regarding the 5 points below, and an email follow-up, marked as "Team communication", or similar to confirm what was agreed, it can be easy to forget what was agreed when you're busy!
>
> 1. **Agree on a few ways that you and your developer are both happy to communicate**. You can change them later if you want to.
>
> 2. **Provide your developer with an emergency contact number, and tell them the best way to reach you if they need a quick response,** then make sure you check this regularly. You don't want to find that you were sent an urgent message hours ago, that you've only just noticed!
>
> 3. **Ask your developer about the best way to contact *them* in an emergency.** If your app goes down, or there is an unexpected problem, you'll want to be able to make contact quickly.
>
> 4. **Set some personal boundaries** and tell each other which hours are off-limits (unless there is an emergency, of course!)
>
> 5. Even if you communicate in a range of different ways, **maintain one master storage system for your requirements.** Don't spread tasks across several different tools. This is a guaranteed recipe for confusion! It will become a headache to manage and will make your build process more inefficient.
>
>   Make sure your developer isn't wasting precious time hunting for requirements in multiple places.

CHAPTER 22
How to manage your software project

Fig 86. An example of the Slack messaging tool. https://slack.com

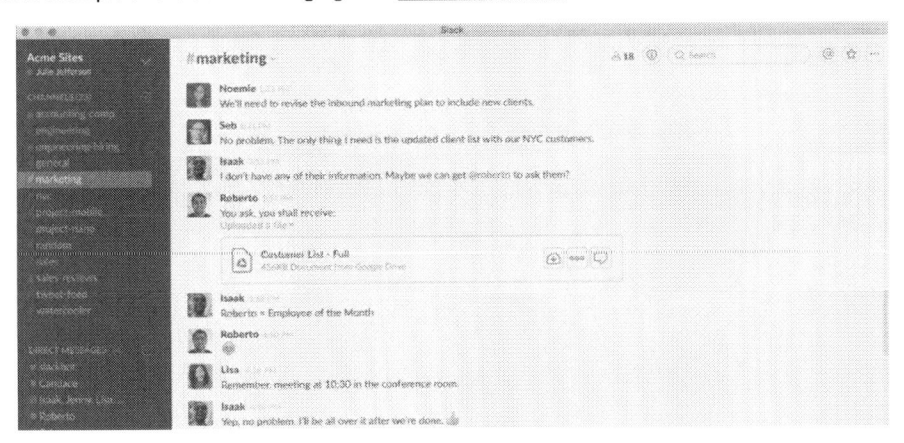

Decide which activities will you commit to when managing your team.

Project and task management tips

In addition to managing development related tasks, you may find it useful to store, organise and remind yourself about other tasks related to your project, or business. If you're using Trello, you'll be able to set yourself reminders by creating cards and setting due dates for them, as demonstrated earlier in the chapter, or by putting reminders in your Trello calendar using the calendar *Power-Ups* functionality.

CHAPTER 22
How to manage your software project

Fig 87. Turning on the calendar Power-Ups functionality in Trello.

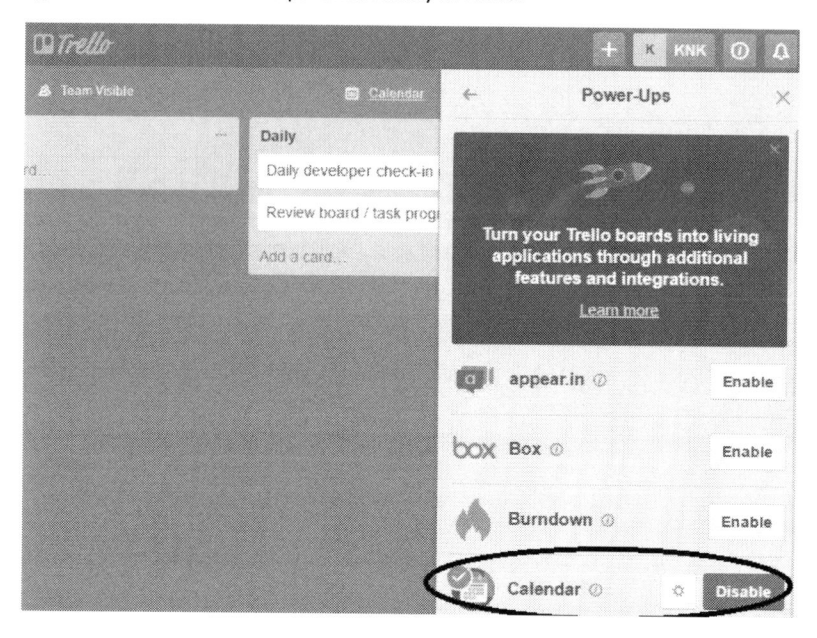

Fig 88. Set a due date as shown in Fig 84 to see the calendar due dates displayed on the front of your cards in Trello.

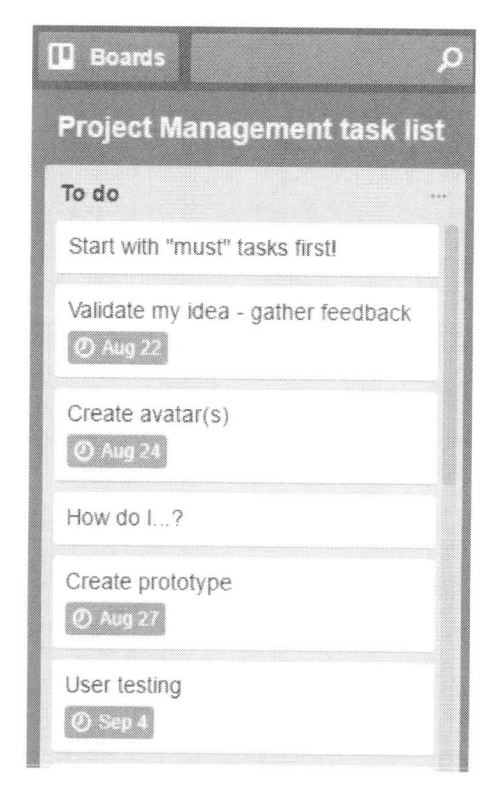

332

CHAPTER 22
How to manage your software project

Fig 89. Trello calendar "monthly view" including the four cards with due dates. (It's also possible to get a weekly calendar view.)

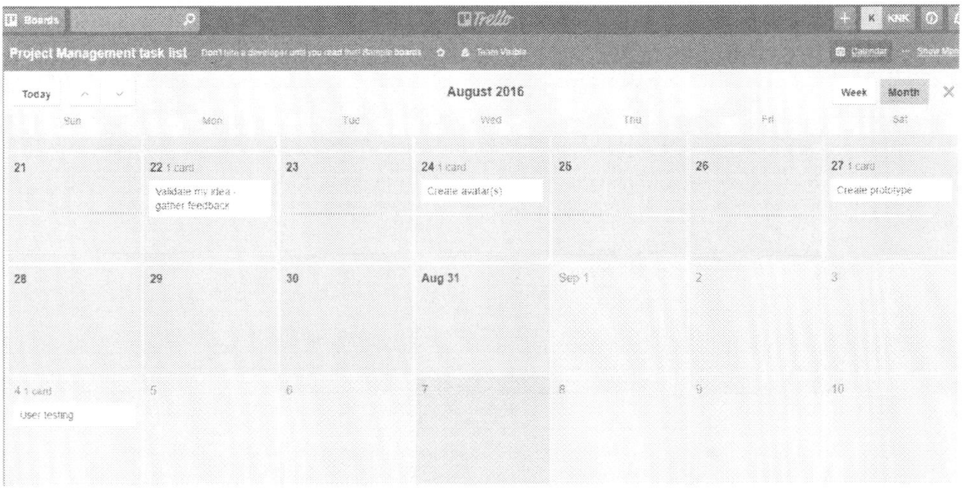

You can access my Trello boards here:

http://www.mylanderpages.com/donthireasoftwaredeveloperuntilyoureadthisbook/free-resource-2-trello-boards

"Google" your calendar for a quick summary

If you use Google Calendar, then a quick and easy way to access all your tasks and appointments is to Google the words "calendar today", "calendar this week", "calendar this month" or "calendar [insert the month you want]" to see your events appear in your search results. You can also search for "calendar last month" to view a summary of your past activities. Using the word "agenda," plus the month you want also works.

CHAPTER 22
How to manage your software project

Fig 90. Use Google to see a list of the events you've added to Google calendar.

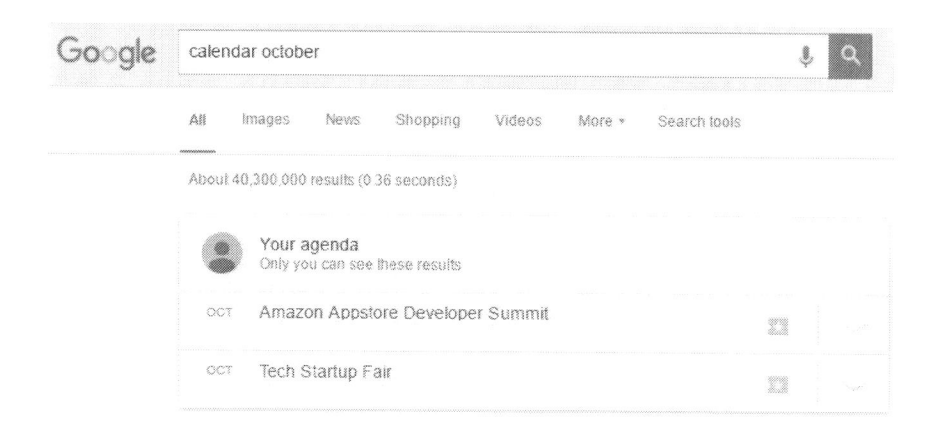

Documenting repetitive tasks can increase your productivity

Try documenting important processes that should be performed periodically, or in a consistent manner in the form of checklists. It's efficient and there'll be less chance of forgetting important steps (which *could* lead to things going wrong).

You may wish to document how to use any tools or software relevant to your app, or how to release new functionality to your live environment (this will come in handy in chapter 24.) Once these procedures are safely stored you can refer to them when you need them and make them available to staff and freelancers if you wish to outsource these tasks in future.

Google Drive lets you create and share your documents for free (or for a monthly fee via the Google for work software), https://www.google.co.uk/drive/

Google Keep can be used to store notes or checklists. Make a copy of your original list and then you can strike through the tasks in the copy without affecting the master version: https://keep.google.com/

CHAPTER 22
How to manage your software project

Fig 91. Using Google Keep to store important tasks or repetitive processes.

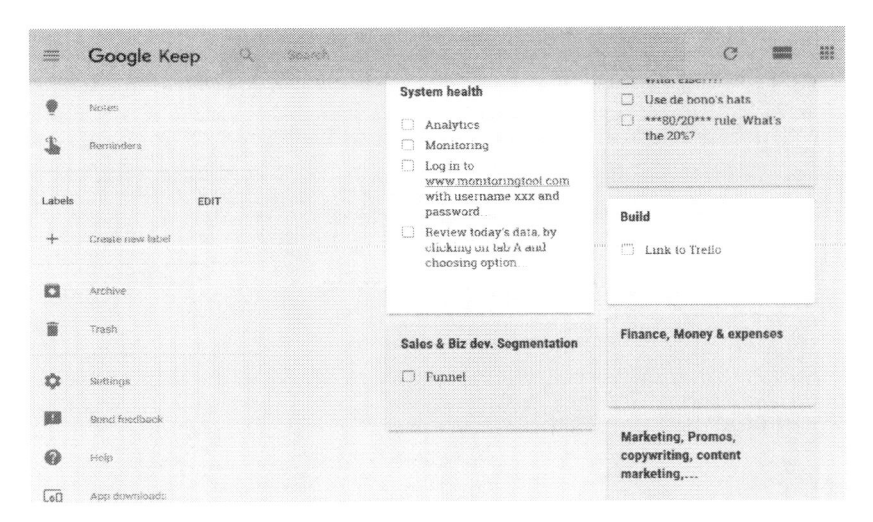

Process Street provides checklist software for businesses. There's a free plan that provides a maximum of 5 active templates and 5 checklists
https://www.process.st/

Wunderlist, allows you to create lists, assign tasks, attach documents. There is a free version available: https://www.wunderlist.com/pro/

Evernote is free for up to 60 MB of storage. You can create and share notes and checklists, which can be synced across 2 devices. Functionality increases with the paid annual plans, which cost £29.99 and £44.99 per year at the time of writing: https://evernote.com/

Carrying out regular user testing

Another important habit that should become "the norm" during your project and afterwards, is user (usability) testing. Untested assumptions and guesswork are costly - you may find later that your initial guess wasn't right and functionality that you believed would be popular with customers isn't.

As a result, you may have to waste time and money on rework, or worse you could run out of money to make the necessary amends.

How often should you perform a new round of customer research or user testing?

Be prepared to do research whenever you're not sure about a product decision.

This could involve speaking to your target market about your ideas, as you did back in chapter 3, or testing new prototypes, which we covered in chapter 13. You might even run an A/B test or request feedback via a questionnaire.

User tests should be repeated as products evolve. Additions or changes to functionality, wording, layouts, user journey sequences and even the position of call to action buttons and app colour schemes can have a strong effect on the usability and desirability of your product.

Make sure that any changes you make definitely improve your product for the better – from your customer's perspective, rather than your own!

If the opposite is true, you'll want to know. Have you heard of a phenomenon called *website redesign backlash*? Keep your customers happy!

As your product becomes more complex, your user testing will also become more involved.
You will be able to do more detailed testing of your user journeys and specific areas of your app, be able to invite users to enter data into your app and display information on screen for them to interact with. See chapter 13 to recap on the questions you can ask during user testing and how to run a user testing session.

In the next chapter, we'll be focusing on a range of ways to perform tests on your app to make sure it's ready to be released for beta testing.

CHAPTER 23
Break your app - before your customers do!

In this chapter:
- Why technical testing is fundamental to your success
- How to make sure your app gets approved into the app marketplaces by Apple and Google. This is NOT automatic!
- Testing your product
- Keeping track of bugs
- Common types of software testing
- Testing tools and software

Whether you do your own testing or hire a professional tester, an awareness of the technical tests available, and their uses and benefits, will help you maintain the quality of your product. There are many different types of technical test! We'll be reviewing a number of them in this chapter, but before we do that, let's review why testing is so important.

More testing, less problems.
There is no way to be sure that all your functional and non-functional requirements have been delivered without fully testing your app.
In addition to this, if you don't test thoroughly, you won't know the extent of any problems that you have. You can't deal with issues that you aren't aware of, so test all your functionality carefully, identify problems and resolve them as quickly as possible.

Bugs fixed today are cheaper than bugs fixed tomorrow.
Numerous studies have shown that bugs cost more to fix the longer they go undetected.
You DON'T have to fix every bug that you find, but you *should* have a "zero tolerance" policy on bugs that have a negative impact on your customers' ability to use your product, or ones that will cause them to lose confidence in, or abandon it. Bugs of that type should go into your "must" queue to be resolved - allow them to fester, and they may create bigger issues for you in the future.

CHAPTER 23
Break your app - before your customers do!

Fig 92. Relative cost to fix bugs based on time of detection. Source: National Institute of Standards and Technology (NIST).

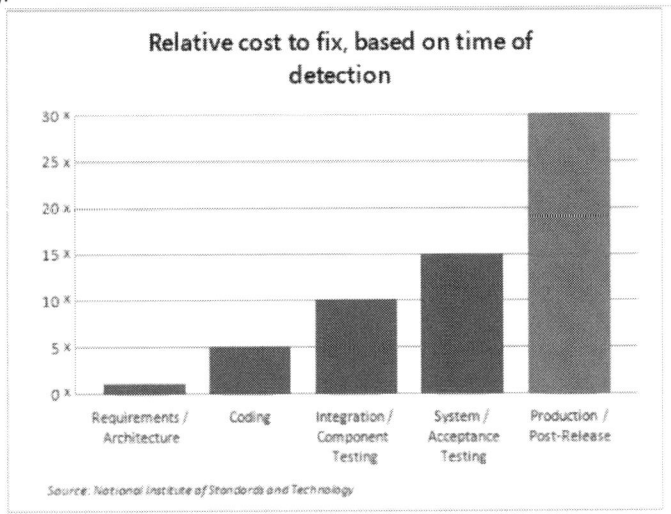

If you allow your customers to become your testers, they won't thank you for it.

Following on from the previous point, let's explore the impact of bugs on your customers.

Without adequate testing, your customers will be the first to find the bugs and issues lurking within your product. This is obviously bad for business.

It's also a compelling reason to get your product in front of as many people as possible *during* the development process and immediately *before* you launch your product. This will help identify as many issues as possible before you have customers using it full-time.

Even with a brilliant concept, if there are too many issues, the most loyal customers may eventually lose patience. Issues with your product can diminish trust and cause people to stop using or paying for your product, visiting your website or lead to them uninstalling your app. You may also face reputational issues if customers complain publicly.

Users won't be gentle with your app so you can't afford to be either!

There's no use in "politely" testing your app and using it only as you intended it to be used.

Your product should be robust, and able to handle whatever is thrown at it "out in the wild."

CHAPTER 23
Break your app - before your customers do!

Do some *exploratory* and *destructive software testing* and actively try to break your app. Be rough with it, so you know where it's vulnerable. We'll talk more about these types of tests later in this chapter.

The gatekeepers at the app stores will refuse you entry if your app doesn't meet their standards.

If you want to submit your app to one of the app marketplaces, you'll need to carry out rigorous testing to get rid of any bugs and issues first. Each app marketplace has its own standards and quality checks and you'll need to pass all of them. The app stores will keep rejecting your app until they are satisfied that it does not violate any of their rules and policies, *and if you fail to get approval, you'll have to start the process all over again.*

Do your best to avoid the cycle of pain - submitting your app, waiting up to a week for a response, receiving a list of issues back, taking several days to fix issues, submitting your app again, receiving more amends to review... by reading the app store submission checklists and marketplace terms and conditions carefully and having your developer do the same before submitting your app. The App Store is known for being very particular!

Your app will be checked for malware (short for "malicious software"), including viruses, spyware and other undesirable elements, which could be introduced to millions of mobile devices via the app stores.

Allow at least 4 weeks to resolve any issues and to get your app approved.
I say this because the app stores will test according to their own timescales. You really can't do much to hurry them in testing and re-testing your app and giving their feedback, so be aware that you may need to delay the launch of your app if you receive a long list of amends.

Here is some guidance provided by the app marketplaces:

The App Store

Some common reasons for apps being rejected by Apple can be found here:

https://developer.apple.com/app-store/review/rejections/

Here's an App Store submission checklist https://developer.apple.com/app-store/review/guidelines/#before-you-submit,

Apple's terms and conditions are here: https://developer.apple.com/terms/

How to submit your app for review to the App Store:

https://developer.apple.com/library/content/documentation/LanguagesUtilities/Conceptual/iTunesConnect_Guide/Chapters/SubmittingTheApp.html#//apple_ref/doc/uid/TP40011225-CH33

Google Play Store

Google Play / Android's terms and conditions are here:

https://play.google.com/about/developer-distribution-agreement.html

Here's a submission checklist for the Google Play store:

https://developer.android.com/distribute/tools/launch-checklist.html

Testing your product

Tests for you, or a QA to do

There are many ways to test an app! Factor in as much time as you can to cover the bases in these key areas:

First, test the acceptance criteria on your cards:

Review *Step 5, Test* in chapter 22 for a recap.

Next, get creative with some exploratory and destructive testing

Exploratory testing is ad-hoc testing of your app. Set at least an hour aside (or several 1-hour sessions for large or complex apps) with 1 goal: to find as many bugs and oddities as possible in the time available. Unlike the testing done on your cards, which is focused on checking that specific functionality exists and works properly, with exploratory testing there is no structure to follow, so just go crazy!

Destructive testing is where you get tough with your app - abuse it, test its limits and try to break it! Try to do the *opposite* of normal and see how well it copes.

Try to perform activities out of sequence. Go against the instructions provided by the app. Do the opposite of whatever you consider to be logical. Try and progress to the next stage in a user journey before you've completed all the required steps on the stage you're currently at. *Can you damage your app, or cause it to malfunction, or "meltdown"?*

Try to move, drag, tap, swipe or click haphazardly to see how your app handles this. If you repeatedly click or tap the buttons or links, does it crash? (Users often get impatient and click buttons multiple times, but this can make the software run even more slowly. Apps can be built so that the first click counts and multiple clicks are ignored so the app is not processing unnecessary actions.)

Insert the "wrong" types of information into your data entry fields, enter numbers where there should be letters and letters where there should be numbers. Put telephone numbers in your email address field, enter email addresses without the @ sign in it. Leave fields or options that you were meant to respond to completely blank and try and progress to the next page or screen and see what happens. If you have date of birth fields, if your system is expecting *structured data* in a set format, such as MM/DD/YYYY representing the month, day and year of birth, what happens if you try YYYY/MM/DD or DD/MM/YYYY? Where possible, make it difficult (or even impossible) for people to enter data in the wrong formats. This makes life easier for everyone.

Look out for typos in your on-screen text and try to find errors in your copy!

Performing regression and integration testing

These are tests that you should do later in the project as your app becomes more mature.

Regression testing. Unfortunately, in software development you can't assume that any functionality that was working yesterday, will work today if changes have been made to the code base. A change can include a bug fix, new functionality, *refactored* (improved) *code* or changes to the behind-the-scenes technical settings (called *configuration settings*) which affect the app. The building blocks of the app are interconnected and alterations can sometimes affect existing parts of the app in unexpected ways. *Regression testing* verifies that software previously developed and tested still works. These tests may be done on parts of a system or even an entire app, especially before releasing software to customers.

CHAPTER 23
Break your app - before your customers do!

Integration testing. *Systems integration* is the process of bringing together different parts of an app, system or software application so that they act together as a coordinated whole. *Integration testing* reviews how well the different "parts" work together as a system and whether there are any "weak links" across that system.

APIs and other components not built by your developer may be integrated or bolted on to your app to save time. They can help you avoid re-inventing the wheel if certain functionality already exists that you can purchase or adapt. The challenge is to make sure that the parts built from scratch *and* the "borrowed and bought" parts work together smoothly. From a user experience perspective, the app needs to *feel* unified, and not like a Frankenstein's monster composed of different parts, which together result in a "choppy", disjointed experience.

Keeping track of your bugs

No matter what type of app you're building, if you think you've found a bug:

Reproduce it. This means proving that the steps needed to cause a bug to appear can be repeated. A bug needs to be *reproducible* in order for your developer to properly investigate, trace its cause and fix it and a reproducible bug is one that can be triggered at will.

You may also find *deficiencies* - items that are not exactly what they should be, or other issues which mean that the work delivered is not acceptable and needs some form of adjustment.

Prioritise it. Decide whether you want to spend any of your budget on fixing the bug, or dealing with the issue. Your decision should be made based on the impact of the bug or issue on your product. If you decide to fix it, then...

Log it. When you find a bona fide bug, capture the details on a card. The more information you can provide the better. Note down the actions to take to reproduce the bug and add screenshots of the issue to the card if possible, because visual examples aid understanding. Add information about what *should* have happened - in other words, the correct behaviour you expected to see, to the card. For example: *"When I click the start button, the app should display the profile page, NOT the payments page."*

CHAPTER 23
Break your app - before your customers do!

You can create a "bug card" by clicking on the card and amending the label. I've assigned a red colour code to my bug cards. This can be done in Trello using the following process:

Fig 93. Cards in Trello can be colour-coded and named using the label functionality.

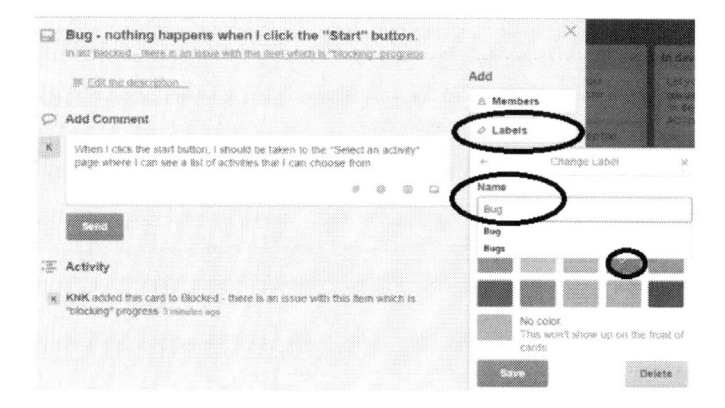

Figs 94 and 95. The bug label is now visible on the inside and outside of the Trello card.

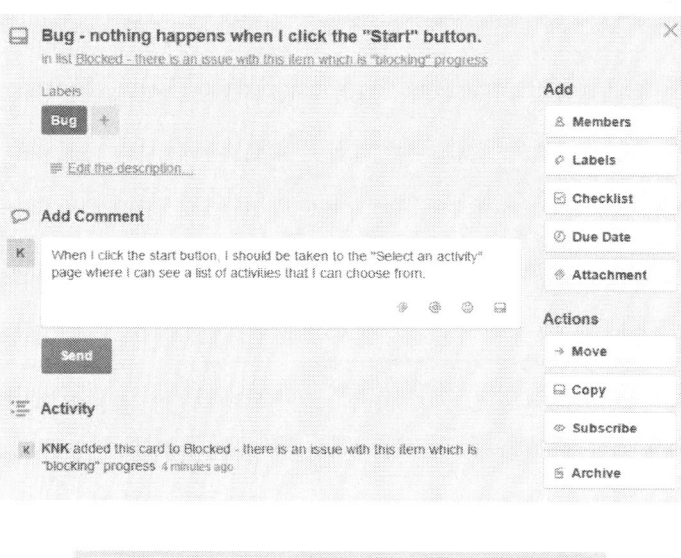

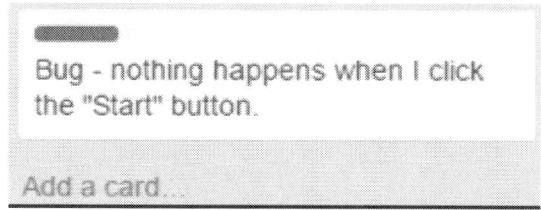

344

Tests for your developer (or a specialist software tester) to do

If you've put performance, security and other NFR related cards in your MVP queue, then a developer, or specialist software tester will need to run some specific tests on your app:

Concurrency testing, (also known as *multi-user testing*) simulates user activity in an app to identify any issues that arise when multiple users access your app. It must be able to cope with large numbers of users performing the *same activities at the same time*, if not, issues will arise and it may crash, or run very slowly. Your developer will need to make provisions for this and should ask you how many users you're expecting to have as your customer base grows. They will convert this into expected figures for user activity per hour or even per minute and may translate this into *requests*, (in other words the taps, clicks, requests for data etc. that users are generating) to understand the demand that will be placed on the system.

Stress testing (or peak testing) is performed to determine a system's behaviour under "stress" conditions. The amount of *load* is *systematically* increased over time until the system can no longer cope, which will allow you to understand its limits. Your monitoring tools should be switched on when this is done so your developer can gather data about what happens within the app whilst it is performing under strain, and can assess which elements of the app need adjusting to help it perform more efficiently.

Spike testing involves subjecting the app to a *sudden* high volume of load to see if it can cope. As an example, a website that suddenly receives a large number of visits due to publicity or a special promotion can crash if no provision has been made for sudden spikes in traffic.

You and your developer should factor in future *growth in customer numbers,* and *spikes* in traffic when setting up your app, so you have some safety margins in place between normal ranges and more extreme ones.

Soak Testing (or endurance testing) is a type of performance test that verifies a system's stability and performance over an extended period of time, for instance over several days. This confirms an app can handle a "normal" (i.e. expected) level of use over time.

Page load and mobile app performance tests. These performance tests look at the *speed* of your app rather than how efficiently it performs under stress. This could include gathering data on page load speeds on the web, mobile app performance, and performance when specific activities take place such as clicking or tapping buttons or links, or retrieving and displaying the data held in your database. If performance issues are found, your developer should *performance tune* the app by looking at ways to maximise the speed at which different activities can be performed. Monitoring tools that include speed focused testing will be very helpful in gathering performance related data for you.

Penetration testing. It's time for some ethical hacking! *Pen testing* as it is also known, is the process of assessing (and even attacking) your own app to identify vulnerabilities that could be exploited by malicious third parties.

When all the functionality in your app has been fully tested and no further issues have been found, this stable version of your MVP (which is ready to be released to the public), is called a *release candidate.* The release candidate is no longer usable if you find significant issues with it. In this case, more fixes will need to be made and the app will need to be tested again. When you find another stable, bug-free version of your app, this can become your new release candidate.

The Power of Automated Testing

Testing becomes a bigger job as more code is written and there is more functionality to test. Therefore, you might consider having automated testing as your first line of defence and regular manual testing of your cards as your second.

Automated testing adds a degree of reliability to your app as it grows. Specialist software can be used to control the execution of *tests* and the comparison of actual outcomes with expected outcomes. The tests specify what *should* happen when the tests are run and the test software compares this with what *actually* happens, generating alerts or failure reports if any discrepancies are found. Your developer can then investigate what went wrong.

Automated tests can be written (or amended) to cover a*ll functionality and features and to cover gaps* where bugs have arisen before. Tests can also be written *to cover some or all of the user journeys* that exist within your app. The number of tests in place across the code that makes up your product is described as the *test coverage.* Gaps in test coverage can leave your product exposed.

Unit testing is a software development process in which the smallest testable parts of an application; the units, are individually tested. Unit testing can be automated or covered by manual testing.

Automated testing is extremely useful, but there are a few drawbacks to consider;

- **Manual (human) testers still have the edge over computers in some respects,** especially when it comes to testing creatively, deciding whether your product is pleasant to use and noticing visual issues such as problems with page layouts or the misalignment of widgets on a page. Therefore, automated testing is not the answer in every scenario.
- **It can be time-consuming to write (and run) automated tests.** As a system grows and more tests are added, the *test suite,* (i.e. the entire set of tests to be run) takes longer and longer to finish, which delays how quickly a release can be made. I once worked on a team where it took over 2.5 hours for the whole "suite" of tests to run, which meant a long wait for a release that we could manually test!

If writing tests for everything poses a challenge, work smart by automating the *key user journeys* that customers use and value the most, then decide whether your developer should write other automated tests too. Try to find a good compromise between *test coverage* and practicality.

The importance of cross-browser and cross-device testing

When testing, you will need to consider all the popular web browsers, operating systems and devices that customers might use to access your app, for example:

- *Web browsers* (Google Chrome, Internet Explorer; I.E. Firefox, Safari etc.)
- *Operating systems* (such as the Microsoft-based ones; Windows 7, 8, 8.1, 10, XP and Mac operating systems 10.4 - 10.12. Linux is also a player, but has a much smaller user base.) For a recap on operating systems, see chapter 13.)
- *Devices and computers* (different brands and types of device such as smartphones, tablets, PCs, Macs and laptops). *Phablets*, extra-large smartphones are now on the rise too!

There are dizzying array of devices, operating system and browser combinations that you could test (imagine testing the just one version of the Chrome browser across every operating system in the list, on every device and then repeating this for all the other web browsers in their most popular versions!) Your customers could be using these in any combination, so cross-browser and cross-device testing is an important part of the software delivery process. Knowing your target market will be helpful in making decisions about where to focus your testing energies - you may come to realise that certain browsers or devices are more popular with them than others, which will help you to prioritise. For example, if you have a *web app* intended for business use then the *I.E. / Windows / Desktop (PC)* combination *may* be the one to prioritise for testing, as the Microsoft suite of products still dominate the business computing market. However, you should always confirm assumptions like this with your target market!

Cross-browser testing. Your *web app* may work perfectly on some web browsers, but be partially or completely unusable on others.

It's not unusual for parts of an app to be misaligned, broken or even missing in different web browsers. If this is the case with your app, then you should be the first to know.

When it comes to personal use, the three most frequently used browsers worldwide are Chrome, Firefox and Internet Explorer *for desktop use only*, followed in much smaller numbers by Safari, Edge and Opera.

The order shifts to Chrome, Safari, I.E and Firefox when we look across *desktop, mobile and tablet devices worldwide*.

CHAPTER 23
Break your app - before your customers do!

Fig 96. Worldwide Desktop Browser Usage Share. Source: StatCounter, http://statcounter.com/.

Worldwide Desktop Browser Usage Share

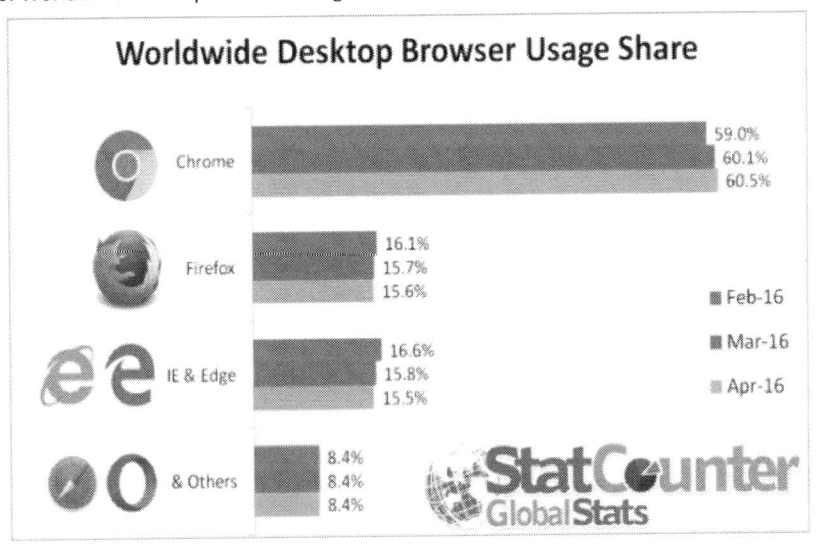

- Chrome: 59.0% (Feb-16), 60.1% (Mar-16), 60.5% (Apr-16)
- Firefox: 16.1% (Feb-16), 15.7% (Mar-16), 15.6% (Apr-16)
- IE & Edge: 16.6% (Feb-16), 15.8% (Mar-16), 15.5% (Apr-16)
- & Others: 8.4%, 8.4%, 8.4%

Fig 97. Worldwide stats including desktop, mobile and tablet. (If you're curious, UC Browser is a mobile browser created by the Chinese company UCWeb.) Source: StatCounter, http://statcounter.com/.

StatCounter Global Stats
Top 9 Browsers from Apr 2015 to Apr 2016

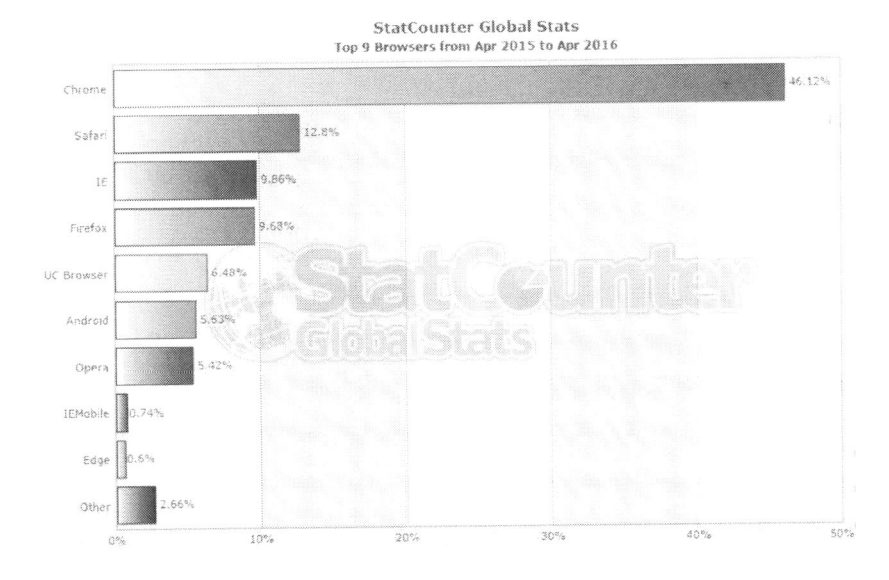

- Chrome: 46.12%
- Safari: 12.8%
- IE: 9.86%
- Firefox: 9.68%
- UC Browser: 6.48%
- Android: 5.63%
- Opera: 5.42%
- IEMobile: 0.74%
- Edge: 0.6%
- Other: 2.66%

Cross-device testing takes into account laptops, PCs and different mobile devices including smartphones and tablet devices.

Remember that native mobile apps need to be tested on smartphones and tablets and web apps need to be tested on laptops / PCs, Macs, smartphones and tablets via different web browsers.

Your app and its content may be displayed (or rendered) differently on each based on the dimensions of each device and the different pixel widths of the screens.

Fig 98. In a commercial environment, a range of devices may be used for testing, this is sometimes called a *device farm*. Devices. Source: Brad Frost. https://www.flickr.com/photos/brad_frost/7387824246,

Testing tools and software

I know! It all seems pretty terrifying and you're probably wondering how to handle all these testing combinations.

Now for the good news. Thankfully there are some solutions to this problem!

There are ways to test your app across different device, browser and operating system combinations using *remote access device farms.* This means that you test on devices accessed online, rather than doing this manually with lots of physical devices piled up around you! In some cases, the devices you are testing via the web will be "real" physical devices too. Here are some options:

- You can test your website's functionality and design across a range of browser and operating system combinations from $39 per month using CrossBrowserTesting.com. http://crossbrowsertesting.com
- The AWS *device farm* is a mobile testing service from Amazon. You can test your app on physical devices via the Amazon Web Services cloud. The service will give you 250 minutes of testing for free: https://aws.amazon.com/device-farm/

CHAPTER 23
Break your app - before your customers do!

- STF (Smartphone Test Farm) lets you test physical devices from your web browser: http://openstf.io/

Emulators (also known as *Simulators*) are tools which will display a representation of a mobile device on your computer so you can develop, and test mobile apps without a physical device.

Here's an Android emulator example:

https://developer.android.com/studio/run/emulator.html

The App Store has a simulator, which comes with the Apple developer pack: https://developer.apple.com/programs/whats-included/. This will allow you to make your app available to **25 internal testers** per app via the TestFlight service. This would allow you to get a copy of your app on your own mobile device for testing – you might use the rest of your allocation for user testing.

There is a summary video, that will walk you through the process, here

https://itunespartner.apple.com/en/apps/videos#testflight-beta-testing

Fig 99. This emulator shows a device with the text, "Hello World", a popular test program used by developers. https://i.stack.imgur.com/7q9g6.png

CHAPTER 23
Break your app - before your customers do!

Although useful, testing using emulators isn't quite as accurate as using physical devices, so tools that allow you to test with real devices, even if done remotely, should be slightly more accurate.

In the next chapter, we'll talk about the steps involved in launching your app!

SECTION 8

LAUNCH IT!

CHAPTER 24
How to launch your MVP (as a beta)

In this chapter:

- Why beta testing can get you off to a great (and safe) start
- Who else runs beta tests?
- The 5 decisions you'll need to make if you want to do beta testing
- How to set up and manage your beta
- Project pitfalls
- Releasing your MVP and "going live" with your product!

Doing a "soft launch" of your MVP to a small segment of your target market as a *beta test* is the ultimate in risk management. You can dip your foot (probably not a toe, you're a bit more committed than that!) in the water without having to get right in and you'll *still* have time and a degree of "breathing space" to make adjustments and deal with issues calmly whilst customer numbers are still small.

Beta tests really can help you maximise your chances of success in serving and pleasing your audience. Even if you're a start-up without an existing reputation, you'll want to create a positive impression and build trust with your customers from day one. Running a beta will also help you test out your customer care processes, (more on this later in this chapter, and in chapter 25) and ease yourself into all the operational tasks involved in managing a business.

What do you think? Does this sound like a sensible approach?

How does Beta testing work?

When running a *beta test*, an early "finished" version of your product is made available to customers and they are free to use it in their own environment and on their own device(s) for a period of time.

They won't have any tests to perform, and you won't be there to observe their experiences as you did when you were doing user testing. The objective of the beta test is to gather more feedback and pick up any remaining niggles or teething problems which did not surface during user testing. It is the "acid test;"

customers will use your product whenever and however they please, without the boundaries and confines of scripts, or time-limited tests.

The beta should also provide data about your app's reliability and expose any technical issues or "fine-tuning" that needs to be done behind the scenes. If your app struggles to cope when multiple people are using it, you need to know this *before* it becomes widely available. If you've chosen any monitoring tools which can be used to check the "health" of your app, then set these up and have them up and running for the beta. Activate any analytics tools you have too, so you can gather statistical data to help you understand your customers' behaviour. (There are a selection of analytics and monitoring tools available for you to review across chapters 6, 21 and 25.) These are exciting times!

I should clarify an important point before we go on.
Whatever functionality you plan to make available to your beta users, it should not be buggy or unreliable. Launching a product with minimal functionality is not the same as launching a poor-quality product.

You should have done enough technical, functional and usability testing to weed out major issues. As a result, you should not *expect* to find problems during beta testing, but the beta should expose anything that might have been overlooked or that was not obvious earlier in the development process. Therefore, you should be *prepared* to deal with challenges and to actively monitor your product's performance (and your customers' experiences with it) very closely.

Are Beta tests common?

Yes, they are, for all the reasons given! If you run a Beta test, you'll be in very good company:

Google has run Beta tests with Gmail, as well as other Google applications; http://www.geeky-gadgets.com/wp-content/uploads/2009/07/google_beta-2.jpg, Chrome and the Google mobile app, and did you catch the 2007 Beta version of Spotify?

https://tctechcrunch2011.files.wordpress.com/2015/07/spotify-beta-2007b.png?w=600

CHAPTER 24
How to launch your MVP (as a beta)

Firefox and Instagram have also beta tested their products.

Figs 100 and 101 - Instagram beta (former logo) and Firefox® beta logo.

A few decisions

Setting up a beta test

Naturally, there is some prep work involved, but beta tests can be fairly simple to set up. Initially, you will need answers to several questions:
- Who should be involved in beta testing...and how will you invite people to get involved?
- How many people should participate? You need enough to really put some "pressure" on your product and provide a decent amount of feedback, but not so many that the beta becomes overwhelming for you.
- How long should the beta period last?
- Should you charge for the beta?
- How will you launch your product for beta testing?

O.K. Let's address these questions!

Who will be involved in beta testing... and how will you invite people to get involved?

First, you'll need to "invite" a subset of your target market to try your product for a set period of time. Here are some suggestions:

CHAPTER 24
How to launch your MVP (as a beta)

Reach out to people via social media. Ask them to get involved and spread the word to others too. Here's the list of popular social media sites from chapter 3:

- Facebook
- YouTube
- Twitter
- LinkedIn
- Instagram
- Pinterest
- Google+
- Snapchat
- Tumblr
- Reddit
- Flickr
- Meetup.com

You might also want to try Quora, Medium and Product Hunt.

Be super-efficient when contacting your future beta testers online using *social media management* tools that let you publish to multiple sites at once:

Hootsuite, will allow you to connect and post to up to 3 social media sites from a choice of Instagram, Facebook, Twitter, LinkedIn, Google+ and YouTube and there's a dashboard available to monitor your activity. Here's a link to their free service: https://hootsuite.com/create-free-account. Buffer app covers all of the social media sites serviced by Hootsuite, with the exception of YouTube, https://buffer.com/pricing.

Pair this up with another social media tool like *Likeable Hub* (Facebook, Twitter and LinkedIn) https://likeablehub.com/ or Everypost http://everypost.me/pricing/ to cover a large number of sites at once from a mobile app or online.

You can, of course use these tools for your general business marketing too.

If you want to know when you should post to different social media sites for maximum impact, take a look at this great post from HubSpot, who own a marketing and sales product by the same name, http://blog.hubspot.com/marketing/best-times-post-pin-tweet-social-media-infographic.

Refer to your customer profile(s). Do you recall the customer profile(s) you created back in chapter 3? Gather all the data about where your target customers are and work through the list.

Attract people using a website. You could also advertise the Beta on a website and try asking them to sign up online.

You could set up a landing page for this purpose and direct traffic to it from social media posts, social media ads, or Google Adsense ads. In the past, Yahoo! Mail has recruited visitors arriving on its home page to join its Beta test with a prominent "Try it now" button, a few selling points covering the benefits of the new version of the app and some encouraging testimonials.

Add any positive feedback from your user testing sessions to your landing page for extra credibility.

Convert user testers to beta testers. Why not ask your user testers if they'd like to become beta testers too? As beta users, they'll be free to use the product how and when they like!

Consider advertising for beta testers by placing ads in the local paper, or through websites such as Gumtree and Craigslist.

Post flyers in public places. Put the word out in gyms, sports clubs and at yoga classes… What other places can you think of?

Contact the people in your email contact lists. Explain what you're doing and when and ask them to reply if they're interested or have any questions. Be prepared to follow up to check that the emails were received, and to chase up anyone who hasn't gotten around to replying to you. Note that emails with large attachments, and ones with HTML and images are more likely to get dumped into the folder of obscurity by recipients' email service providers!

Make a few good ol' fashioned phone calls… or send SMS, *WeChat* or *WhatsApp* messages to your contacts list.

Pay professional beta testers. As a last resort, you might pay for Beta testers via a freelancer sites like Upwork or Freelancer.com. Bear in mind that the people that you pay to do Beta testing may not be truly representative of your audience, although you may still get some useful feedback from them. You will be paying *them,* whereas a beta tester may be paying *you* (if you are intending to charge people to use your product during the beta.) In addition to this, if they aren't part of your target market, their needs may not be the same and they may not be able to provide the quality of feedback that your target market would give you. Still, they are people with opinions and you also need to test the infrastructure that supports your app, so there will still be some benefits to this approach.

Finding business beta users

If your app is for businesses, begin cold-calling, emailing and networking.
Visit websites to collect contact information and try a combination of LinkedIn, conferences, associations, trade or membership groups. Promote your product by focusing on the *WIIFM* "What's in it for me?" for your target customer group. Don't just state what the product does, emphasise the *benefits* it will bring and how it will remove those painful problems or allow the customer to enjoy those benefits that you identified back in chapter 3. This is a sales technique called *telling* a feature and *selling* a benefit, which keeps the focus on customers' needs. Factor 50 sun cream may be a blocker of UVA and UVB rays from the sun, but these are just the features. Using it correctly will greatly reduce your risk of: i) premature aging and ii) getting skin cancer. These are the *benefits,* and they're very powerful ones! Demonstrate how your product will improve their lives or rid them of problems, and ask them to trial it.

There is also a sales technique called *SPIN selling,* which is very popular. This stands for: **S**ituation, **P**roblem, **I**mplication and **N**eed-payoff. SPIN can be used to deconstruct the issues that your customers are facing and present an appropriate solution to them - your product! It would be fairly straightforward to prepare a pitch and presentation using SPIN to make a compelling case.

You can find an overview here;

http://www.sellingandpersuasiontechniques.com/SPIN-selling.html it's a basic page with a few sales prompts on it, but you can ignore those if you just want to read the content.

Be aware that this process could take anything from a few weeks to several months. You'll need to connect with the relevant *decision makers* or *influencers* from each business, with the authority to get the beta approved, build relationships with them, and deliver some form of pitch to convince them of the value of the product before they are likely to consider a beta testing agreement. Do you know anyone who works in or has connections to the industry or market that you are targeting? Could they connect you to the right people?

How many people should participate?

If you have a B2C (Business to Consumer) app, I would try between 10 and 30 people.

If you're testing a B2B (Business to Business) app, then between 2 to 5 businesses will give you a range of feedback *across different* companies, as well as a range of individual users. This is assuming that your product is suited to only a portion of the people in each company. If the companies are large or there are a large number of people who might use your product, keep the range of businesses wide, but limit the number of people involved from each company if possible. Why?

Because different companies may have different internal processes and may run your product on different devices and operating systems. This is great for finding out how your product performs in *all* these different environments and if these variations affect the way(s) your product can be used.

Of course, you could try an *open beta,* which is open to anyone at all, but there is a risk of being inundated with problems to resolve if unforeseen issues arise. *If you're unable to deal with issues quickly, or to acknowledge and respond to customer feedback, your beta testers may be discouraged from continuing to use your product.* You really need people to have a good experience during the beta, so they are more likely to convert into paying customers.

How long should the beta period last?

I think anything between ten working days to a month is a nice time-period for a beta. You could cut this back if you really wanted to, although I'm not sure why you would. It will be beneficial if all the beta testers have used your app at least several times during the beta period and if the beta period is too short, this may not be the case. If you have monitoring tools in place, consider using these to help you identify those who have not used your app yet. Contact them with a polite reminder of how important their feedback is and when the beta trial ends!

Should you charge for the Beta?
The answer is, it depends!

If you are planning to charge for your product from day one, then your beta should test out your theories about pricing too. You could consider offering your product as "try before you buy" - free for a set number of days, or offer it at a discount for Beta testers. However, if you have validated your idea (chapter 2), know who your target market is, along with their wants and needs and how to market to them, (as we discussed in chapter 3) and the product has been user tested with people from your target market, (chapters 13 and 22) then you already know that there are people who need your product and are willing to pay for it, so go ahead and ask! (See chapter 8 for a recap on software pricing models.)

If you've chosen a business model that doesn't require you to charge customers to use your app, or you are planning to adopt a freemium model, then offering the product for free makes sense.

How will you launch your product for beta testing?

Android / Google Play beta testing

You have the option of *inviting specific people* to the beta test (a *closed beta*), which you can do via their Gmail account or a Google group, or you can launch a beta version of your app on Google Play which anyone will be able to access. You can find instructions here:

https://developer.android.com/distribute/engage/beta.html

This is a *launch checklist* for Android apps:

https://developer.android.com/distribute/tools/launch-checklist.html

iOS / App Store beta testing

This can be done via a tool called TestFlight. You can make your app available to 25 internal users via TestFlight, but you can invite up to 2,000 people to test your app via email for beta testing, and they can test on their smartphones or tablets.

The Beta period is set for you at 60 days;

https://developer.apple.com/testflight/. There are some TestFlight instructions here:
https://developer.apple.com/library/content/documentation/IDEs/Conceptual/AppDistributionGuide/DistributingYourAppUsingTestFlight/DistributingYourAppUsingTestFlight.html#//apple_ref/doc/uid/TP40012582-CH37-SW1

Here's a link to the TestFlight app on iTunes:

https://itunes.apple.com/gb/app/testflight/id899247664?mt=8

If your beta is open to **anyone**, you will need to go through Apple's Beta App Review process and comply with the full set of app store guidelines before Beta testing can begin, however, if your beta is by "**invite-only**"**,** there is no need to go through this extra step.

https://developer.apple.com/app-store/review/guidelines/

This has its advantages and disadvantages. If you avoid the Beta App Review process, you'll save time, but you won't know how much work you still have to do to get your app accepted into the App store. You could transition from a closed beta to an open beta if the app is stable and things are going well.

If different users test on different versions of the iPhone and iPad, or different Android smartphones and tablets, then that will help you identify strange behaviour across different devices.

Launching your *web app* for beta testing

If you've built a *web app*, you can invite beta testers to access your product by sending them a link. If you give out a link, (or a link and password), bear in mind that these could be shared with people outside the beta group. If this is a concern, ask your developer if they can suggest any other options. It is possible to stop Google from including websites in its search results using methods like the *robots exclusion standard* (commonly known as *robots.txt),* which tells Google whether to index a page or not, but this will only prevent people browsing the web from accidentally discovering your beta site. (See chapter 9 if you'd like to revisit SEO and indexing.)

Don't forget about cross-browser and cross-device beta testing!
Try to get some users to test on a smartphone, others on a tablet, others on a PC or laptop and some Mac users too, if you can! If you do this, you're likely to have beta testers using a range of different browsers so your beta will cover off cross-browser and cross-device scenarios too!

Project managing your beta

It's time to put your project management hat on again and consider the things which might go wrong, and how you would handle them. Think *smooth and well organised...* that's the impression that your customers should have during your beta.

Here are some points to consider:

Provide information, instructions and an outline plan. Don't assume that people know what a Beta is and what's involved in taking part in one. When you first ask people to join your beta, explain the concept and let them know how long the beta will last and what you expect them to do during the beta period. (Use the app, provide feedback and write you an online review or testimonial, or an app marketplace review if you have a mobile app). Outline all the great things your app does and reconfirm the cost of your product (if there is one) and any discount you are offering. Provide your contact details (telephone, website, social media profiles etc. where relevant) and ask people to reply if they have any questions.

Decide whether a beta agreement is required. *Beta Agreements* (also known as *Beta Testing End User Licensing Agreements,* or *Beta Testing Software Licensing Agreements),* are terms and conditions for your participants. Clauses might include: an agreement to take part in, and to abide by the terms of the beta test, product and company disclaimers and limited liability statements, and any confidentiality clauses that are relevant. You may also wish to include a statement which confirms you as the owner of the software along with any restrictions on its usage that you feel are relevant.

Simply-Docs provides legal documents, contracts and templates. They have a beta agreement for a *closed beta* (invite-only.) http://simply-docs.co.uk/Software_Development_and_Testing_Agreements/Beta_Software_Terms_and_Conditions_Closed_Beta and here's a link to the open beta agreement document;

http://simply-docs.co.uk/Software_Development_and_Testing_Agreements/Beta_Software_Terms_and_Conditions_Open_Beta

If you are building an iOS mobile app, Apple provide terms and conditions for TestFlight users;

http://www.apple.com/legal/internet_services/itunes/testflight/sren/terms.html

As always, please seek legal counsel if you have any queries about the creation or use of a beta agreement.

Stay in contact. Request people's contact details in advance of the beta. A telephone number and email address should be gathered as a minimum. Send out a reminder to beta testers a week before the beta is due to start, including an overview of how they will access the product and reminding them of all the important details needed to participate in the testing. Prepare another reminder for the day before the beta with any important instructions about how to access or log in to your app.

Manage expectations. Make beta testers aware that they might find issues. This is not an excuse for releasing a poor-quality product, but it *is* a caveat – anyone doing beta testing should know that it would not be *unreasonable* to come across bugs or functionality that needs minor improvements.

Provide access details and supporting information on launch day. On the day that your beta begins send, the email out again with any links or information required to access your app. (If you send the link in advance, a proportion of people *will* click on it, so don't send it until you're ready to go live, or going live will happen sooner than you planned!)

Include a set of FAQs (Frequently Asked Questions) in your email, based on the things you think people will want to know to help them get the most from your product and from the beta period. Reconfirm the best way(s) to contact you if they have an issue or want to give you feedback.

Have a system for logging issues. When you capture issues relating to your Beta, try to do this in a consistent format. A log for tracking issues might look something like this:

- *The date and time that the issue occurred.* (Cross referencing issues back to the time they happened can help your developer analyse the root cause of problems. Your app monitoring tools may be useful for this type of task.)
- *The beta tester's name and contact details.*
- *The device used to access your app* e.g. a smartphone, tablet, PC, Mac or laptop.
- *The web browser and the version used,* if you're beta testing a web app.

- *The operating system used* e.g. Android, iOS, Windows, Mac OS X etc.
- *An issue category,* so you can see what types of problems are arising most frequently. Useful categories might include: bug, question (or query), suggestion / request, complaint, issue.
- *A description of the problem and how to reproduce it.* Note down what happened, the part(s) of the app affected and whether the issue is still going on. Ask for a screen shot of the problem wherever possible; it's much quicker to grasp what's happening if you can see the issue for yourself. Even if the problem appears to have gone away, don't be lulled into a false sense of security, bugs lurk! Sometimes only a very precise set of steps in a given order cause them to show up, so try to *replicate* the issue by repeating the steps the beta tester took. Can you make it happen again? If so, capture the step-by-step details of how to *reproduce* the bug on a bug card, and add it to your *Ready for build* queue for your developer to fix. (See chapter 22 for more details.) Add suggestions, requests and other issues to the TBC queue on your backlog or to the "must", "should", "could" or "won't" queue depending on your assessment of each one. Another option is to add all feedback to a new board for managing customer service related topics, and then to decide what to do with them. I'll show you how to do this in chapter 25.
- *A severity rating.* As an example, you could use ratings of "low", "medium", "high" and "severe" or a rating of 1-5, where 1 is the most severe and 5 is the least (or vice-versa). The more users are inconvenienced or impacted by problems with your app, the higher the severity rating should be. If you have multiple issues, use your rating system to help you decide which you should resolve first. Watch out for issues which aren't serious, but are annoying a large proportion of people. If it's relatively easy to deal with these items, you could consider getting them fixed and out of the way.
- *A customer care reminder / follow-up.* Use this to confirm whether you have thanked users for their feedback and addressed their issue(s) as part of your customer care process.

Please note that you may only be able to recreate certain issues if you use the right combination of device, operating system and web browser that the beta tester was using. This is why it is important to gather these details.

For a copy of this issue management log, in spreadsheet format, click the download button below:

http://www.mylanderpages.com/donthireasoftwaredeveloperuntilyoureadthisbook/resource-8-issue-log-for-beta

Customer care. Be available to support and help your beta testers for the entirety of the beta testing period. Look out for emails from beta testers and be prepared to respond quickly. With business users, you'll need to provide support during office hours, but consumers may use your product at all hours of the day, night and weekends, so if you can't offer support during certain hours, then let your beta testers know when you'll be available.

If you receive lots of "how do I?" questions, then there is an issue. People should be able to navigate their way around and complete tasks without help. This may indicate that:

- **Your FAQs do not cover all the basics** (or were not noticed).
- **The buttons, icons, options or call to actions in the app are not obvious enough**. (Adding contextual or inline help - see chapter 11, changing the size and colour contrast of the buttons and screens, or adjusting the positions of buttons or icons on the screen may help.)
- **Your user journeys, or the layout, or positioning of the functionality on your screens may need reorganising** to make them easier to follow.

Update the FAQs document as you receive more questions and make sure that customers know where to find it in your web or mobile app.
If users are confused, you will need to get the root cause of the problem, or you will end up "fixing" the wrong things. Carefully review the feedback received and contact customers if necessary to make sure you really understand the problem(s), then create cards for the work and drop them into the correct queues on your backlog, according to priority.

CHAPTER 24
How to launch your MVP (as a beta)

> *Pro Tip*
>
> **Resolve issues quickly to avoid "abandonment."**
> Even if they have agreed to test your product, people may abandon it and revert back to a more familiar tool if they experience any issues. It will always be easier to use a familiar tool than to wrestle with problems with a new one. Encouraging *user adoption;* (the acceptance of new products) is important if you want the people testing your product to continue to pay you, or to convert to paying customers after your beta.
> Make sure you find out what kind of experience your beta testers are having and resolve issues quickly, so that test users have a positive experience with your app and quickly become accustomed to using it.

Gather and share feedback. Aside from handling customer service and having your developer check that your app is coping, following on from the points in the pro tip, you should also reach out to your beta testers to remind them to provide you with feedback.

Email them or call them and if people are happy, ask for testimonials for your web app and reviews in the relevant app marketplace. Share positive feedback within the beta testing group.

Decide how you want to receive feedback. Do you want to receive emails, or will you send out a feedback form? Should people contact you via Social Media? You might also use:

SurveyMonkey, https://www.surveymonkey.co.uk/
Google Forms, https://www.google.com/forms/about/
Typeform, https://www.typeform.com/pricing/ or
SurveyGizmo, https://www.surveygizmo.com/plans-pricing/, to send out simple questionnaires or forms. All 4 offer free basic plans.

Surveys may be useful to get an overall summary of people's thoughts and feelings about your product, but personally, I would also call a proportion of users during the beta. (It's generally easier to talk than to write, so you will get more feedback!) If you have business users, make a good impression and check in with them on a daily basis to find out what has been happening and to address any issues.

Releasing your MVP

Before you release your MVP to your Beta users, regardless of the size of your team, there are some important checks and balances to be done. Companies that build software sometimes have a set of criteria used to establish whether or not it is the right decision to progress with a software release. This is often called a *go / no-go decision*. A review date is set, which acts as a deadline for assessing the state of your product and deciding whether it is ready for launch or not. Your decision should also take into account your team's state of readiness – ideally, you will have prepared all your FAQs and help content and have all your support processes in place *before* you go "into beta". Go / no-go criteria might look something like this:

- **Have all the technical, functional and non-functional items on your "must" list been completed?** Did you finish building all the cards and user journeys needed for MVP?
- **Was feedback from recent user tests positive?** If you've received strong feedback which suggests that more work needs to be done on your app, there is no point going into beta without considering what this feedback is telling you, and what action(s) should be taken before you launch.
- **Is the product stable?** Have you finished testing all the cards and user journeys in your app? Is it free of serious issues? Is the product successfully integrated with any 3rd party tools required to make it operational?
- **Has contingency planning been done?** Do you have an idea about how you will avoid, mitigate or transfer any risks that you might face? Which risks are you willing to accept? (See Chapter 19 for a recap on managing project risks.)
- **Are your beta testers prepped and ready?** Have you given them sufficient notice about the beta? Do they know how they will access your product? Business customers will expect to be given a lot of advance warning.
- **Are the 3rd party products, services or systems involved in making your product (and launch) a success in place?** If you need a 3rd party to perform any tasks for you, inform them as far in advance as possible and be very clear about what you need and what the delivery deadlines are. Allow extra time just in case!
- **Are you prepared and ready to manage the launch?** Do you have a plan in place for supporting your beta testers? Chapter 25 contains examples

of ways you can set up your own customer care and support infrastructure.
- **Have you and your developer planned the release and done a dry-run?** There may be a number of steps involved in releasing your product to an app marketplace, or to the web. A *release checklist* can be used to capture all the steps involved in the release. Create one and store this somewhere safe (see Chapter 22 for a list of apps), so that the checklist can be used on release day to reduce the chance of important steps or activities being forgotten. *Call a meeting with your developer before the beta and plan out all the tasks involved in the release and what the timings for these should be.* After you capture all the steps, ask your developer to run through them to check for errors or omissions.
- **Will there be monitoring and analytics tools in place to provide important data about the app?** I mentioned these earlier in the chapter - if you have 'em, switch 'em on!

Pro tip!
Avoid launching on Mondays and Fridays.
Professional software delivery teams avoid releasing software on Mondays or Fridays.
This is done to manage risk.
Why are Mondays avoided? Products due to be launched are often monitored carefully several days before the scheduled go-live date. A release on a Monday would prevent this from happening, unless the product is monitored on a weekend.
Why are Fridays avoided? Releasing on a Friday means that if there are issues on the weekend after the release, or your system starts to show signs of stress during that time, there may not be anyone "on duty" to investigate and fix any problems found.
Of course, you can change your working schedule during the beta, which will give you more options.

Don't forget that making changes to your app close to launch is on the "suicide mission" list! See chapter 19 for the list of project pitfalls.
Best practice is to release the final code (functionality, fixes, changes) needed for a release, test it carefully, *regression* and *integration test* the whole product thoroughly, (see chapter 23 to review what these types of test are), confirm all is well, monitor the app for a day or two and *then release.*

CHAPTER 24
How to launch your MVP (as a beta)

Once the release has been made...

Be sure to do *post-release tests*. *Post-release tests* are done by checking the live version of the app and testing the major user journeys and functionality immediately after a release has been made. If you have a mobile app, do this by downloading the beta version of your app onto a smartphone and tablet and testing it out. If you're using TestFlight, this should be quite straightforward. If you have a web app, then go online, log in and test your app on a laptop, smartphone and tablet to cover the bases.

Look out for issues and be ready to respond!

What happens at the end of the beta period?

At the end of the trial period, you may choose to:

- Call the Beta period to a close - revoke access to the app and reflect on next steps.
- Leave the beta to run for an extended period to gather more data.
- Increase the number of Beta users.
- Remove any barriers that prevent non-beta users accessing your web app, or submit your app to the Google Play or App Store, and go fully "live"!

Your decision should be made based on your level of optimism based on the feedback you have received, and your observations during the beta. Before you launch fully, or extend your Beta to cover a wider group of users, run through the go / no-go questions again and ensure that any significant issues from the beta have been dealt with. Decide whether your app can support more users - speak to your developer and discuss the data collected from your monitoring tool(s.)

Also, consider where you may need to improve your customer service processes to give customers the support and information that they need.

In the final chapter of this book, we'll talk about customer care and other *post-launch activities*.

CHAPTER 25
Life after Launch

"I did then what I knew how to do. Now that I know better, I do better."
- Maya Angelou

In this chapter:
- Developing your customer care and support infrastructure
- Dealing with issues and negative events
- Collecting data and responding to feedback

You've launched! Congratulations!!! What happens next? Now you have a commercial product out in the world, you'll no doubt be thinking a lot about marketing, sales and how to grow your business. However, by focusing on customer care and continuing to learn about your customers' behaviour, requirements and expectations, you will be able to retain existing customers *and* have a firm foundation for expansion.

Developing your customer care and support infrastructure

Here are some simple, but effective ways to take care of your customers:

Create a self-service website. With the right information, your website or web app can play the role of a customer service agent. Regardless of the type of app you're building, there's no reason why you can't have a website with some FAQs, "how to" screenshots or videos available on it. Not only does this information help customers who are stuck to resolve their own issues, it reconfirms your product's features and benefits, and educates them about how to get the most out of using it. Reduce frustration amongst your customers by making sure they can find this information quickly and easily by using clear descriptions and labels.

Decide how customers will be able to contact you. If you've ever played "hunt the email address" on a company's website, you'll know how frustrating this is!

CHAPTER 25
Life after Launch

Even if you can only offer customer care by email in the early days, make your contact information easy to find, whether you:
- Publish your email address on your website
- Have a contact form on your website
- Include your contact details in your mobile app or
- Display your contact information on your app marketplace page.

If you're able to provide telephone support, or services like live chat, then make sure these are made obvious to your customers. Startup-friendly companies you can approach for live chat tools include:

Zopim; https://www.zopim.com/pricing/ the "Lite" plan is free, the basic plan is $14 per operator per month.

Snapengage; https://snapengage.com/live-chat-pricing/ from £45 per month for 4 agents.

LiveChat; https://www.livechatinc.com/features/ from $19 agent per month

Olark; https://www.olark.com/pricing from $17 per agent per month.

A 24-hour response policy for emails is generally acceptable (48 hours worst case), but customers will, of course, want you to get back to them much sooner than that if possible.

Have an *email auto-responder*, which acknowledges the receipt of all emails you receive and replies back to customers confirming how quickly they can expect a response.

Monitor feedback and respond to it. Check your app store and online reviews and take swift action to rectify any problems. Reply to users who report issues, and let them know what you are doing to fix them. If you're going to make improvements, or fix issues based on customers' input, communicate the good news and let them know that you are listening to their feedback.

Use tools to help you manage customer care and communication. Consider using a helpdesk tool to categorise and "triage" contact from customers.

Freshdesk, https://freshdesk.com/pricing is a helpdesk management tool which is free to use for up to three customer service agents.

You could create categories such as "bugs", "questions", "complaints" and "suggestions" and group customer feedback in this way inside the helpdesk tool. You could also include other categories such as "issues" and "testimonials." This is a very simple, but effective way to see what is happening in your business and to organise customer feedback.

CHAPTER 25
Life after Launch

It will also help you to understand the major reasons why customers contact you. Trello can be used as a helpdesk tool (is there no end to its many talents?) You can use it to create a queue for each category type, or add colour-coded labels to each card to categorise them.

Reduce questions and suggestions (which will increase your workload), by communicating common queries and comments via a blog, social media, or by regularly updating your FAQs to cover all the questions that your customers are asking.

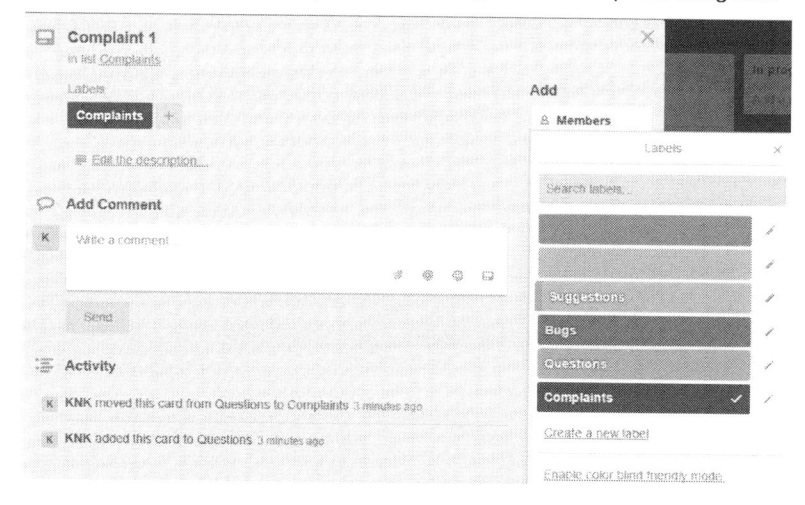

Fig 102. Using Trello as a customer care system and setting customer response categories.

Fig 103. Sample customer service board.

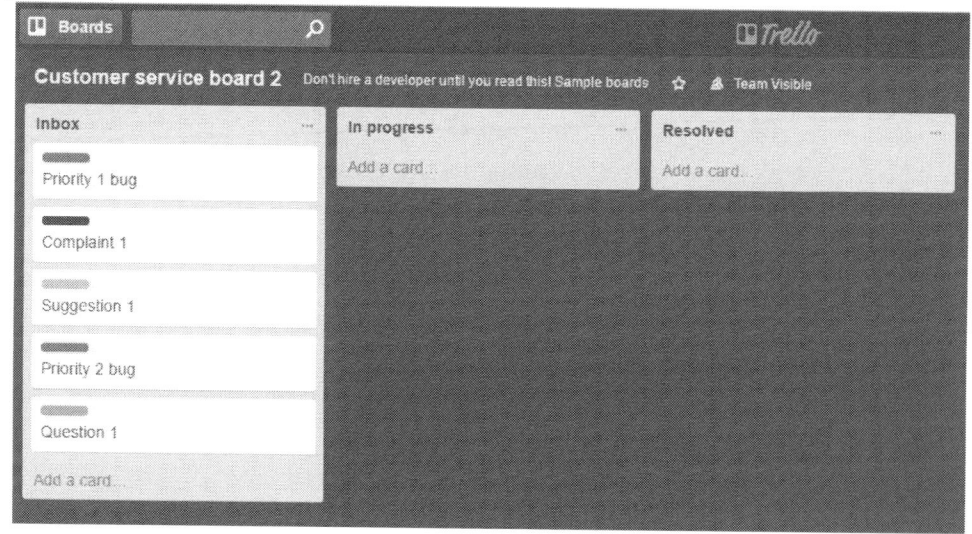

CHAPTER 25
Life after Launch

You can make copies of my Trello boards for a quick start. Just click the link below:
http://www.mylanderpages.com/donthireasoftwaredeveloperuntilyoureadthisbook/free-resource-2-trello-boards

Dealing with technical issues or negative events

You've done your best, but just in case things don't go according to plan, follow these tips for dealing with customer issues in an effective manner.

It's good etiquette to keep customers informed if a major issue occurs that will disrupt your service or seriously impact them. This also stops you receiving lots of messages from customers about the same issues.

If a significant issue has been discovered that you *weren't* aware of, switch into investigation mode and check, (or ask your developer to check) your app for issues and look at your monitoring and analytics tools, if needed. Find out the severity and extent of the problem, including how many of your customers have been affected and what problems they have experienced. Gather as much information as you can as quickly as possible, to help your developer diagnose the problem. Once you have the facts, communicate with your customers without delay, explaining:

- What the problem is.
- The cause of the issue.
- When the problem started, or was first identified.
- Which parts of the app are (or aren't) affected?
- Any recommended workarounds or temporary solutions available to overcome the issues. Workarounds are offered to reduce any frustration or inconvenience felt by your customers whilst the problem is being resolved.
- How long it will take to fix the problem. (Get an estimate from your developer.)

Clearly send out the message:
"We care, we're sorry. We're getting on top of this and are working towards a solution."

Keep customers updated on your website or via email, but **beware of overpromising**. If a fix takes longer than you say it will, then this will only frustrate people more. For example, if your developer believes the issue will be fixed in four hours, then it would be better to say that you're working on the problem and it will be fixed "later today" rather than saying it will be fixed in four hours. If the fix ends up taking five hours, or six, you'll have to keep going back on your word, which may damage customers' confidence in your business. I am not advocating staying silent, as this can also be damaging - just don't commit to specific dates or times until you are certain that you can deliver.

This information is particularly relevant if your software will be used by businesses, because if a major issue occurs during office hours, they are likely to be using your product. With an app for consumers, some people may not even know you had an issue, whilst others will be affected. Use your analytics and monitoring tools to decide how many people have been impacted and whether to contact everyone, or just to reply to anyone who contacts you.

If a serious issue is found after you go live and an emergency bug fix is needed, your product should be tested to see that the emergency fix hasn't broken any other parts of your app, before you send an update out to customers, so be conservative when telling people what will happen and when.

Collecting, analysing and responding to data and feedback

Embrace the "business in a Petri dish" life of an entrepreneur! Continue to learn about your market and your customers. Now you have people using your product "in the wild", you can start collecting information about customer behaviour, so you can make smart data driven and evidence based decisions. Let's review some *data analytics* tools for web and mobile apps that you can use:

Google Analytics (GA) is a very useful tool for understanding customer behaviour on websites / web apps. It will tell you where visitors to your website arrive from and which pages they exit from, as well as where they are in the world. You will also be able to see which pages on your site are most popular and your *bounce rate,* (the number of people who come to your site, but leave soon after, having only visited one page and without interacting with it), and much more! There's some set-up work to do in adding the GA code to your site, but it's a fairly simple task. You can learn more about the free version of GA here: https://analytics.google.com/analytics/web/

GA can also be set up alongside Firebase (owned by Google), to provide analytics for your iOS or Android mobile app: https://firebase.google.com/.

CHAPTER 25
Life after Launch

https://support.google.com/firebase#topic=6386699 and

https://support.google.com/analytics/answer/1008015?hl=en

Fig 104. A Google Analytics Dashboard.

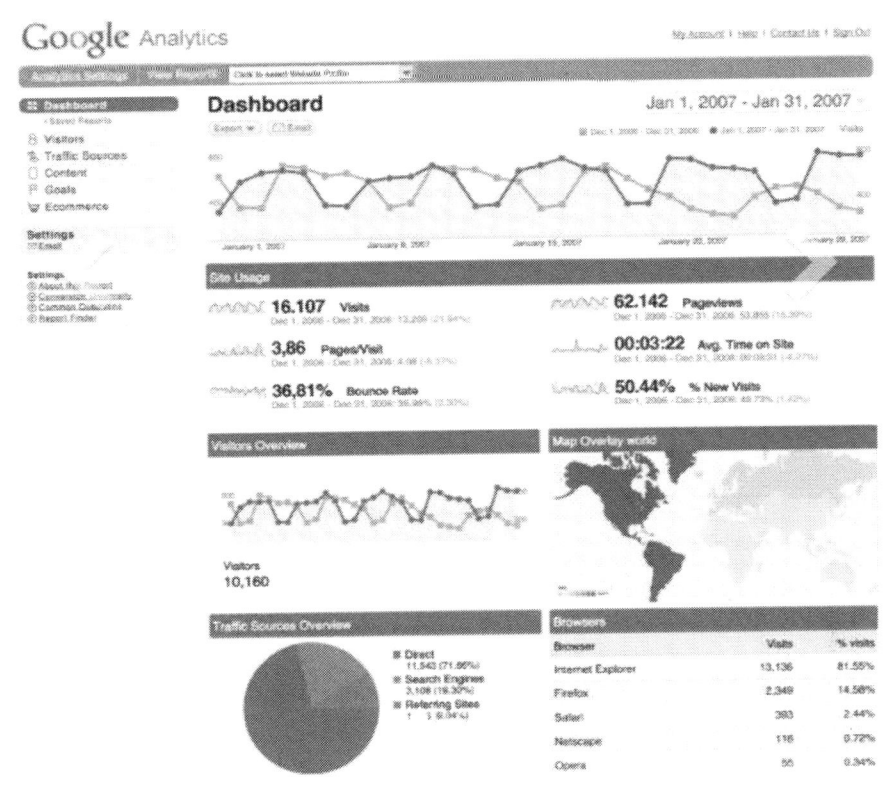

Crazy Egg, https://www.crazyegg.com/pricing offer a number of products, including heatmaps and overlays that indicate where customers are clicking on the page - and the parts of your website or web app that are most (and least) popular. Prices start from $9 USD per month.

CHAPTER 25
Life after Launch

Fig 105. Crazy Egg – visualising where your visitors click.

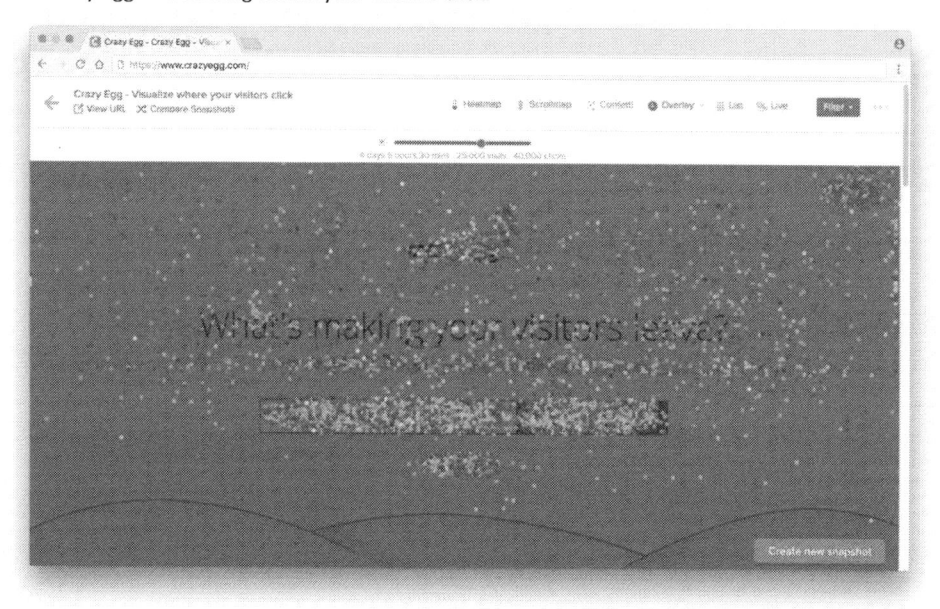

Piwik Pro offers data on mobile and web app usage and costs from 29 Euro for 100,000 actions a month: https://cloud.piwik.pro/

GoSquared offers web analytics and *feature usage* metrics so you can see how customers are using your app. It also has a CRM system, which can help you track and manage customer relationships. It's free to use for 1000 data points per month. https://www.gosquared.com

As well as gathering data via analytics tools, continue to gather *qualitative data*: run user tests and arrange customer interviews as you extend or update your product. Ask customers what they think of your product and how it can be improved – email them, call them, send them questionnaires and ask for feedback via your website. They are the key!

I hope this book has been useful and informative, and I wish you every success on your journey. Please turn to the next page to find out what comes next!

THANK YOU

Thank you for taking the time to download this book. I greatly respect your drive and desire to get your software built! My purpose has always been to share quality information about building software that is not easily accessible to non-technical business people, and I hope I have achieved that.

What comes next?

1. **Use the free resources** that come with this book. The download links are on the next page.
2. **Get your free bonus chapters.** They are a thank you gift for buying this book. The link is on the next page.
3. **Say hi / request a free Skype session** with me. I'm offering the first 4 readers to email me *each month*, a free 25 minute Skype session, where we can chat about any queries you have about the software delivery process. Email: http://www.purposefulgroup.com/contact-us.html and ask for a **Free session** in your message.
4. **If you liked the book, please leave me a review.** Just click on the *Write a customer review* button on the Amazon sales page for the book: https://amzn.com/B01LY5C1IK, or visit your local online Amazon store. I'd *really* appreciate it!
5. **Spread the word.** If you have friends, family or co-workers who would find this book helpful, please share the link: https://amzn.com/B01LY5C1IK.

I have one last quote for you, my favourite by Anais Nin:
"Life shrinks or expands in proportion to one's courage."

With my best wishes,

Kay

DEDICATION

For Irene - with all my love and gratitude now, and forever.

I'd also like to say a big thank you to the people that have cheered me on, and given me both moral and practical support.

I appreciate you all!

ABOUT THE AUTHOR

K.N. Kukoyi has a passion for translating concepts into professional software used by businesses and consumers worldwide, and has spent over a decade leading and working in technical teams, delivering mobile apps, websites and a range of other digital products for companies of all sizes, from small businesses to multinationals, helping them to achieve their strategic goals through the use of software.

Before embarking upon a career in IT, she spent several years working as an IT recruiter, reviewing the CVs of thousands of software developers from around the world on behalf of her clients.

The author has diplomas in Internet Marketing and coaching and the CSM Agile certification. She has trained both technical and non-technical teams in Agile processes, and enjoys coaching and mentoring individuals and entrepreneurs to help them improve their performance.

K.N. Kukoyi has founded several small businesses and has first-hand knowledge of the challenges faced by small enterprises with limited resources.

She is the founder of Purposeful Products, a business and software consultancy that helps clients to transform their ideas into commercial software products.

http://www.purposefulgroup.com/contact-us.html

CREDITS

	Table of credits and references
	Introduction
1	Fig 1. CB Insights - The top 20 reasons why startups fail. www.cbinsights.com/blog/startup-failure-reasons-top/
	Chapter 1
2	Fig 2. Types of IP. Source, The Intellectual Property Office (IPO)
3	Fig 3. Patents and computer programs. Source, The Intellectual Property Office (IPO). http://www.ipo.gov.uk/blogs/iptutor/stem-patents-and-trade-secrets-part-1/
4	Fig 4. Discussing your invention. Keeping Schtum! Source, The Intellectual Property Office (IPO)
5	Fig 5. The Toshl app I-III.
	Chapter 2
6	Fig 6. A comparison search using Google Trends, based on web searches from July 2015 - July 2016
7	Fig 7. Running a keyword search for the term "computer games" using the Wordtracker tool.
8	Fig 8. Star ratings for a game available in the Google Play Store
9	Fig 9. Put Google Alerts to work for you and receive alerts via email or RSS
10	Fig 10. Find the latest academic research on your topic of choice using Google Scholar
11	Fig 11. SWOT analysis table. https://commons.wikimedia.org/wiki/File:SWOT_en.svg, Xhienne Entrepreneur definition, SMALL BUSINESS ENCYCLOPEDIA
	Chapter 3
12	Fig 12. YouGov customer profile for customers of The Independent newspaper
13	Fig 13. YouGov customer profile for Instagram customers
14	Fig 14. Customer profile form.
15	Fig 15. The inner world of your target customer.
16	Fig 16. Freepik avatar creator tools. http://www.freepik.com/free-vector/male-avatar-creator_822151.htm
17	Fig 17. Freepik avatar creator tools. Woman avatar creator. http://www.freepik.com/free-vector/woman-avatar-creator_824042.htm
18	Fig 18. Freepik avatar creator tools - business team avatar examples. http://www.freepik.com/free-vector/business-team-avatar-collection_874660.htm

	Chapter 4
19	Fig 19. The Waterfall model. The concept stage marks the start of the project and the release stage marks the end
20	Fig 20. The Agile development cycle. A single iteration includes all the stages from requirements gathering and analysis to release. https://upload.wikimedia.org/wikipedia/commons/5/50/Agile_Project_Management_by_Planbox.png. Aflafla1 - Iterative development model V2.jpg
	Chapter 5
21	Fig 21. Iconography example. The hamburger menu item. Chris Messley. Flickr / Thinkstock
22	Fig 22. Where there's a Project Manager, a Gantt chart is probably not very far away. By Vheilman. [CC-BY-SA-3.0 (www.creativecommons.org/licenses/by-sa/3.0)], via Wikimedia Commons. https://commons.wikimedia.org/wiki/File:Gantt_chart_example.png
	Chapter 6
23	Fig 23. Http status code table
24	Fig 24. A "500" internal server error page
25	Fig 25. A 404 page created by Blue Fountain Media. http://www.bluefountainmedia.com
26	Fig 26. Example of the Uptrends monitoring console. https://www.uptrends.com.
27	Fig 27. A website with an SSL certificate.
	Chapter 7
28	Fig 28. "m." websites, an old-school approach requiring two different URLs. Source. Google Webmasters, mobile friendly website advice.
29	Fig 29. How content should "respond" when displayed on different device sizes. Diseño web adaptativo, http://www.dobuss.es/, JOSE LUIS DOBUSS
30	Fig 30. "Why make a website mobile friendly?" by Google. https://developers.google.com/webmasters/mobile-sites/
31	Fig 31. The number of apps in the top 4 app marketplaces in June 2016. Source of data, Statista.com.
32	Fig 32. Worldwide Smartphone Shipments by OD, Market Share, and 5-year CAGR 2015-2020, Source: IDC Worldwide Quarterly Mobile Phone Tracker, September 2016. http://www.idc.com/getdoc.jsp?containerId=prUS4142561
	Chapter 8
33	Fig 33. Pricing table plugins compatible with websites built using WordPress. https://wordpress.org/plugins/pricing-table/
34	Fig 34. Responsive pricing tables for WordPress, screenshot. https://wordpress.org/plugins/dk-pricr-responsive-pricing-table/screenshots/

35	Fig 35. AdSense ads by Google. https://www.google.com/adsense/start/.
36	Fig 36. Top 5 selling apps. Google Play store. July 2016. https://play.google.com.
	Chapter 9
37	Fig 37. WhatsApp Inc's store listing page
38	Fig 38. App launcher icons.
39	Fig 39. Market share held by the leading search engines in the United Kingdom (UK) as of June, 2016. Source Statista.com https://www.statista.com/statistics/280269/market-share-held-by-search-engines-in-the-united-kingdom/
40	Fig 40. Page titles and meta descriptions, plus image and video search rankings.
41	Fig 41. Page heading titles are used to structure your content and indicate the relevant importance of each heading and section of content.
42	Fig 42. A mobile app requests permission to send push notifications to a customers' mobile device.
43	Fig 43. Example of a web browser requesting permission to send push notifications to a customer.
44	Fig 44. Inside the Landerapp landing page builder.
	Chapter 10
45	Fig 45. The parts (and parts of parts) of a product
46	Fig 46. User journeys for an office administrator and an HR Manager. Freepik business team avatar
47	Fig 47. Using a simple diagram to represent each step
48	Fig 48. Flowchart symbols: http://brailleatm.com/ZGVjaXNpb24gZmxvd2NoYXJ0IHN5bWJvbHM/
49	Fig 49. Lucidchart template. www.lucidchart.com
	Chapter 11
50	Fig 50. Make sure users know where they are within your app at all times. https://upload.wikimedia.org/wikipedia/commons/7/78/Traquair_House_Maze.jpg. Hedge maze in rear garden, Traquair House in Scotland. By marsroverdriver
51	Fig 51. A simple, user-friendly interface. https://mailshake.com/
52	Fig 52. Touch Gesture Reference Guide, by Luke Wroblewski. http://static.lukew.com/TouchGestureGuide.pdf
53	Fig 53. A hand drawn wireframe for an imaginary news app.
54	Fig 54. Mobile app gestures log.
55	Fig 55. Radio buttons
56	Fig 56. Checkboxes
57	Fig 57 i. Dropdown menu. Fig 57 ii. Selecting items (in this example, US States) from a list using a mobile device. http://wiki.processmaker.com/3.0/JavaScript_Functions_and_Methods by ProcessMaker. Fig 57 iii. jQuery date picker for mobile devices. (It can be used to select times too.) http://www.jqueryscript.net/time-clock/Stylish-jQuery-Date-Time-Picker-For-Mobile-Devices-mobiscroll.html

58	Fig 58. An example of text appearing in a tooltip in response to being "hovered over" by a user.
59	Fig 59. Iconography. Common symbols for web and mobile apps.
60	Fig 60. Using Lorem Ipsum to focus attention on graphic elements in a webpage design proposal. Lorem ipsum design.svg. UED77; SVG by Mysid. https://en.wikipedia.org/wiki/File:Lorem_ipsum_design.svg
61	Fig 61. Taco, the Trello mascot
62	Fig 62. Zendesk's "The Mentor"
63	Fig 63. The Tunnelbear mascot
64	Fig 64. Page loading notifications (or page loading "spinners"). From top, W Brett Wilson, Lazarevic Ivan, http://workshop.rs/2012/12/animated-progress-bar-in-4-lines-of-jquery/ and others,
	Chapter 12
65	Fig 65. A hand drawn wireframe of a mobile news app.
66	Fig 66. A hand drawn wireframe of a landing page for a web app.
67	Fig 67. Device and browser templates. http://www.interfacesketch.com/
68	Fig 68. An example using the POP app
	Chapter 13
69	Fig 69. "Why You Only Need to Test with 5 Users" by Jakob Nielsen (March 19, 2000). Article: https://www.nngroup.com/articles/why-you-only-need-to-test-with-5-users.
	Instagram story. TechCrunch, Investopedia: http://www.theatlantic.com/technology/archive/2014/07/instagram-used-to-be-called-brbn/373815/, https://techcrunch.com/2010/11/08/instagram-a-pivotal-pivot/, http://www.investopedia.com/articles/investing/102615/story-instagram-rise-1-photo0sharing-app.asp
	Chapter 14
70	Fig 70. The "My App" product backlog, prioritised using MoSCoW
71	Fig 71. When explaining what you need from a developer, consider the full range of requirements. https://commons.wikimedia.org/wiki/File:Iceberg.jpg. By Uwe Kils. http://www.ecoscope.com/iceberg/
	Chapter 15
72	Fig 72. Diagram showing the interrelation of Application Software Operating_system_placement.svg: Golftheman, derivative work: Pluke
73	Fig 73. Programming languages, SDKs and IDEs compatible with Android and iOS app development
	Chapter 19
74	Fig 74. Trello project plan / roadmap example, part 1.
75	Fig 75. Trello project plan / roadmap example, part 2.
76	Fig 76. Work plan template. http://www.tools4dev.org/resources/work-plan-template/
77	Fig 77. Risk assessment quadrant. Risk and Impact. https://opentextbc.ca/projectmanagement/wp-content/uploads/sites/3/2014/06/risk-and-impact.jpg
78	Fig 78. Risk management options. By Barron & Barron Project Management for Scientists and Engineers, http://cnx.org/content/col11120/1.4/
	Chapter 20
79	Fig 79. Trello board with t-shirt sizes assigned to cards
	Chapter 22

80	Fig 80. Inside a Trello card with the checklist option activated.
81	Fig 81. The top priority card from the Must queue on the product backlog is moved to the Development board.
82	Fig 82. The card is transferred between boards using the Move Card functionality.
83	Fig 83. Software versioning.
84	Fig 84. Setting a due date in Trello
85	Fig 85. A yellow marker indicates that a task is due to be delivered within 24 hours
86	Fig 86. An example of the Slack messaging tool. https://slack.com
87	Fig 87. Turning on the calendar Power-Ups functionality in Trello.
88	Fig 88. Set a due date as shown in Fig 84 to see the calendar due dates displayed on the front of your cards in Trello.
89	Fig 89. Trello calendar month view
90	Fig 90. Use Google to see a list of the events you've added to Google calendar.
91	Fig 91. Using Google Keep to store important tasks or repetitive processes.
	Chapter 23
92	Fig 92. Relative cost to fix bugs based on time of detection. Source: National Institute of Standards and Technology (NIST).
93	Fig 93. Cards in Trello can be colour-coded and named using the label functionality.
94	Figs 94 and 95. The bug label is now visible on the inside and outside of the Trello card.
96	Fig 96. Worldwide Desktop Browser Usage Share. Source: StatCounter.com.
97	Fig 97. Worldwide stats including desktop, mobile and tablet. (If you're curious, UC Browser is a mobile browser created by the Chinese company UCWeb.) Source: StatCounter, http://statcounter.com/.
98	Fig 98. In a commercial environment, a range of devices are often used for testing, this is sometimes called a device farm. Devices. Source: Brad Frost. https://www.flickr.com/photos/brad_frost/7387824246, https://creativecommons.org/licenses/by/2.0/
99	Fig 99. This example shows an emulator displaying a device with the text, "Hello World", a popular test program used by developers. https://i.stack.imgur.com/7q9g6.png
	Chapter 24
100	Fig 100 Instagram beta logo. (Former logo.)
101	Fig 101 Firefox beta logo.
	Chapter 25
102	Fig 102. Using Trello as a customer care system and setting customer response categories.
103	Fig 103. Sample customer service board, created using Trello.
104	Fig 104. Google Analytics example.
105	Fig 105. Crazy Egg product example.

Made in the USA
San Bernardino, CA
13 September 2017